T0329634

DEMOCRATIZING FINANCE

Democratizing Finance

The Radical Promise of Fintech

MARION LABOURE

NICOLAS DEFFRENNES

Harvard University Press

Cambridge, Massachusetts & London, England / 2022

Library of Congress Cataloging-in-Publication Data

Names: Labouré, Marion, author. | Deffrennes, Nicolas, 1983– author.
Title: Democratizing finance : the radical promise of fintech /
    Marion Laboure, Nicolas Deffrennes.
Description: Cambridge, Massachusetts : Harvard University Press, 2022. |
    Includes bibliographical references and index.
Identifiers: LCCN 2021034384 | ISBN 9780674987227 (cloth)
Subjects: LCSH: Financial institutions—Effect of technological innovations on. |
    Financial services industry. | Equality—Economic aspects. | International finance. |
    Consolidation and merger of corporations.
Classification: LCC HG173 .L34 2022 | DDC 332.0285—dc23
LC record available at https://lccn.loc.gov/2021034384

Contents

Abbreviations

AI	artificial intelligence
ATM	automatic teller machine
AUM	assets under management
B2B	business-to-business
B2C	business-to-consumer
BATX	Baidu, Alibaba, Tencent, and Xiaomi
BEPS	base erosion and profit shifting
C2C	customer-to-customer
CB	central bank
CBDC	central bank digital currency
CDU	Christian Democratic Union
CDS	credit default swaps
CEO	chief executive officer
CGAP	Consultative Group to Assist the Poorest
COD	cash on delivery
CPI	Consumer Price Index
CSU	Christian Social Union
DLT	distributed ledger technology
EA	euro area
EC	European Commission
ECB	European Central Bank
EGDI	E-Government Development Index
ERP	enterprise resource planning
ETF	exchange-traded fund
EU	European Union

FATCA	Foreign Account Tax Compliance Act
Fed	Federal Reserve System or Federal Reserve
FI	financial institutions
Fintech	financial technology
FRED	Federal Reserve Economic Data
FX	foreign exchange
G2C	government-to-consumer
G2P	government-to-person
GAFA	Google, Apple, Facebook, and Amazon
GDP	gross domestic product
Global Findex	Global Financial Inclusion Database
GNI	gross national income
GST	goods and services tax
HIV	human immunodeficiency virus
HNWI	high net worth individual
ICT	information and communications technology
ID	identity document
IMF	International Monetary Fund
IoT	Internet of Things
IPO	initial public offering
IRA	individual retirement account
IRS	Internal Revenue Service
IT	information technology
KYC	Know Your Customer
MFI	microfinance institution
MSME	micro, small, and medium enterprises
NICT	new information and communications technologies
NGO	nongovernmental organizations
NYSE	New York Stock Exchange
OADR	old-age dependency ratio
OECD	Organization for Economic Co-operation and Development
PE	private equity
P2P	peer-to-peer
PBoC	People's Bank of China
PM	prime minister

PPP	Paycheck Protection Program
QR Code	quick response code
RFID	radio frequency identification
SEC	Securities and Exchange Commission
SEPA	single euro area payment
SMB	small and medium business
SME	small and medium enterprise
SMS	short message service
STP	straight-through processing
SWIFT	Society for Worldwide Interbank Financial Telecommunication
TIAA	Teachers Insurance and Annuity Association
TFP	total-factor productivity
UAE	United Arab Emirates
UIDAI	Unique Identification Authority of India
UK	United Kingdom
UN	United Nations
UNICEF	United Nations Children's Fund
UNRISD	United Nations Research Institute for Social Development
US	United States
USD	United States dollar
VAT	value-added tax
WB	World Bank
WFP	World Food Programme
WHO	World Health Organization
WID	wealth and income database

DEMOCRATIZING FINANCE

Introduction

A financial technology revolution, still in its infancy, is beginning to reshape societies and economies by ushering in the global democratization of finance. While digital currencies and robo-advising have attracted attention in the popular media, little has been written about how financial technology, or *fintech,* is affecting the overall economic outlook of nations.

In this book we explain how fintech promises to impact a range of economic and social outcomes, including financial inclusion, income and wealth inequality, economic growth, and investment. As we will examine, decisions and innovations by governments and technology entrepreneurs will affect the international balance of power between nations and the rates of economic inclusion among underserved populations. The fintech revolution will influence every person in the world.

The term *fintech* has been used to refer to a wide variety of financial technologies, but for our purposes in this book we will use it to refer to any new technology and innovation that has been developed or is being developed in the twenty-first century to compete with traditional methods of delivering financial services. Examples of fintech, according to this definition, include mobile banking with smartphones, digital investing services, and cryptocurrencies like Bitcoin. These technologies have a common goal: they are designed to make financial services more accessible to the public. Today's fintech revolution enables consumers to transfer funds, raise money for business start-ups, and manage personal finances without the help of an intermediary or professional. Fintech is also improving economic inclusion, providing access to banking and commerce in rural areas, and allowing individuals to receive social security transfers. In summary, modern fintech is democratizing finance.

Financial Services Have Reached an Inflexion Point

Since the late twentieth century, banks and insurance companies have grown massively. We have seen intense merger and acquisition activity as national banks and insurance firms have been gobbled up by regional players, who are themselves devoured by global companies. Mergers and acquisitions in the banking sector peaked in 1998 and 1999, and then again in 2007, with more than $450 billion of transaction value for each of those years. This consolidation process has enabled banks to expand into adjacent financial services, such as asset management or insurance, and has fueled enormous economies of scale in three critical areas that pertain to financial services.[1]

First, the mutualization of funding gives large and diversified financial services companies access to "cheaper" money. For example, funding mutualization allows big banks to more easily attract deposits to lend to its consumers and customers, and large insurance companies can reinvest revenues from policy sales to its own asset manager.

Second, a large network and product base benefits from being able to offer every financial service that consumers might need (loans, current accounts, payments, insurance, and so on) with one account and at one branch. Across most developed countries, we now see oligopolies dominated by just three to seven banks and/or insurance companies, each with a widely distributed network of local branches.

Third, massive companies benefit when they can absorb the cost of managing and analyzing data, which are core functions of a financial services company. To accomplish these functions—storing, processing, and analyzing consumer data, making credit decisions, and tracking account movements—without a more expensive third party, banks and insurance companies need to scale up.

The three factors mentioned above, coupled with the rise of new technologies, have helped fuel a process of consolidation leading to the emergence of financial service behemoths. These giant firms are now capable of capturing a significant slice of the global economic pie. The share of GDP held by the financial services sector has nearly doubled since the 1980s, growing from less than 4 percent of US GDP to 8 percent just before the 2008 financial crisis. The major financial services companies have become so large that they are now considered to be "too big to fail."[2]

However, we believe the consolidation tidal wave is losing its steam. Since 2010 the yearly value of mergers and acquisitions has been, on average, around $100 million, which is less than one-fourth of its peak value in the previous decade.[3] The 2007–2008 financial crisis significantly modified the supply–demand equilibrium in financial services. Large financial institutions were all weakened by the crisis and were forced by capital or liquidity constraints, or by regulators, to significantly reduce their activity. This left new areas of unmet demand, in particular within the lower income quartile of the population and among small businesses.[4]

In response, the spectacular development of digital technologies has offered new solutions and models for conducting financial services. Online brokers have been increasingly competing with bank and insurance branches. Digital wallets and mobile payments have offered consumers alternatives to exchanging and storing cash. Peer-to-peer platforms have emerged as a new way to match deposits and lending activity. Cryptocurrencies have reduced the intermediary role of banks in money exchange. Blockchain and other data-management technologies have begun to significantly disrupt back-office processes and organizations.

We should recognize that it will be easier to analyze the impact of these technologies after they have matured. Many of today's innovations will not impact our world as much as the paper bill or credit card. Some may become fads or be replaced by newer, more ambitious technologies. Some technologies might not be as widely adopted as expected, but they could still serve as seeds for a future, life-changing ecosystem. Nevertheless, we can already see that fintech is democratizing finance and extending affordable banking services to the world's 1.7 billion unbanked adults. Our goal in this book is to provide an accessible summary of these impacts and, despite uncertainty, to offer an informed assessment of the potential impacts of a wide range of fintech innovations.

The Human Impact of Fintech

What might that democratizing trend mean for people around the world? As we demonstrate in this book, fintech has already helped millions escape the poverty trap.

During the twentieth century, those with extensive access to financial services had an unfair advantage over those in developing nations who lacked access to even the most basic financial services, such as bank accounts and government identification cards. This disparity in access had been one of the leading drivers of inequality.

Thomas Piketty has famously argued that the rate of return on capital over the past three centuries has been significantly greater than the economic growth rate, and that, therefore, income from capital investment has outpaced income from labor activity. At the very top of the distribution, incomes skyrocketed. Between 1980 and 2016, the top 0.001 percent rose by 650 percent in the United States, and by 200 percent in Europe.[5] Unequal access to financial services has played a critical role in bringing about these outcomes. Anthony Atkinson and his colleagues have shown, for example, that the wealthiest individuals have access to investment products—asset management funds and hedge funds, for example—with significantly higher financial returns than the mainstream products available to most people. Small investors, by contrast, are typically directed to so-called vanilla investments, such as low-yield bank deposits and government bonds. The role of capital in driving inequality is reinforced by the fact that an increasing share of wealth is inherited, which is unequally distributed.[6]

Over the past decade, the income of the middle class, which represents the largest share of the population in advanced countries, has stagnated or declined. Only a third of households in developed countries saw their incomes rise between 2005 and 2014. In the aftermath of the 2008 global financial crisis, the traditional banking industry has left "subprime" individuals and many small businesses either underbanked or without any banking options at all.

Fintech innovations today are beginning to disrupt those twentieth-century systems of access to financial services. Frustrated by limited access to quality financial services, middle- and lower-class populations are looking for other options—and fintech innovators are providing them. Peer-to-peer platforms in transportation (Uber) and hospitality (Airbnb), for example, are serving as models for new peer-to-peer lending marketplaces that are disintermediating banks. The changing landscape of health care and retirement funding, driven by digital innovation and algorithmic solutions, may offer alternative retirement solutions, especially for millennials.

As for the billions of underbanked people trapped in poverty, we will show in this book that fintech innovation is providing improvements in health care, government infrastructure, farming, and manufacturing. These advancements often give poor people an opportunity to launch their own businesses. Fintech can help small-scale entrepreneurs in their struggle to escape poverty by providing them with basic banking services through which to grow businesses and store wealth. Fintech can improve infrastructure for financial transactions, such as saving, spending, and borrowing money. Through these services, underbanked individuals can better weather economic shocks and health setbacks, which leads to greater long-term financial stability.

The scope of fintech improvements is vast because there are so many unbanked people in the world. According to the World Bank's Global Financial Inclusion Database, about 1.7 billion adults in 2017 did not have an account at a financial institution. Women are disproportionately excluded from the formal financial system, constituting 56 percent of all unbanked adults. Nearly half of the world's unbanked population is concentrated in just seven developing economies: Bangladesh, China, India, Indonesia, Mexico, Nigeria, and Pakistan.

Most people in poor households in these countries own smartphones, but they almost always use cash, physical assets (jewelry and livestock), or informal money lenders and cash couriers to make payments or save. Informal banking mechanisms can be insecure, expensive, and usurious. In addition, they offer limited or no help after a personal catastrophe, such as a serious illness or a poor harvest.

A growing body of evidence suggests that access to secure financial tools at critical moments in life can help poor families move out of poverty or absorb financial shocks without being forced deeper into debt. Unfortunately, today's brick-and-mortar banking system was not designed to aid the poor. Banks, utility companies, and other institutions pass to consumers the costs of storing, transporting, and processing cash. This creates a vicious cycle, one that can lock poor people into the cash economy and prevent them from advancing toward electronic transactions and savings.[7]

Digital banking can help millions of unbanked poor people in both advanced and developing countries to overcome daily financial problems like those described above. The mobile phone and internet revolutions have already reached most corners of the world, including in Africa's developing economies, and rapid advances in digital payment systems have fueled the emergence of online financial services that allow for virtual saving and instantaneous transfers.

A Roadmap for the Reader

At the outset, it is important to emphasize that this book does not present a simplistic view of fintech's potential impact on global economic inequality. While many claim that technology, globalization, and finance are primary sources of rising inequalities, we offer a research-based view of how the fintech revolution will influence societies and economies. Our research shows, for example, that technological disruption simultaneously widens inequalities in developed markets while reducing poverty in less-developed economies. Countries advance when they implement technology, and they stay behind when they do not pursue technological development. This occurs because fintech provides people in emerging markets greater access to information and labor markets, thereby offering increased opportunity to join global competition. In some circumstances, the expansion of opportunity in developing nations may crowd out people in established markets.

By presenting our extensive research on the existing and potential impacts of fintech, this book will serve as a helpful study for policymakers and entrepreneurs. To date, existing research on the problem of increasing inequality has centered primarily on fiscal policy. By contrast, this book presents an in-depth study of the connections between financial technology and inequality. From this solid foundation we can build our understanding of the fintech revolution and its socioeconomic implications.

The structure of the book strongly emphasizes the differentiation between the challenges of fintech in advanced and emerging economies. In advanced countries, fintech helps to improve the existing financial framework and tackles a wide range of issues, such as convenience in payments, retirement and financial planning, and the delivery of government services. In emerging countries, fintech innovation mostly solves an issue of financial inclusion and access to financial services. This is similar to how telecom infrastructure enabled some countries to leapfrog landline phone systems to cellular phone systems, including smartphones.

Chapter 1 discusses today's serious economic challenges that the millennials in particular are facing: low growth, unsustainable public debt, high pension liabilities, and a job market that is more unstable than ever. These macro trends have accelerated the development of a new generation of financial services that we commonly name *fintech*. Chapters 2–4 describe the disruptive impacts of fintech: first, how banks are facing new competitors; second, how fintech affects consumers and financial planning; and third, how governments are responding to technological progress. Chapters 5–7 highlight the key issues and restrictions that emerging economies must overcome to expand their economies. We explain how fintech develops hand in hand with other economic and physical infrastructure, which government should proactively develop to promote commerce and trade. Chapters 8–9 present a practical overview of recent developments in payment systems and digital currencies.

More specifically, Chapter 1 describes the coming revolution in banking. Entering the workforce in the aftermath of the 2007–2008 financial crisis, millennials will have to cope with stagnating or declining household income, an unstable economy, a job market impacted by a new digital economy, and elevated housing prices—a perfect storm. Many have started their careers with low savings, high student debt, and unstable self-employment incomes. They will struggle to save for property purchases and pensions. Many new emerging financial services (fintech) have been designed to solve these new challenges—by, for example, offering more convenience, new ways to save money despite unstable job income, and improved access to credit.

Chapter 2 first briefly considers four major economic revolutions, the fourth of which we are experiencing today, and discusses the dramatic impact of the 2007–2008 global financial crisis on the general economic environment. We then look at how the world's banking sector is being dramatically transformed by new and innovative technologies that are likely to have a lasting impact on banks. By the end of the chapter, readers will have a satellite view of the fintech terrain, a good orientation for the deeper analysis in subsequent chapters.

Chapter 3 demonstrates how services like "robo-advisors" make investing easier and more affordable for people with limited financial literacy and little or no investment exposure. This chapter also discusses the changing landscape of health care and retirement financing, along with the cost and performance differences between robo-advisors and human advisors. It also presents a thorough and nuanced picture of fintech products being developed by entrepreneurs, venture investors, and traditional financial specialists.

Chapter 4 concentrates on how governments at all levels need to modernize fiscal policies to be aligned with the new era of peer-to-peer employment platforms and cross-border digital commerce. Blockchain, already adopted by large banks and start-ups, offers a great backbone for centralizing and managing citizen data, simplifying back-office processes, tracking government-public financials, and taxing transactions. Opportunities for better services are vast, and some countries, such as Estonia and the UAE, have embraced the digitalization of their government processes and interactions with citizens.

Chapter 5 explores the interconnections between economic development and inequalities, thereby providing the macroeconomic context for more-specific analysis of fintech in subsequent chapters. It focuses on the issue of the unbanked population in emerging economies and explains the relationship of financial inclusion to broader social and political phenomena. Examples from South Africa, China, and Colombia illustrate the importance of policy efforts to help broaden access to financial services as an economy develops.

Chapter 6 provides detailed analyses of the current development of financial services in emerging markets and the unfulfilled needs of the population. The chapter specifically focuses on how essential it is to fulfill these needs in order for individuals to climb out of poverty. We explore how fintech companies such as Paytm, Jumia, and Lazada have managed to design new products and models to offer low-cost financial services even to people in the most remote rural areas.

Chapter 7 addresses the specific fintech tools that governments of emerging economies can deploy to promote economic growth and financial inclusion. Governments can use private-sector innovations—digitization, blockchain, and artificial intelligence are examples—to foster greater financial inclusion, improve public service payments, expand government identity documentation, and distribute wealth and social welfare benefits. As we demonstrate, there is an inextricable link between digitized payments and the quality of publicly delivered services such as roads, electricity, and health care facilities.

Chapter 8 focuses on the digitization of money, including an analysis of twentieth-century innovation and the more recent rapid growth of global digital payment systems. It describes the strategic battle between banks, card companies, and tech innovators as the mobile phone becomes the next credit card. For this chapter and for Chapter 9, we did an exclusive survey of over 3,600 customers in China, France, Germany, Italy, the UK, and the United States, some of the results of which are given in Appendixes A and B.

Chapter 9 provides a detailed overview of digital currencies, including Bitcoin, Facebook's Diem, and sovereign digital currencies in India and China. It explores the factors that are moving these currencies into the mainstream and what is at stake for regulators. Overall, this chapter provides the reader with an understanding of the latest issues that will shape currencies and payments by 2030.

Covid-19: A Catalyst for Fintech Transitions

As we finalized this book in early 2020, we were confined in our homes and teaching courses online rather than at Harvard's campus in Cambridge, Massachusetts. We could not foresee all the ways the pandemic would change the world, but we knew there would be a "before and an after."

With regard to fintech, we could already witness profound changes in the way people were handling payments. Many governments saw cash as a potential transmitter of Covid-19. The Federal Reserve quarantined physical dollars flowing into the United States from Asia to avoid spreading the pathogen. China and South Korea quarantined and disinfected banknotes to stem the spread of the virus. Concern over spreading the disease caused many people to increasingly use contactless payment methods. Even the elderly, who typically shun technological change, began to use new forms of fintech.

Based on what we see today, we think that Covid-19 will be a catalyst for bringing digital payment methods into mainstream use. In Asia, and specifically in China, the pandemic may accelerate trends among younger populations to switch to digital payments. China's electronic payment system is relatively advanced. At of the end of 2020, around 86 percent of internet users in China used online payments services (up from 18 percent in 2008).

In advanced economies, elderly people are most at risk of contracting the virus, but also the most attached to cash. Extreme circumstances and fear may push them to try card payments, increase their use of e-commerce, and reduce in-store purchases. The hardest step toward change is always the first, but once people have tried a new technology or service, they are often quick to adopt it permanently.

The coronavirus may accelerate efforts by governments to deploy central bank digital currencies (CBDCs), a topic we discuss extensively in Chapter 9. In early 2021, 86 percent of central banks were working on a government-operated digital currency, 60 percent were experimenting with proofs of concept for a CBDC, and 14 percent, mostly in emerging economies, were running pilot projects. Central banks in China and India, where one-fifth of the world's population resides, are likely to issue a general-purpose, government-authorized digital currency in the near future.

At the time of this writing, we are in the middle of the storm, but economists are forecasting a deep global recession and governments have already announced massive stimulus packages to preserve companies and workers. The US Federal Reserve has contemplated using a "digital dollar" and digital wallet to send payments to individuals and businesses. Extraordinary circumstances and the need for fast responses will force governments to rethink the distribution of social transfers.

Nobody has a crystal ball, but we can assume that today's extreme circumstances will catalyze change. The 2008 financial crisis is an example; it acted as an enabler for innovative companies to launch and thrive. Likewise, the coronavirus crisis may act as a catalyst, or perhaps a fertilizer, for these technologies to become mainstream.

Despite many uncertainties, it is clear that fintech will continue to cause massive changes in the world's economies and cultures.

CHAPTER ONE

Millennials—The Subprime Generation?

Following the 2007–2008 financial crisis, advanced economies have been constrained by monetary policy, strained finances, and low productivity growth. Middle-class wages have been stagnating over the last decade. In this chapter we provide a snapshot of the current macroeconomic context in which low economic growth, low productivity, difficult-to-access credit, low savings levels, and high housing prices coexist.

In this context, in which a large number of young people face severe economic burdens and more unstable income, a new generation of financial services has emerged. It is no coincidence that most of the new fintech giants we will discuss in this book have emerged in the few years following the financial crisis.

The Subprime Generation?

In this section we will analyze in detail the changes in the economic environment between two generations and how it impacts the Millennials' financial planning.

The Great Middle-Class Stagnation

After World War II, the US and European middle-classes experienced a long period of increased purchasing power. Just a few decades ago, most parents in these advanced economies believed their children would be better off than they were. This confidence rested on the fact that most Western households had benefited from strong economic growth and sustained employment. Specifically, the baby boom generation saw greater revenues and stronger social benefits than those received by their parents.

The economic situation of industrialized nations has been characterized by growing inequality, job insecurity, and income disparities. Over the past decade, incomes among the middle class, the largest group in advanced countries, have stagnated or declined (Figure 1.1). Given the lingering effects of the global fi-

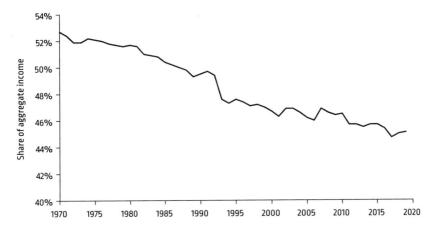

Data source: US Census Bureau, "Current Population Survey 2020: Annual Social and Economic (ASEC) Supplement," https://www.census.gov/data/tables/time-series/demo/income-poverty/historical-income-households.html.

FIGURE 1.1   Share of aggregate income going to the middle 60 percent of households

nancial crisis, as well as the current political environment, we should not expect any near-term reversal of this trend.

During the global recession and financial crisis, economic growth contracted, unemployment significantly increased, and median incomes diminished as a result. Since 2008, purchasing power has significantly dropped, wages have stagnated, and the middle class has experienced a declining share of national income.[1]

Detailed McKinsey household survey data collected from twenty-five advanced economies show that the incomes of 98 percent of households increased between 1993 and 2005. However, between 2005 and 2014, incomes rose for only one-third of households; the remaining two-thirds saw incomes stagnate or decline. These figures vary significantly between countries. For instance, between 2005 and 2014, the income share grew for 37 percent of citizens in France, 19 percent of citizens in the United States, and 3 percent of citizens in Italy. In stark contrast, 80 percent of households in Sweden experienced rising incomes. The study confirms that the (relative) "losers" of this period were people in the middle and lower segments of country income distributions; the "winners" were among the top 1 percent globally.[2]

Long-term structural trends have also played a considerable role in driving inequalities. We need a deeper understanding of those structural trends—such as why companies find it profitable to relocate and outsource abroad—to understand the recent history of economic inequality. We will examine them in the following pages.

First, trade and financial barriers have declined. At least two components contribute to higher demand for foreign labor. The skills of foreign workers and their ability to replace domestic workers are a function of trade and financial openness, each of which has changed within the period under consideration. This is in part due to the actions of the World Trade Organization. Second, as the labor markets of more-advanced economies have evolved, demand for low- or medium-skill workers has declined. This is partly explained by the rise of technology, and partly by the fact that companies have relocated abroad and outsourced work to lower-cost laborers. Thus, over the past decade, low- and medium-skill workers have faced stagnating or decreasing wages, whereas highly skilled workers have seen their wages increase.

The demographic landscape has changed significantly in advanced economies. The percentage of elderly people is growing due to increased life expectancy and low fertility rates. This results in a reduced number of working-age people and therefore less revenue to fund the economy. This also increases governments' expenditures on benefits, particularly around health care and pensions. Recent indebtedness and other public financial constraints have added to the demographic shift and severely limited the ability of governments to increase social benefits and transfers.[3]

Sweden is an outlying example. Sweden has been very successful at reversing the great stagnation trend. As mentioned above, incomes increased for 80 percent of Swedish households between 2005 and 2014. The government reformed its system, mainly in response to the crisis in the early 1990s, by reducing taxes on capital, income, and labor in order to encourage work and investment. Along with other measures, these actions increased the flexibility of the pension system.

Governments in some advanced countries, specifically in Europe where pensions are public, have started to cope with this new demographic shift and challenging economic environment. They have readjusted and decreased social benefits. For example, some countries have raised or indexed the retirement wage, and increased the pension contribution rates paid by retired people.

An aging population implies (a) lower fiscal revenues from the working population, (b) higher spending on public pensions, and (c) higher spending on health care. The combination of these three factors will make it increasingly difficult for governments to maintain the same social benefits for the millennial generation. Millennials will need to proactively ensure proper private savings as a substitute for lower public contributions. This will not be easy in light of student loan debt levels and unstable employment situations.

The Housing Lift Is Out of Service

After the dot-com bubble of the early 2000s, the US Federal Reserve maintained low interest rates. This, in addition to the "savings glut" created by commodity-producing countries that stored reserves, provided ample market liquidity. The excess liquidity was invested, which contributed to the increase of several asset prices. Between the mid-1980s and 2008, most asset classes exhibited limited volatility. Leading economists, such as Harvard University's James Stock, Princeton University's Mark Watson, and later Ben Bernanke (who served two terms as chairman of the Federal Reserve, from 2006 to 2014) called this period the "Great Moderation."

However, the underlying risk of mortgage assets at the time were highly underestimated by ratings agencies that granted the best ratings to several mortgage-backed securities. In *Irrational Exuberance,* published in 2005, Yale University professor and Nobel Prize–winning economist Robert Shiller explained that the housing boom in large US metropolitan areas had little to do with economic fundamentals and no precedent in real estate history. Nonetheless, in the early 2000s housing prices crept upward as people began investing heavily in real estate.[4]

Shiller highlighted that median home prices were valued at up to nine times the median income in some areas of the United States. He warned about "the enormous home price boom that many countries were experiencing." Cheap access to credit encouraged many to refinance their homes or take out a new loan against their home equity, which was likely invested years before at a lower value and then partially or fully repaid. Remortgaging a home often generated large amounts of cash that could be reinvested for buying a new home.[5]

A recent survey on international housing affordability demonstrates how the above-mentioned factors have made cities less affordable. Hong Kong has seen its median multiple increase from 11.4 at the end of 2010 to 20.7 at the end of 2020, making it by far the least affordable city in the world. The same trend can be observed in Vancouver (13.0), Sydney (11.8), and Auckland (10.0), cities where median multiples have all increased since 2010.[6]

The repercussions of the housing bubble and subsequent credit crunch can still be felt today. The increase in post–World War II housing prices led to high prices compared to salaries, despite the 2008 credit crunch. Loan terms have tightened since the bank crisis and borrowers now expect to pay larger down payments. Banks also more closely scrutinize the total indebtedness of individuals. Consequently, millennials face even more constraints. They typically have less savings, in part because they are more likely to owe student loans. According to the National Association of Realtors, the median age of US homeowners increased from forty-two to forty-five years old between 2012 and 2017.[7]

In the United Kingdom in 2015–2016, there were 654,000 first-time-buyer households. This was a slight decrease from 2005 to 2006 (675,000 households) and a large fall from 1995–1996 (922,000 households). Like the United States, the age of the UK's first buyers is rising. Because two incomes are often required to buy property, many people buy with a partner. First-time buyers need higher incomes and more help to fund down payments—an average cost of $70,000—than people needed twenty years ago.[8]

To make matters more difficult, the economic fundamentals that normally lead to increased home values have significantly weakened. First, urbanization is now mostly complete in advanced economies and demographic growth has slowed down significantly (enough for housing demand to drop). Second, global economic growth has slowed significantly and will likely stabilize at a fraction of what it was in the previous century. Third, interest rates are currently at or near zero in many advanced economies, making it likely that they will rise. It will be the job of policymakers to determine how quickly and to what extent interest rates should be increased.

So, despite a few exceptions in certain areas with unusual dynamics, house prices will not benefit from the same tailwind that people enjoyed in the past. Housing will become increasingly difficult to afford, making it harder to invest in a home early in life as part of one's wealth creation plans.

A New Way of Life

Technology is revolutionizing job markets and the way people live. It's possible that artificial intelligence and robotics will eliminate many jobs, especially in industrialized countries. The labor market in these countries is experiencing massive shifts, changes that could leave the most fragile part of the population behind.

Since the post-recession economic recovery, more than 99 percent of job growth went to workers with more than a high school education. Workers with a high school diploma or less saw virtually no jobs recovery. Out of the 11.6 million US jobs created in the post-recession economy, 11.5 million jobs went to workers with at least some college education. People with graduate degrees gained 3.8 million jobs, those with bachelor's degrees gained 4.6 million jobs, and those with an associate degree gained 3.1 million. By contrast, workers with a high school diploma or less gained only eighty-thousand jobs.

These trends among low-education workers are partly explained by increased technological innovation and abundantly cheap foreign labor. Wages for employees with low education levels stagnated or decreased over the past decade, whereas wages for highly skilled workers grew. The situation is not expected to improve. The Bureau of Labor Statistics estimates that automation could take 55 percent of the jobs currently executed by a person without a high school degree, 52 percent of the jobs now conducted by those with a high school degree and work experience, and 44 percent of the jobs now filled by those with some postsecondary education. By contrast, automation may take only 22 percent of the jobs performed now by those with a bachelor's or graduate degree.

Unfortunately, education costs have continued to rise. In 1997–1998 in the United States, tuition per year averaged $16,233 for private colleges, $8,840 for out-of-state students at public universities, and $3,168 for in-state students at public universities. In 2017–2018 these figures were $41,727, $26,010, and $10,691, respectively. Stated another way, the average tuition rose by 157 percent for private colleges, 194 percent for out-of-state students at public universities, and 237 percent for in-state students. These education prices will most likely remain a barrier against those trying to enter college and make it more difficult for students hoping to pay tuition long enough to graduate. Can technology and web-based training counterbalance this trend? Perhaps. Many expect that the next model of education will emerge from online education.[9]

The Global Freelance Network

The number of freelance workers around the world is increasing as worker mentalities change and as people seek more job flexibility. The rise of the freelance workforce is also blurring the lines between clients and contributors, workers and consumers. This is the new era of the networked economy.

Besides the trend favoring high-skill workers (mentioned earlier), the increased use of flexible employment contracts is fundamentally shifting the labor market. Companies are now more open to hiring independent contractors instead of full-time employees. As a result, the number of freelancers has exploded over the last decade. Estimates of the size of the US freelance workforce vary, ranging from 20 percent to about 34 percent of the total working population, depending on the precise definition of "freelance." Regardless, these workers use an increasing number of freelance platforms (UBER, Upwork, and so on). The share of independent workers is expected to rise even more. Similar trends can be observed across Europe and elsewhere.[10]

Several factors are driving this trend. First, on the supply side, the peer-to-peer economy has created jobs for a wide range of skills, in many locations, and on a flexible basis, but governments have been unable to create such jobs. On the demand side, increased job competition has made workers less able to be selective in the jobs they accept. In other words, there is an increased likelihood that people will take "parking jobs" while they wait for something better. This also contributes to the surge in independent contractor jobs with less career visibility and shorter contracts.

Because the "gig" economy relies on freelance contracts, workers have no income security or employer benefits, such as health insurance, pension plans, and maternity leave. Temporary contracts are very convenient for companies, but they raise legitimate concerns for workers—that the lack of security will become the "new normal." Labor market migration and contract flexibility weaken the bankability of the young generation and increase risks related to future career and income.

The Big Job Migration

In many ways the insecurity of freelance workers today is not unique. Throughout history, new technologies have stoked fear and indignation. In 1589 Queen Elizabeth I expressed her reluctance to grant a patent to the inventor of the stocking frame because she feared it would have a negative impact on the welfare of knitters. In the early nineteenth century, textile workers in the United Kingdom and France protested the arrival of steam-powered presses. The term *Luddites*— meaning people who fear new technologies—derives from the anti-technology protests of Luddites in Nottingham, England, in 1811, and of Canuts in 1831 in Lyon, France. Luddites fought against the implementation of textile machinery during the Industrial Revolution.[11]

Economists David Ricardo, Karl Marx, and John Maynard Keynes also expressed concern about the impact of technology on employment. In the early nineteenth century, Ricardo worried that machines would make labor redundant. In the 1850s, Karl Marx envisioned a world in which labor would be transformed by "an automatic system of machinery." And in 1930, John Maynard Keynes coined the term "technological unemployment" to describe jobs lost to technological advancement. Keynes promoted state intervention as a means of overcoming persistent technological unemployment. In the 1970s—the golden age of capitalism—several works were published that warned against technological unemployment, including *Peoples' Capitalism: The Economics of the Robot Revolution* by James S. Albus in 1976, and Jeremy Rifkin's *The End of Work* in 1995.[12]

Technology has forced workers into major geographical migrations. For example, the first industrial revolution forced many people to move from the country into cities as the share of agricultural employment sharply declined. Agriculture accounted for 58 percent of total employment in 1850. Today it accounts for only 2.5 percent. Workers in other sectors, such as miners and household workers, were less affected by mechanization.

In other cases, technology has required workers to shift into entirely new types of work, such as when populations moved from manufacturing and toward the service sector. Since 1960, manufacturing employment has fallen from 27 percent of total US employment to 9 percent today. This sharp decline was caused mainly by automation and a surge in global trade as competition from lower-income countries increased. The rising demand for services transformed the manufacturing sector.[13]

Historical examination shows that new technologies raise productivity growth, enabling firms to lower consumer prices, pay higher wages, and distribute profits to shareholders. Thus, they stimulate demand across the economy and lead to job creation. Following this trend, the overall effect of mechanization has been job creation. Employment has grown over the past few decades, even with the increased size of the workforce. In the United States, for instance, the number of women entering the workforce increased twofold (working age women constituted only 32 percent of the workforce in 1950 compared to 60 percent in the late 1990s).

There is strong evidence of a positive correlation between productivity, technology, and employment. At the macro-economic level, we observe that technology often increases employment, which also typically raises productivity. However, it is also true that, at the industry level, mechanization and automation can lead to job destruction (Figure 1.2). For instance, Daron Acemoglu and Pascual Restrepo (2017) have shown that for every industrial robot employed, six US workers in surrounding metropolitan areas lose their jobs.

This chain of events can be explained as follows: Automation raises productivity; the aggregate workforce and/or shareholder income rises; consumption increases due to higher ability to pay for goods and services across the economy. Thus, productivity gains ultimately create more jobs than they destroy. It is a cycle with bidirectional causality. However, these technological advances also force workers to migrate from one industry/sector to another, as we discussed earlier.[14]

Innovation's Gains and Losses

It is still difficult to predict what will create the next generation of jobs. History shows that it is easier to identify initial job destruction than to foresee the wider ecosystem that innovation creates.

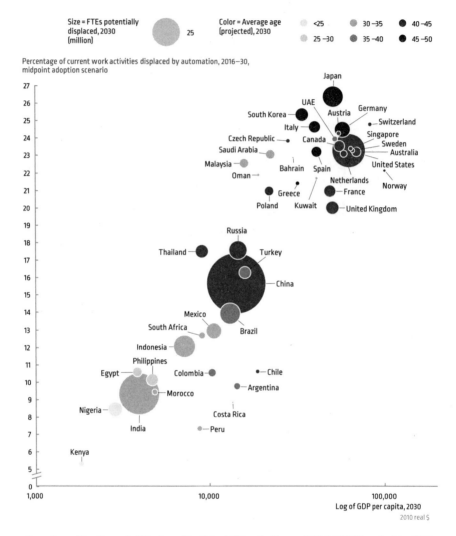

Size = FTEs potentially displaced, 2030 (million) 25

Color = Average age (projected), 2030   <25   25–30   30–35   35–40   40–45   45–50

Percentage of current work activities displaced by automation, 2016–30, midpoint adoption scenario

Log of GDP per capita, 2030
2010 real $

FIGURE 1.2   Impact of automation, by country income level

The first microcomputer, the Micral N, was patented in 1973 by François Gernelle. Ever since, microcomputing has been at the heart of tertiary economic activity. It is no longer about the material that one works on, but about the production, transformation, dissemination, and storage of information. Productivity of the United States rose at an annual pace of 1 to 1.5 percent since the early 1970s, and it steadily averaged 2.9 percent between 1995 and 2000. Many economists, including Alan Greenspan, credit the increased workplace productivity to computer technology.[15]

In *Jobs Lost, Jobs Gained: Workforce Transitions in a Time of Automation,* published in 2017, the McKinsey Global Institute estimated that computers created 15.8 million net jobs since 1970 in the United States, or 10 percent of the 2015 civilian labor force. In total, 3.5 million jobs were lost while 19.3 million were created.

The personal computer first eliminated the need for some workers who specialized in editing and retyping documents. Demand for jobs related to typewriter manufacturing, secretarial work, and bookkeeping declined. Typists and secretary positions in the United States, for example, fell by 1.4 million between 1990 to 2015.

However, the personal computer also created millions of jobs across a wide range of occupations and sectors. Jobs in manufacturing and semiconductors represented 1 percent and 3 percent of the net jobs created, respectively. Businesses that relied on computers (customer service call centers, e-commerce) created many jobs.[16] But computers created the largest share (18 percent) of new net jobs. They include professions such as computer scientists, IT system administrators, and app developers. Today's computer software and service companies (such as IBM, Microsoft, and Oracle) employ 3 million people in the United States alone.

There is an entire ecosystem of people manufacturing computers and programming software to solve problems and improve efficiency. We can offer new services thanks to software that enables web communication, online booking, and so on. These technologies have also paved the way for other technology revolutions, such as video games, e-commerce, and new business models.

The next revolution may do more than displace low-skill workers; it could influence the way high-skill professionals at the "top of the food chain" do their work. For example, radiologists in the late 1980s had to examine 20 to 50 images for each CT and PET scan. Now there can be as many as 1,000 images captured per scan. Examining those images can be tedious for radiologists, who are prone to errors. Artificial intelligence could act as a diagnostic aid by flagging specific images and thereby allowing radiologists to use their time more efficiently. In other words, future solutions need not be binary (either human or machine). Instead, we will certainly see humans and machines working together.

There is ample reason to expect that many jobs will involve humans and machines, but some jobs will certainly be lost. To what extent? The answer will depend on the type of job and how easily it can be mechanized.

The first, and easiest, category to automate will be jobs that include "deductive computer processing" based on logic and algorithms. A large share of jobs in this category can already be automated by computer processing, such as printing boarding passes or calculating basic taxes.

The second category deals with inductive computer processing based on probability forecasting. Such systems can predict the risk of housing defaults. Although this category is more complex than deductive computer processing, the technology is gaining momentum. Call centers that use voice recognition and probability forecasting are already being replaced with machines that ask questions and recognize responses.

The third and most challenging job category deals with code principles, which is primarily a domain of humans. This category remains the most difficult to automate because it deals with complex environments, such as moving furniture into a third-floor apartment or writing a convincing legal speech. This type of work requires more complex coding and machine learning techniques.

Today's automation technologies threaten both low- and high-skill workers. The largest disruptions are expected in advanced economies. Occupations such as office support will be hard hit. Clerks and administrative assistants are being replaced by AI scheduling tools. However, not all jobs have a technology equivalent. A personal assistant with the ability to book multiple meetings, arrange travel tickets, and take care of personal tasks is unlikely to be replaced with AI soon. Services for aging populations are expected to increase, and robots lack the emotional capabilities needed to interact with others. Thus, positions that rely on human interaction (psychologists or family doctors) and offering personal counsel won't be replaced by AI, at least not in the near future. Moreover, most new jobs—such as creatives, managers and executives, and care providers—will require human interaction and relationships.[17]

Automation will likely reduce the number of middle-income jobs. However, low-wage jobs (childcare workers, nursing assistants, retail salespeople) and high-income jobs (software engineers) are likely to persist and expand. This suggests that income polarization and inequality could worsen in advanced, high-income economies where labor is more expensive. High-wage countries, such as Japan and Germany, will be more significantly impacted by automation.[18]

In emerging economies, the opposite effect will probably occur. More jobs will be created among middle-income workers in the service sector and in the construction industry. As the middle class grows, more demand for middle-class jobs will be created. Educational requirements will also increase, which will increase the percentage of workers who have a secondary education.

Location is another variable that will affect how many jobs are lost, changed, or created. Jobs that can be relocated to emerging economies will likely be transferred out of advanced economies. Thus, careers in countries with advanced economies are more likely to require an advanced degree.

Students for Life

Big Data companies are (a) improving, accelerating, and streamlining decision-making processes across management levels within large organizations; (b) making jobs for well-educated people more interesting; and (c) eliminating white-collar jobs among people who invested heavily in MBAs, medical, accounting, and law degrees.

White-collar workers will be impacted also by the increasing number of people who speak English around the world. Approximately 1.5 billion people— 20 percent of the global population—speak English.[19] This fact, along with the internet (remote working) will give companies the opportunity to seek workers from abroad at lower costs. The number of cross-cultural exchange students and summer school programs has risen over the past thirty years. The London School of Economics has expanded its summer schools to Beijing (run by Peking University) and to Cape Town, South Africa (run by the University of Cape Town). Harvard University is running summer schools in France, Italy, China, Japan, South Korea, Senegal, and Argentina. In pursuit of educational advancement, people around the world are taking online courses from anywhere in the world. Examples include the Harvard Extension School, EdX, Coursera, and other Massive Open Online Courses (MOOCs). As a result of these trends, all workers will need to constantly pursue more education and knowledge.

To adapt this new economy, our workforces must be willing and able to transition and retrain. People in all occupational sectors will need to invest time to learn new skills. Future work activities will require more advanced social, emotional, creative, and reasoning capabilities. Conversely, fewer workers will be needed in routine, predictable, physical activities, such as food preparation or basic data-processing positions that can easily be automated.[20] As stated earlier, jobs that require a low level of education have a higher likelihood of becoming automated.

How does one gain job security in the age of automation? Through educational attainment. We cannot be certain what specific new jobs will be created, but it is nearly certain that tomorrow's occupations will require a highly skilled and adaptable workforce. In advanced economies, educational requirements will increase, resulting in a greater proportion of the workforce seeking advanced education.

Coming Next: Welcome Back Subprime?

As we have seen, millennials are entering the workforce in a new economic context. As a result, their borrowing and saving potentials are much lower than those of previous generations and their income is more volatile, which makes them a far less bankable "subprime generation."

Prohibiting subprime loans may have made banking safer, but it has also exacerbated the problem of financial inclusion. Even in developed economies, a non-negligible part of the population has little or no access to financial services. Millions of people (not only millennials) in advanced economies lack bank accounts. In 2015, 7 percent of households did not have access to a checking or savings account. This suggests that about 15.6 million adults and 7.6 million children in the United States were unbanked. These individuals cited their main reasons for not having a bank account, in order of importance: lack of money; no perceived need for a bank account; only allowed to share an account held by another family member; account fees too expensive; long distance from financial institution; lack of necessary documentation; lack of trust in the financial institution; and religious views.[21]

In the European Union, according to MasterCard, 139 million adult citizens remained financially excluded in 2016, which is about 19 percent of the total population. The study emphasized that 35 percent of financially excluded people were in the age group eighteen to thirty-four, 33 percent were employed full time, 12 percent were retired, 9 percent were students, and 87 percent, surprisingly, had lived in one country their entire lives. According to the World Bank's Global Findex, Romania suffers the highest no-account rate (39 percent), followed by Bulgaria (37 percent), Slovakia (23 percent), Hungary (28 percent), and Poland (22 percent).[22]

So, What Does It All Mean?

This first chapter brings some context to Chapters 2–4. First, we have seen that the financial crisis has significantly weakened banks and has slowed the process of consolidation that previously led people to believe that large banks were "too big to fail." It has left significant room in the system for new entrants. Chapter 2 will discuss the profound changes to the financial services sector, changes that are forcing banks to adapt and leading to the emergence of new players.

Second, we have highlighted the challenges of a fast-changing job market in developed countries. The current technological revolution is displacing jobs and moving more traditional employer–employee contracts toward freelancing and a "pay-by-the-task" relationship. Chapter 3 outlines how these changes in the job market can affect individual savings and the new digital solutions that are emerging to facilitate financial planning in the twenty-first century.

Last but not the least, we show that governments are being disrupted on two fronts. First, they need to adapt their approaches to data gathering and fiscal policy to the changing job market. Second, most of the disruptions impacting banks' back offices (automation, blockchain) are transferable to government functions, such as tax collections, identity administration and official documents, and distribution of social benefits. Chapter 4 will highlight the profound mutation of government services in the digital age.

CHAPTER TWO

Banking in the Digital Era

In this chapter we explore how digital banking could replace the traditional banking system and will examine some of the most significant recent financial innovations, such as microcredit, crowd lending, peer-to-peer lending, and crowdfunding. We will also offer a broad and analytical view of the "uberization" of retail banking; specifically, how the evolution of banking has affected the costs and risks associated with financial transactions, and how fintech has synergistically boosted economic productivity within the finance industry and beyond.

The Four Industrial Revolutions

In the West, three "industrial revolutions" paved the way for our present era— an era of digital, Internet revolution. A brief history of these three socioeconomic disruptions can help us comprehend the ways in which fintech innovation is situated in history, and how fintech might impact the future.

The first industrial revolution occurred in western European economies during the eighteenth century. Abundant and cheap coal, combined with a supportive institutional environment, were critical conditions for this era's mechanization advancements. These conditions, together with financial reforms, led to the emergence of large factories and corporations, such as the Marshall Mill in Leeds, and the stock market that financed companies.

During the second industrial revolution, in the late nineteenth and early twentieth centuries, the United States led the way in mass production, which was energized by the invention of the combustion engine, electricity, the telegraph, and production assembly lines. World-renowned companies such as Ford, Goodyear, ExxonMobil, and Edison International emerged. During this period, railroads in the United States sparked an unprecedented social upheaval. They fueled a consumer economy and facilitated a massive population movement from rural areas into increasingly crowded cities. They connected the country from coast to coast and made the transportation of people and freight easier and cheaper. Railroads also reshaped the agricultural system, and eventually farmers found other work.

In the long run, however, the explosive growth of the railroad industry also yielded considerable new opportunities. Waves of new, well-paying jobs emerged for an expanding working class and spurred the rapid growth of other industrial sectors. For instance, the metallurgy industry boomed to meet the demand for iron rails and coal-powered steam locomotives. The coal mining industry grew exponentially. The labor demand for laying thousands of miles of track and staffing trains, depots, and company offices also grew rapidly.

The third industrial revolution, which was characterized by automation and computerization, began in the mid-twentieth century. Deep capital markets and intellectual property rights, established by the World Intellectual Property Organization in the 1960s, facilitated the creation and global expansion of firms like IBM, Microsoft, Apple, and Google.

After the train and the telephone, perhaps the most powerful innovation to disrupt and improve our modern world has been the Internet. In little more than a generation it has completely reshaped or even replaced most traditional communication platforms, including the telephone, radio, television, the print media and especially paper mail and the conventional postal system. The Internet has given rise to a set of entirely new communication services, such as blogging, social networks, and video-streaming websites. Online shopping has grown exponentially for major retailers, small businesses, and entrepreneurs. This has enabled firms to extend beyond their "brick and mortar" presence to serve a larger, often global market, and even to sell goods and services entirely online. More recently, online marketplaces and peer-to-peer platforms have disintermediated entire industries, matching buyers with sellers on a massive scale.

This fourth industrial revolution, which is still under way, has enabled the rise of gigantic transformational companies like Google, Amazon, Facebook, Apple, and Alibaba. While these examples are the largest and best known of the new tech companies, CBInsights reports that over 700 privately held Internet "unicorns" valued at $1 billion or more have emerged as of July 2021.

Today's digital revolution is driven by advances in data collection and management, and artificial intelligence (AI). At the heart of the digital revolution are new financial technologies. Also known as *fintech*, these technologies are profoundly transforming the way businesses, governments, and individuals interact economically.[1]

Finance Reborn

With that broad historical context in mind, it is important to focus on how the 2007–2008 financial crisis increased fintech's influence in the global economy. That financial crisis transformed the banking sector and shook the foundations of the financial industry. The market capitalization of several large financial institutions and insurance companies plummeted, forcing them to merge or go bankrupt. Governments responded to the crisis by imposing new banking regulations, and banks responded with innovations to serve consumers. As a result, the crisis upended old ways of organizing and operating banks.

Seeing cracks in the traditional system, some investors turned to new financial technology companies. We will further address the reasons they pursued fintech solutions later in this chapter. For now, it is important to say that the 2008 pivot toward fintech has since propelled another wave of disruptive fintech innovations, such as Stripe (online payments), SoFi (a lending platform), and Alipay (online payments in China). In part because of fintech, the financial industry has discovered new vistas.

The swell of economic turmoil, new regulations, and innovation during and after the crisis has perhaps revealed a deeper transition in the financial sector. That transition is driven by unprecedented industry innovations, including the rise of digital payments, cryptocurrencies, and alternative forms of banking—all of which pose systemic risks to the financial sector.

Earthquake Aftermath

Prior to the financial crisis, the markets peaked in the early 2000s. The five major investment banks—Goldman Sachs, Merrill Lynch, Morgan Stanley, Lehman Brothers, and Bear Stearns—also experienced significant market cap increase. These investment banks and others were involved in "securitizing" mortgages. They pooled mortgages distinguished by default risk into tranches and then traded these securities to other investors. Large insurance companies also participated in this kind of lending practice. The underlying justification was the belief that pooling high-risk mortgages into one asset would reduce risk and therefore make the asset more valuable. In retrospect, it is hard to comprehend how this could have occurred, but few believed that all the underlying mortgages *could* default. Tragically, the unfathomable occurred. The countless assets contingent on those mortgages became worthless.

*   *   *

The mortgages underlying those securities did, in fact, collapse in 2007 when house prices stabilized. Because the mortgage-backed securities constituted a significant portion of many banks' balance sheets, the systemic consequences were far reaching. In 2008, Bear Stearns and Lehman Brothers, two of the five Bulge Bracket Banks, went bankrupt, as did American International Group (AIG), the largest insurance company in the United States. On the weekend when Bear Stearns went bankrupt, Bank of America acquired Merrill Lynch. Within a month, Goldman Sachs and Morgan Stanley became regulated commercial banks. By November 2008 none of the Bulge Bracket investment banks remained. The world experienced the largest economic downturn since the Great Depression.

One root of the problem was that lenders granted mortgages to people who had little or no means of paying the mortgage, especially if housing prices fell. As house prices steadily climbed in the early 2000s, banks lowered their lending standards. Some waived income verifications or down payments. NINJA loans (no job, no income, no assets) became common. Banks, investment banks, and rating agencies all accepted large fees to create securitizations. The repurchase agreement "repo" market, traditionally based on US Treasuries, grew so fast that it began to run out of securities. Public policy encouraged, even demanded, lenders to grant more loans to lower-income borrowers. These risky mortgages were employed to "support" the value of the tranches of securities.

In retrospect, we can identify three main contributing factors behind the 2008 crisis: falling capital risk, rising repo haircuts, and increased counterparty risk. As people in the financial sector saw danger ahead, the market responded with four mechanisms by which the global crisis unfolded.

The first mechanism relates to liquidity spirals. As the assets on banks' balance sheets decreased, lenders restricted credit. This, in turn, pushed asset prices down and caused a downward spiral. Second, risk-averse banks began to increase reserves and restrict lending access to capital markets. Third, Lehman Brothers and Bear Stearns faced "bank runs" as investors rapidly withdrew massive amounts of capital. That resulted in a multiplier effect that shook public confidence in the overall banking system. Finally, concerns over counterparty risk—defined as the likelihood or probability that one of those involved in a transaction might default on its contractual obligation—led to systemic gridlock. The ensuing panic had consequences beyond subprime bonds. It created "genuine fears about the location of subprime risk concentrations among counterparties."[2]

In response to the financial crisis, governments chose to provide bailouts to financial institutions they deemed "too big to fail." They believed that these bailouts would prevent further deterioration of the entire financial system and spare citizens from greater harm. In the United States, bailouts were offered to AIG, Fannie Mae, and Freddie Mac. The US government also created the Troubled Asset Relief Program (TARP) and passed the 2008 Emergency Economic Stability Act to purchase $700 billion of impaired bank assets. Through one new program or another, the Federal Reserve eventually supported nearly every major financial institution. Even foreign banks received indirect bailouts. The Federal Reserve rapidly went from a simple balance sheet and a very conservative policy to unprecedented interventionist measures. The Fed's balance sheet also grew 500 percent to $4.5 trillion. The balance sheet, at the time of this writing, remains close to this level.

The government then increased spending, as part of its expansionary fiscal policy, to stimulate a GDP rebound. It also enacted further policy measures to prevent a future crisis. In 2010, Congress passed the Dodd-Frank Wall Street Reform and Consumer Protection Act. Among other things, this act gave the Financial Stability Oversight Council the ability to break up banks that contributed to systemic financial risk. The act also stipulated the Volcker Rule, which restricted a bank's ability to engage in speculative trading.

All of this had a profound impact on the financial industry. Banks never regained their former power.

Fertile Ground for Disruption

As a result of banking and financial services having been debilitated by the financial crisis, many new fintech players saw an opportunity to disrupt the financial sector. These firms have used digital technology to improve efficiency and reduce costs. In the last ten years, private investment in global fintech has multiplied (Figure 2.1). The top fintech investment destinations are led by China and the United States.

Investment in Asian fintech companies grew steadily to a record $8.6 billion in 2016. Within that context, fintech investors have focused mostly on China, in part because of China's influence in all of Asia. China has a chance to lead in AI because it adopts new technologies quickly;[3] traditional financing and investment opportunities are rather limited, both in China and abroad, which opens the door for fintech companies; a steady increase in housing prices has made investment in traditional risk assets riskier; and Chinese firms face limitations when investing overseas.[4]

Interestingly, more than half of China's total fintech investment so far has come from a single deal: the $4.5 billion funding round of Ant Financial (Alibaba's payment and lending division). Thus, while most countries have experi-

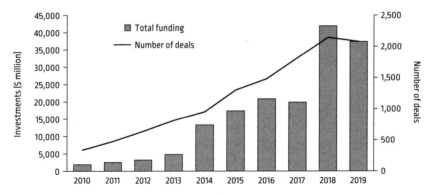

Data sources: CBInsights, "The State of Fintech Q2 2020 Report: Investors and Sector Trends to Watch," 2020, https://www.cbinsights.com/reports/CB-Insights_Fintech-Report-Q2-2020.pdf?utm_campaign=marketing _campaign_q3-2020_finserv&utm_medium=email&_hsmi=92686104&_hsenc=p2ANqtz-8AwkoBElatz BOQpwe-z4akad14Hp60SEWVg7Bdzukum0yyNA6SU9Lhaun5Y4x3gqm3XtaQdV1Big7noP0XxxBrMY F7kg&utm_content=92686104&utm_source=hs_automation; Business Wire, "Global Venture Capital Investment in Fintech Industry Set Record in 2017, Driven by Surge in India, US and UK, Accenture Analysis Finds," February 28, 2018, https://www.businesswire.com/news/home/20180227006642/en/Global-Venture -Capital-Investment-Fintech-Industry-Set.

Note: From 2010 to 2015, we used the data representing "deal value."

FIGURE 2.1   Global investment activity in global fintech companies

enced investment declines, China's fintech investment doubled in 2016, earning them a central place in the fintech market.

If we look beyond questions of geography, we see that fintech companies have been targeting four key technological areas: artificial intelligence, cybersecurity, blockchain, and disruptive insurance technologies (insurtech).

ARTIFICIAL INTELLIGENCE

Many menial tasks performed by financial professionals will soon be handled by computer algorithms. This will likely result in lower costs, higher quality, and more diverse financial product offerings. Entrepreneurs are creating new fintech companies that use machine learning and Big Data. These new online banking products include trading automation (high-frequency trading) and more efficient customer services, sometimes using robo-advisors.

CYBERSECURITY

AI has also exposed cybersecurity vulnerabilities, a reality that became particularly salient following the 2016 bank heist of Bangladesh's central bank via the

Swift payment system. Criminals stole $81 million, which at that time was the largest successful bank robbery in history. The financial sector's justifiable fear of losses has continued to drive increased investment in cybersecurity. In 2017, cybersecurity start-ups raised a record $7.7 billion across 552 deals, including a record of ten mega-deals worth more than $100 million. Among other deals, ForgeRock, the identity management start-up, announced an $88 million Series D investment. Cybereason, a Boston cybersecurity firm specializing in endpoint detection and response to digital security breaches, announced it had secured $100 million in funding. Signifyd, which specializes in preventing e-commerce fraud, closed a $56 million Series C investment.

BLOCKCHAIN

Blockchain, a nascent technology, works like a digital ledger that records financial (or other types of) transactions across a decentralized, openly shared network of computers. We will address blockchain's functions more in subsequent chapters. For now, it is important to know that opinions about blockchain are mixed. In 2016 the entire financial industry seemed euphoric about blockchain technology, but the hype has been increasingly replaced by a cautious and studious approach. Most large financial groups believe blockchain has the potential to revolutionize the financial industry. A few central banks have considered creating digital currencies based on blockchain technology. Several banks—including HSBC, Deutsche Bank, Rabobank, and Société Générale—have agreed to collaboratively develop blockchain technology for financial trading. One of the most successful initial digital coin offerings was Filecoin, a blockchain-based cryptocurrency and digital payment system located in the United States. It raised $257 million in 2017. Tezos, a new blockchain currency aiming to be more reliable than Bitcoin or Ethereum, raised $232 million in 2017. Sirin Labs, a Switzerland-based company that plans to build a blockchain-based smartphone, raised $157 million in 2017.[5]

INSURTECH

The term *insurtech,* denoting the combination of insurance and technology, designates all services and innovations that combine digital and insurance activity. Insurtech firms aim to serve the B2C segment (individuals, companies, professionals) and B2B (insurers, insurer banks, mutual, social protection groups). Insurance companies rely on digital technologies to introduce innovations that drive the emergence of new economic models, new processes, and new products. These models and products have the capacity to modify the behavior of all market players, policyholders, insurance intermediaries, insurers, and rein-surers—a profound transformation.

Digital disruption in the insurance sector lags behind the changes in other financial sectors. However, start-ups like so-sure, Friendsurance, Lemonade, Guevara, and Brolly have emerged with transformative sectoral models. Other companies have focused on operational efficiencies and cost-effectiveness. Further investment in insurtech is expected to continue as start-ups identify new needs and solutions.

We mentioned above that China has gained a leading role in developing and implementing fintech innovations. So next we look more closely at China's influence.

Will China Lead the Change?

The United States and China together host more than 80 percent of the world's unicorns. Late in 2019, China surpassed the United States to become the world's biggest hub for unicorns, becoming the fintech equivalent of Silicon Valley. The tech firms Xiaomi, Baidu, Didi Chuxing, Meituan, and Toutiao are all head-quartered in Beijing. China's e-commerce giant, Alibaba, is based in Hangzhou. Shenzhen is home to Tencent, a multinational conglomerate that is investing heavily in AI. Despite its relative youth, Tencent already has market capitaliza-tion higher than General Electric, and Baidu is larger than General Motors.[6] The two largest unicorns are Ant Financial, valued at about $200 billion, and Lu.com.

China's meteoric economic catch-up is often attributed to its ability to leap-frog innovative technologies, but this explanation does not account for China's impressive progress in finance and technology. Important cultural factors seem to be driving China's recent expansion. These include its ability to quickly adopt new technologies, its massive centralized business platforms, and its relatively weak privacy norms. Ironically, internal investment is aided because it is so dif-ficult for Chinese firms to make international investments.

China's ability to rapidly adopt new technologies may secure its spot as the global AI frontrunner. Just as millions of Indians skipped over landlines and flip phones to immediately adopt smartphones, Chinese consumers are bypassing older technologies and jumping directly to new technologies. For example, Chi-nese shoppers have skipped credit cards to embrace e-payment platforms. Al-though Apple Pay has not yet gained full momentum in the United States, its Chinese equivalent, Tencent, facilitates more than 600 million cashless trans-actions every month.

Tencent and other Chinese firms' massive, centralized platforms give them an edge in AI research and development. They have huge stores of data to train machine-learning algorithms. These platforms enjoy near-monopolistic power that will help China monetize applications in the future. Tencent's many services include social media, music, e-commerce, mobile games, Internet services, payment systems, smartphones, and multiplayer online games—all of which are among the world's biggest and most successful in their respective categories. Offerings in China include the well-known instant messenger Tencent QQ and one of the world's largest web portals, QQ.com. Its mobile chat service, WeChat, has helped bolster Tencent's continued expansion into smartphone services and has been credited as one of the world's most powerful apps. It also owns most of China's music services (Tencent Music Entertainment), which has more than 700 million active users and 120 million paying subscribers, making it one of the world's largest and most profitable music services.

Moreover, Chinese firms benefit because Chinese citizens are not very concerned about privacy. In the West, privacy is regarded as a personal right, which restricts the ability of companies to collect consumer information. By contrast, in China privacy is generally associated with being suspicious or secretive. People assume that an honest person has nothing to hide from the public domain. Thus, Chinese consumers are often willing to give up their data. While India is adopting a "right to information" and the European Union has codified a "right to be forgotten," China allows its technology firms to collect a wide range of user data for many purposes, such as for credit-scoring systems like Alibaba's Sesame Credit.

Still, limited financing and investment opportunities—at home and abroad—could slow China's momentum in AI and related fields. Chinese savers have little incentive to park money in Chinese banks because the inflation rate is higher than the real rate of return on deposits. This, coupled with China's high consumer-price volatility, feeds resistance to locking up savings. There is little reason to invest in the Shanghai Corporate Index because economic growth rates outpace stock-market performance. Investors still have the market turbulence of 2015 fresh in their minds. They keenly recall how this turbulence led to government intervention, sharply falling prices, and several trading stagnations.

As briefly mentioned earlier, it is difficult for Chinese firms to make international investments. In addition to the Chinese government's controls on capital, the US government has been considering tighter restrictions on Chinese investments in strategically important sectors, particularly those relating to AI and machine learning. In fact, US regulators recently blocked Alibaba's attempt to acquire MoneyGram, citing national security concerns.

The prospect of a China-led fintech and artificial intelligence revolution poses both opportunities and challenges. From the perspective of the West, these advancements could allow for more collaboration with one of the world's most dynamic economies. At the same time, China's expansion will likely give rise to new clashes between Chinese firms and foreign regulators.

The New Bank Branch Is Digital

In light of the fintech innovations mentioned above, and geopolitical concerns, it's reasonable to ask what bank branches will look like in the future. It is hard to imagine a city center without bank branches or insurance offices, but brick-and-mortar branches may soon be replaced by digital equivalents. This section explores how "platform" banking innovations are reshaping the retail banking landscape and leading to the dominance of online and mobile financial services.

From Branches to Mobile Banking

Online banking begins with consumer trust. There would have never been an e-commerce boom without consumer faith in online payment security. Early in the rise of e-commerce, consumers may have been comfortable making small online purchases of things like books. But before long, people began to make online purchases across many product categories. They gradually became accustomed to booking hotels and plane tickets on the Internet. People are now so confident in the reliability of online purchases that everything from house sharing to ride hailing can be done with handheld devices. All payments are seamlessly integrated between banks and companies.

Online banking had its precursors. Citibank, Chase, Chemical, and Manufacturer Hanover attempted to offer home banking through videotext (Minitel in France) as early as the 1980s. However, this service was relatively unsuccessful.

In the late 1990s, big banks recognized the important role the Internet would play in the future of their businesses. By 2000, after a few significant mergers and acquisitions, 80 percent of banks offered e-banking. Bank executives saw the lucrative potential of the new online interface and realized it would help with everything from cross-selling to consumer retention.

However, consumers were still reluctant to transact online in the 1990s and, as a result, initial growth was slow. Banks did not achieve their first million digital consumers until 2001. It took Bank of America an additional ten years to reach two million consumers. It's likely that the parallel growth of the e-commerce sector—such as ordering products from Amazon or eBay—increased consumer willingness to adopt online banking. In the early 2000s, entrepreneurs launched the following new online banks with no physical presence: ING Direct (Netherlands), First Direct (UK), PC Financial (Canada), and E*TRADE Bank (United States), among others.

However, as is often the case, new opportunities presented new threats. Inevitably, hackers targeted the banking sector. The first techniques developed to swindle consumers out of their money included phishing, a method by which hackers created fraudulent electronic exchanges to "bait" consumers. Another approach was pharming, in which hackers created fake websites that looked authentic to trick consumers into sharing sensitive information, such as credit card details. Hackers also commonly manipulated signature banking software to substituted legitimate transactions shown on the consumer's screen with a clandestine, behind-the-scenes transaction that siphoned off money. These were the online equivalents of a Trojan horse, in this case a horse that modified the payment destination and payment amount.

Unsurprisingly, banks quickly developed effective countermeasures and improved the security of their authentication tools, such as digital certificates, SMS payment confirmations, and unique code generators. Heightened security renewed and increased consumer faith in the online banking industry.

The next revolution in online banking germinated in 2007 when Apple launched the iPhone. Online banking gradually migrated from desktop to mobile. By 2009, fifty-four million US households accessed bank accounts with phones. A 2010 survey of consumer billing and payment habits conducted by Fiserv, a financial services technology company, found that consumers were paying more bills with mobile devices and making more person-to-person payments with digital wallets. Today mobile banking is common practice. People automatically assume that every bank has an easily downloadable app that is readily accessible at the touch of a button.

A 2016 study by Bankrate confirmed that with each passing year people were less likely to visit a bank branch for basic transactional services, such as deposits, withdrawals, and wire transfers. Today, local branches remain an important channel for resolving complex issues, but individuals are increasingly turning to online solutions for standard banking transactions (Figure 2.2).

What does this mean for the future of the banking industry? In 2017 the former CEO of Barclays, Anthony Jenkins, claimed that banks were facing an "Uber moment" and that pressure from new technology-based competitors would compel banks to significantly automate their businesses. He warned that the number of frequented bank branches would soon decline by as much as 50 percent.

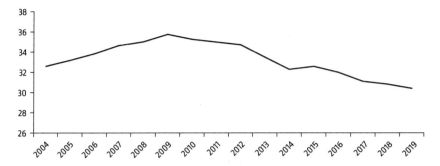

Data source: World Bank, https://data.worldbank.org/indicator/FB.CBK.BRCH.P5?locations=XC.

FIGURE 2.2   Number of bank branches for United States, number per 100,000 adults, annual, not seasonally adjusted

To date, northern Europe appears to have the most advanced online banking industry. Nordic and Dutch banks have already cut their branch numbers by 50 percent. The larger and more traditional markets of Western Europe and the United States are likely to follow suit, cutting 30 percent to 50 percent of existing branches within the next decade.

All said, banks are experiencing a massive technological transformation, one that affects more than the transition away from physical bank branches. The technological innovations responsible for this overhaul will likely impact external and consumer-facing banking services, as well as internal processes.[7]

Next, we look at some of these technological changes and how they are re-shaping financial services for the next generation.

Big Data: Making Decisions Smarter

The term *Big Data* broadly refers to analytical processes that identify correlations and patterns within large datasets, drawing meaningful conclusions from them. Banking is one of the most data-intensive environments there is. In the past, banks have used Big Data to conduct individualized risk assessments and to tailor consumer offerings. While Big Data solutions have been previously applied to front office operations—trading algorithms, customer service, and call centers—consumer banking data is a huge reservoir of untapped opportunities. It comes as no surprise that banks, such as JP Morgan, have set up institutions to analyze credit card payment data with the hope of gaining fresh insights about the US economy. The first retail banks to break into consumer data will have a significant competitive advantage.

Algorithms: Replacing Humans

Algorithms enable computers to learn, to make decisions, and to make predictions based on Big Data. Artificial intelligence (AI) has the potential to emulate the human capacity to learn from and respond to complex situations, make decisions, and initiate productive dialogues. Indeed, most investment trading is currently carried out by computers, not by the "wolves of Wall Street." By some estimates, algorithmic and high-frequency trading accounts for over 90 percent of market volume today, compared to 1990 when it accounted for none of it. Computer algorithms monitor trades for fraudulent behavior patterns. In the future, innovations in AI could be applied to middle- and front-office functions.

The Internet of Things: Dematerializing Banking Interactions

The banking sector is looking toward the Internet of Things (IoT) for growth opportunities. The Internet of Things refers, in part, to the vast network of sensors embedded in everyday objects that are connected to the Internet. Thanks to the IoT, electric cars can communicate with each other. So can household appliances. Everyday gadgets can help us monitor health, which is why health and fitness features are often used on mobile devices today. Some telephones and smartwatches allow users to check heart rate, body temperature, blood pressure, ECG, blood oxygen level, respiration, and many other functions.

Although in its infancy, the integration of online banking with the IoT shows ample promise. It is not difficult to imagine a world in which all identification verification is accomplished using fingerprint and facial recognition technology, and in which transactions are executed effortlessly and seamlessly without cash or credit cards. It could be possible to pay for a meal with just a glance in the right direction or to pay for transportation with a fingerprint. Similarly, with owner permission, cars and household appliances will be able to order replacement parts when needed.

Back Offices: Moving to the Cloud

Computing enables IT resources to be centrally pooled and redeployed on demand. This means that fewer computers and chips are required to achieve the same outcome. It is no surprise that banks rely heavily on computer and IT services. The cloud enables banks to have centralized, up-to-date systems without an army of computers. The cloud also facilitates the quick deployment of new software. These advances can significantly boost cost-savings and efficiency, so long as the transition is done carefully with a mind toward data security and privacy. This is where blockchain comes in handy.

Blockchain: Innovating to New Things

Blockchain was initially used for digital currencies such as Bitcoin. As a shared database of transactions distributed across a network, its application in the banking space extends well beyond cryptocurrencies and could soon include loan syndication, fraud information sharing, master data management, and asset and security issuance. This topic will be discussed later in the chapter.

Now let's look at where technology could have the highest impact in solving the problems of financial integration and financially excluded people.

Leapfrogging Traditional Services in Emerging Markets

In developed markets, the financial services industry is robust and swiftly progressing. By contrast, emerging markets are vulnerable to disruption, in part because banking and insurance are not widespread, meaning that large populations are significantly underbanked.

In recent years, financial services industries in emerging markets have been "leapfrogging" traditional economic infrastructures and moving directly to new fintech models. Mobile phones have long been used as productive tools to help elevate the poorest global communities out of poverty. Starting his operations in 1997, Iqbal Quadir founded Grameenphone in Bangladesh to provide near-universal access to telephone services and to increase self-employment opportunities for its rural poor.

Grameenphone's central social program was created to deliver microloans to impoverished women to help them grow small businesses and micro-enterprises. As the suite of social businesses connected to Grameenphone grew, Iqbal began selling low-cost phones as a productive asset to help poor families (rural and urban) communicate across long distances, improve their business supply chains, and access mobile banks. A sponsored Grameenphone "telephone lady" was placed in each village for a modest fee. She loaned her phone to residents who wished to speak to distant family members. The telephone lady found a new stream of income and the village community benefited from easy-to-access long-distance communication. Thanks to Grameenphone, 115,000 telephone ladies were offering phone services to eighty million inhabitants across 52,000 villages by 2004.

On a much broader scale, a recent telecom boom has abruptly changed the way of life for people in Africa and Asia. Cellphones are no longer luxury items for the wealthy; they are essential tools for life. Today even the poorest families have a smartphone. People can now communicate with improved broadband and without fixed landlines.

Just as emerging markets leaped from having no phone access to using smartphones, they may bypass older banking services and jump directly to the next generation of digital financial services (Figure 2.3). High mobile phone penetration across developing markets—nations with huge populations of underbanked consumers—opens the door to unprecedented financial service opportunities delivered by fintech. The lack of financial infrastructure in these developing economies means there will be less inertia and easier implementation.

In some cases the fintech ecosystem in emerging markets is ahead of developed markets, because advanced mobile technologies were thrust upon emerging markets without precedent. In fact, Africa has been a leader in new payment technologies. In 2007 Vodafone launched M-Pesa, a Kenyan-based mobile phone money transfer solution. This successful mobile-phone-based platform for money transfer, financing, and micro-financing has reduced corruption and lowered the incidence of tax evasion. More recently, the use of mobile payment

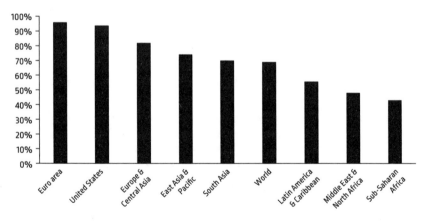

Data source: Asli Demirgüç-Kunt et al., "Measuring Financial Inclusion and the Fintech Revolution," World Bank, Global Findex Database, 2017, https://openknowledge.worldbank.org/handle/10986/29510.

FIGURE 2.3   Percentage of population (age 15+) with a bank account

systems and new blockchain technologies has promised to increase the rate of financial inclusion.

Go-Jek, Indonesia's Uber-like transportation app, recently diversified into financial services by launching an e-wallet. Like other super platforms, Go-Jek offers a menu of services on its platform, including the ability to buy more cellphone data, pay bills, and refill prescriptions. Its competitors do not currently offer services beyond ride sharing and food delivery. Go-Jek captured its user base through an initial value proposition of low-cost ride sharing on motorcycle taxis. The company's potential is significant in part because Indonesia is the fourth-most-populous country in the world, with 264 million inhabitants, 96 percent of whom report having no credit card.[8]

Citigroup's 2017 report "Digital Disruption Revisited: What Fintech VC Investments Tells Us about a Changing Industry," highlights the fast-growing Chinese peer-to-peer lending market. When the report was released, China's peer-to-peer (P2P) lending market was about four times larger than the P2P lending market in the United States and more than ten times bigger than the UK's lending market. The Bank of China now regulates China's P2P lending system by enforcing mandatory registration, minimum capital requirements, and reporting.[9]

India also has great potential for developing new fintech solutions. It has a large population, relatively low historic use of banking, high penetration of mobile phones, and the government's implementation of a biometric ID system. Moreover, in November 2016 Prime Minister Narendra Modi banned rupee notes of denominations 500 ($7) and 1,000 ($14). India's payment solution company, Paytm (backed by Alibaba), has benefited greatly from this demonetization effort. The crackdown on cash, which has been a wonder to behold, has propelled Indians to quickly transition to mobile wallets. Paytm and Ant Financial have set the precedent.

Ant Financial, the most advanced fintech company, has demonstrated that rudimentary payment services can be complemented with loan and wealth management services as more and more people gain access to financial services. All of these trends have called into question the future of the traditional bank branch.

Disintermediating Finance

We have entered a digital generation that will dramatically change financial services. In this section, we will explore some of the most significant recent financial innovations, such as crowdfunding, crowdlending, and Stripe. As we will see, the traditional bank branch and large banking corporations are not the only model for financial services.

Crowdfunding: Financing Your Dream

During the March on Washington for Jobs and Freedom in 1963, American activist Martin Luther King Jr. called for civil and economic rights in his famous "I Have a Dream" speech. Dreams do not always come true, and realizing a dream can be hard. That said, funding your dream can make it more achievable. And crowdfunding is increasingly a way to bring financial support to a project. Crowdfunding is project-based funding for individuals who hope to make their dreams come true.

Crowdfunding is the practice of raising small amounts of funding from a large crowd of investors, typically through the Internet. Crowdfunding developed only recently, but it has had explosive growth in several countries.

Crowdfunding first started as peer-to-peer (P2P) lending in England with the emergence of Zopac.com in 2005, as a form of private lending. Since then many similar sites, such as Indiegogo and Kickstarter (in the United States), have offered similar crowdfunding services. There have also been copycat sites that operate like a donations-to-a-worthy-cause site, as opposed to an "investment."

Kickstarter, created in 2009, is a forerunner in the field. It gives Internet users the opportunity to finance projects that are still at the idea stage. It reduces the heaviness associated with traditional modes of investment. For investors, it is not an investment in the true sense, but a form of "support" in exchange for tangible rewards from the team or person in charge of the project. A reward could be a letter of thanks, a personalized T-shirt, a dinner with an author, or one of the first products off the production line. The reward may vary depending on amounts provided by the supporters.

The business model is relatively simple. A project creator sets a fundraising goal, a deadline, and rewards for support. If the goal is reached before the deadline, the support reward is delivered to contributors via Amazon Payments. If the goal is not achieved, nobody pays. It is therefore an "all or nothing" system that avoids unpleasant surprises. Kickstarter is financed by collecting 5 percent of the donated funds. Amazon captures an additional share of 3 to 5 percent.

We must go back to the early 2000s to understand the genesis of the project. Perry Chen, then a musician, was frustrated at not being able to invite two DJs to a jazz festival due to lack of funds, and he came up with the idea of a funding platform that would let citizens express themselves: "And if the audience of this group could go to a site and commit to buying show tickets? If there are enough of them, the show takes place, and if not, the transaction falls apart." The concept behind Kickstarter was born.

Almost ten years later, and with the help of Yancey Strickler and Charles Adler, the Kickstarter site was launched. Success was immediate. The company quickly raised $10 million from the private equity fund Union Square Ventures and business angels such as Jack Dorsey (founder and CEO of Twitter).

Less than two years after its creation, the *New York Times* described Kickstarter as the "NEA of the people." *Time* ranked Kickstarter as one of the "best inventions of the year 2010" and one of the "best websites of the year 2011." The main competitors were GoFundMe, Dryrock Ventures (for start-ups), and Y Combinator.[10]

The site grew rapidly. In early 2011 more than $7 million per month was committed on the platform, compared to less $2 million a year earlier. By early 2019 Kickstarter reported that it received more than $4 billion in pledges from 16.2 million backers and that it successfully funded 161,000 projects.[11]

Kickstarter is probably the least "tech" of the fintech companies mentioned in this book, but it is no less central in this ecosystem, especially as an early player in participatory funding systems. In the early 2010s, Kickstarter and its competitor, Indiegogo, were the main success stories of the sector. They gave a major boost to the world of fintech. A very large number of entrepreneurs have been influenced by the company's success, philosophy, and simplicity. The start-up accelerated the emergence of crowdlending platforms and pushed large organizations in different sectors to review their models for funding small projects.

From Crowdfunding to Crowdlending

Crowdfunding has several advantages that contribute to economic activation. It encourages financially unsophisticated individuals to participate in formal systems. It allows investors to broaden their asset classes and diversify existing portfolios. It encourages technological advancement by funding promising ventures. And it creates employment opportunities by funding talented individuals and their projects.

This can also happen through increasingly popular peer-to-peer lending platforms. Several platforms have developed to serve specific niches or needs. CommonBond is a simple two-sided marketplace to finance students' tuitions. The technology offers a simple and fast process for getting a student loan and comes with increased job prospects. The CommonBond Family feature ensures that borrowers have networking opportunities, panels, dinners, and career support to help borrowers get jobs after college. CommonBond allows businesses to pay back loans, which helps students reduce debt and makes companies more desirable to the workforce.[12]

Other platforms, such as Kiva, focus on small businesses typically overlooked by banks. A borrower applies for a loan and once the request is verified by the platform, the business and loan details are posted on the Kiva website. Lenders can choose which businesses to lend to. After a period, borrowers can make payments to lenders via PayPal or through Kiva's local field partners who help borrowers through the loan process.

Lending Club allows individuals to invest in consumer credit. Consumers can borrow money for personal loans, business loans, and auto refinancing from other individuals, who earn interest, thereby removing banks and other financial institutions from the lending process.[13]

There are many lessons to learn from these alternate financial systems and community funding ventures. The Internet makes it possible to provide nontraditional finance options based on community funding to people otherwise overlooked by traditional institutions. However, these platforms still need to build more trust with lenders to become mainstream alternatives to banks. But progress in AI should allow for better filtering of loan requests and for enforcing loan repayments.

Stripe: The Giant of the Shadows

Stripe is a ubiquitous giant in the world of online payments that is unknown to much of the public. Its European competitor, Adyen, is better-known thanks to its IPO on June 13, 2018. Stripe, based in San Francisco, launched in 2010 through the American incubator Y Combinator and the collaboration of Patrick and John Collison, two Irish brothers in their twenties.

After their first start-up sold for $5 million, the Collisons focused on the most basic problem of any economic exchange: payments. They saw that too many start-ups failed because they could not recover money quickly and simply from customers. The two young entrepreneurs decided to address the problem by offering a new payment interface that could be integrated with their customers' websites. The company quickly became the first choice of start-ups near Silicon Valley. Then Stripe expanded its customer base to giants such as Google, Uber, Spotify, and Facebook. It is also developing new features and services, such as fraud detection, money transfers, and offline payments. Stripe aims to make it easier for companies to adapt to the regulations of each country. In this context, Stripe has opened eight offices abroad, including in Dublin, Paris, London, Tokyo, and Singapore.

Why is Stripe innovative? Faced with competitors like PayPal, Stripe's main advantage is reduced cost and simple setup for newly launched digital businesses. Stripe charges a fixed commission of about twenty cents and a levy ranging from zero to 2.9 percent (depending on the contract) of the amount of the transaction. Stripe's interface is also much more flexible, more discreet, and easier to use than those of its competitors.

Stripe is also offering teams of dedicated engineers to its largest customers. More than just a payment solution, the company is now at the center of business growth strategies. Stripe offers data processing and other applications that enable companies to track transaction statistics in real time, thereby simplifying management.

Stripe has been an enabler of an ecosystem of e-commerce companies. Many start-ups, particularly in the field of food delivery, owe their success, development, and growth to Stripe's services. In addition to these young companies, the behemoths of the Internet take advantage of Stripe's applications to acquire new customers. With Stripe, there is no need for a bank card or even a bank account to order an Uber or to buy items on Amazon. Stripe can accept payments from anywhere in the world and is available for businesses in forty-four different currencies, including Bitcoin, and through Android Pay or Alipay.

Stripe is another example of how fintech can disrupt traditional players in the financial services sector. It has pushed banks to rethink their models. This could lead to a decline in prices and improvements in banking services. Banks are suffering from aging systems and finding it increasingly difficult to recruit competent engineers, who prefer working for more dynamic companies. J. P. Morgan, with its acquisition of WePay, is one of the few traditional banks to have quickly adopted a new model. As a result, it can offer cheaper rates than most fintech firms in the sector.

All societies today face the challenge of fraud and money laundering. With a growing number of scandals in Europe and elsewhere, Stripe must focus significant resources to preserve its image and credibility. As governments continue to add layers of regulations, they are often lenient with the small fintech companies; however, governments are intransigent with companies like Stripe, whose size rivals that of international banks.

Stripe's global ambitions present it with another challenge. In 2016, the company launched its Singapore office and plans to invest heavily in Asia. But China is not an obvious market, and many disruptive companies have already experienced great disappointment there due to local actors backed by the government.

Are Banks Destined to Disappear?

In the short run, the answer is likely no. Credit cards are still the most popular method of payment in the United States, and it will take time to change the credit-card culture. Because most credit cards are linked to banks, the banks should be safe for now. Moreover, financial services are highly regulated, making it harder for disruptive start-ups to enter the field. And commercial banks will likely play an ongoing and important role.

However, traditional companies like banks must address consumer needs and develop digital services. Given that Apple, Google, and Facebook can collect a high volume of qualitative and quantitative data about their clients, these firms should be able to target the right clients for the right products, thereby generating a more effective distribution channel. In light of these factors, our view is that commercial banks may need to partner more with tech players to remain competitive. Otherwise they will probably be relegated to the background.

In the long term, it is possible that fintech companies could completely replace banks. Forty million Venmo users exchanged $21 billion in the first quarter of 2019, which shows that people (especially millennials) trust nontraditional financial institutions to handle their money. At a time when US banks offer depositors next-to-zero interest rates, there is very little incentive for people to put their money in banks. New technologies like blockchain make it possible for nontraditional financial institutions to function as banks, only with more security. If the digital payment system becomes more prevalent, the need for banks will diminish, as is happening in China. This does not bode well for the future of traditional financial institutions.

We are entering an era of increased competition between incumbent banks and fintech companies. Banking business models haven't evolved significantly over the past few decades, so the services proposed by fintech firms have a relatively high potential to revolutionize the industry. There are several reasons fintech companies could see major advancements.[14]

First, because fintech companies have appeared only recently, the sector is less crowded and less regulated. This makes them more agile, which gives them a greater ability to develop innovative services. By comparison, banking companies are large, highly regulated, and difficult to reform.

Second, fintech companies can broaden financial horizons and surpass geographical barriers, allowing them to reach a wider consumer base than most banks. They can demystify complex financial solutions, making services more accessible to a larger proportion of the population. Robo-advisors that offer investment advice via artificial intelligence, for instance, remove the traditional minimum thresholds imposed by asset managers. This significantly reduces investment costs and enables greater access to higher-quality investment services.

Third, fintech businesses are well informed about their clients. Greater client visibility gives fintech companies the ability to act discriminately and make better pricing decisions. For example, Ant Financial rates consumers through Sesame Credit. App users report that Ant Financial offers loans that are more cost-effective relative to traditional institutions. Similarly, some insurance companies provide clients with fitness trackers. This allows them to monitor exercise habits and reduce insurance premiums for physically active clients.

Fourth, fintech firms provide better client services that are most cost-effective. As a result, their cost base is typically lower than for traditional players, and their client acquisition and servicing costs are also lower. Some companies, such as Earnest, Lending Club, and Prosper, can even avoid using their own capital to offer loans by using investor capital instead.

The financial services industry may follow in the footsteps of the car industry. Over time, car dealers gained independence from car manufacturers. Some began to sell only one brand whereas others became multi-branded. Consequently, the industry split between sellers and distributors on one side and manufacturers on the other. Financial services will likely follow a similar path, with fintech taking an increasing share of distribution and sales while regulated banks act as the "engine factory" that builds and administers financial products.

The emergence of payment apps is likely to create situations in which consumers have funds in various accounts. However, traditional banks have a long history and will continue to benefit from their established reputation as solid and trustworthy places to put savings.

Fintech start-ups are alluring for clients looking for customized services. Due to the large amounts of data they collect, fintech companies have a deep knowledge of their clients' needs and habits, which enables them to tailor relevant services to meet each need. Therefore, to remain attractive to customers, banks must seamlessly integrate their services with third-party services (ride sharing, e-commerce, and so on). To do this, banks might need to outsource their investment activities to players who know their clients better (Amazon, Alipay). With more information, banks can lend money with less risk. As a result, fintech start-ups and banks could assume complementary roles during this period of transition.

The number of alliances between fintech and traditional players continues to rise as several large institutions announce strategic alliances. For instance, in February 2018, Bank of America and Amazon announced a joint venture that offers loans to Amazon marketplace merchants.

However, the integration of banks and fintech companies could be hindered by differences in corporate cultures. Many banks seem to recognize this challenge. In response, they are setting up internal innovation labs that focus on key areas of development (Big Data, AI, cloud storage, automation, IoT, and blockchain). These developments will be scaled up if the early stages prove successful. It's likely that the biggest worldwide "bank" at the end of the next decade will be phenomenal at technology delivery—built on delivery and not on products. As Brett King put it, "by 2025 . . . banks will be competing against technology players like Ant Financial and Amazon. If they are still competing as a bank, it will be like taking on these guys blindfolded."[15]

Although digital-only "challenger banks" are gaining momentum, it is too early to assume that they will cast brick-and-mortar banks into an existential crisis. We should expect a transition during which banks and fintech companies collaborate. We are very much aligned with Tapscott and Tapscott. Is this the end of banking as we know it? That depends on how incumbents react. Blockchain is not an existential threat to those who embrace the new technology paradigm and disrupt from within. The question is, who in the financial services industry will lead the revolution? Throughout history, leaders of old paradigms have struggled to embrace the new. Why didn't AT&T launch Skype, or Visa create PayPal? CNN could have built Twitter, since it is all about the sound bite. GM or Hertz could have launched Uber; Marriott could have invented Airbnb. The unstoppable force of blockchain technology is barrelling down on the infrastructure of modern finance. As with prior paradigm shifts, blockchain will create winners and losers. Personally, we would like the inevitable collision to transform the old money machine into a prosperity platform for all.[16]

Fintech and the Next Financial Crisis

The 2007 financial crisis took root on Wall Street, but the next financial crisis may come from Silicon Valley. A major concern in 2007 was that some banks were deemed "too big to fail." Today banks are better capitalized and regulators conduct stress tests of large institutions. These reforms have adequately addressed the root causes of the 2007 crisis, but they might not account for new and emerging risks, including those presented by fintech.

Since 2007, fintech firms have addressed many consumer needs and reduced transaction costs, and their innovations have become increasingly appealing to consumers. This innovative energy has its positive outcomes, but it inevitably creates risks, including market instability. These risks can be summarized in three categories.

The first risk relates to the vulnerability of fintech due to rapid, adverse shocks. Because most fintech companies are undiversified, small and young, and many operate at a loss. To reach scale, they often depend on current and future capital injections. Most are unlikely to make it. This raises the question: What happens if a start-up goes bankrupt? Could consumers lose their financial investments?

Second, fintech firms are difficult to monitor. Because they function with complex computer algorithms, it is difficult for outsiders to clearly assess risks and rewards. Moreover, many new, innovative technologies fly under the radar of monitoring agencies. It is possible that some companies are creating loopholes for money laundering and fraud? It is difficult to say, for we cannot know what we cannot monitor.

The third observable trend is a lack of commonly held norms like those that guide traditional financial institutions. The fintech industry is so new and its players are so diverse that it's difficult to envision them reaching a point of common guidance and cooperation.

The future of finance—including the risks—will likely move in the United States from Wall Street to Silicon Valley, or to Beijing, Hangzhou, or Shenzhen. As the fintech industry grows, governments and regulators will need to play catch-up to understand, monitor, and cover potential systemic risks.

CHAPTER THREE

The Emergence of Robo-Advisors

In this chapter we explore how newly created robo-advisors (artificial intelligence applied to financial services) increase access to financial products and financial advice while reducing costs. We will discuss the changing landscape of health care and retirement financing, including the differences that exist between countries. We will show how algorithms are rapidly replacing humans, but that new investment solutions and new services could provide a way to ease the tension between a human workforce and artificial intelligence. We also present a thorough and nuanced picture of fintech products being developed by entrepreneurs, venture investors, and traditional financial specialists.

Low-Visibility Economic Struggles

Millennials, or Generation Y—people born between 1980 and 2000—are the first people to be considered "digital natives." The internet and its applications have deeply influenced the way millennials think and behave. It has created informed citizens who expect instantaneous feedback. The Peter Pan syndrome, described by American sociologist Kathleen Shaputis, characterizes millennials as a generation unwilling to grow up, commit, or take on adult responsibilities. For millennials, owning homes and cars may not be a high priority. They are more likely to use Uber than to buy cars, and they prefer Airbnb over renting or buying a holiday home.[1]

Millennials are often characterized as having a different relationship to their jobs than their parents and grandparents had. They favor a flat corporate culture that emphasizes work–life balance and social consciousness. On average, they do not stay in a role more than three years. Online job comparisons and strong social networks offer them a more comprehensive view of the job market than was available for earlier generations. Generation X dreamed of a better work–life balance, but millennials demand it. Flexibility at work has become paramount. If a task can be completed from home or from the other side of the planet, why work in an office cubicle?

Freelance: Where Is My Pension?

Millennials are entering the job market under difficult conditions, particularly in European countries. Jobs are migrating from company-based employment toward peer-to-peer employment via digital platforms (such as Uber). Jobs and work contracts for millennials are increasingly short-term. All of this results in unpredictable income and less ability to save for retirement. It also raises significant questions for health care and pensions.[2]

At present, employers are still usually responsible for contributing to workers' retirement funds and health insurance plans (although this varies by country). In a world where independent contractors become the new normal and where gig employers do not provide health insurance coverage, pensions, or retirement plans, the future of pensions and health care looks bleak. How quickly and efficiently will governments resolve these issues, if at all?

The number of people struggling to pay for health insurance has steadily increased since 2015, according to the Kaiser Family Foundation. Today, 27 percent of the US population have delayed necessary medical care because it is too expensive. Another 23 percent have skipped a necessary medical test or treatment, and 21 percent have failed to fill a prescription.

As more people take part in the freelance economy through online companies, it would be sensible for governments to treat these freelance platforms like any other employer and with the same pension requirements. For example, Harris and Kruger (2015) proposed to structure benefits to make independent worker status neutral when compared with employee status.[3] They also suggested that independent workers—regardless of whether they work through an online or offline intermediary—would qualify for many, although not all, of the benefits and protections that employees receive. These protections would include the freedom to organize and collectively bargain, civil rights protections, tax withholding, and employer contributions for payroll taxes.

For example, a US company like Uber could be required to offer workers a 401(k) or other retirement plan. This proposal could be unpopular, but it could also help freelancers better prepare for retirement and therefore be less likely to need government financial aid when they are older, an outcome that would be helpful for retirees and governments alike.

Interestingly, over the past few years several gig companies began partnering with online investment and wealth management companies as a way of resolving independent contractor complaints about retirement and other benefits. For example, in late 2015 Lyft formed a partnership with the investment firm Honest Dollar to give drivers an opportunity to sock away some of their earnings for retirement. The plan does not require Lyft to pay for its drivers' retirement savings or divert drivers' earnings into a separate retirement fund.[4]

In 2016 Uber followed suit by opening a company-wide retirement plan through Betterment, an online investment and wealth management company. This plan was first implemented in Seattle, Chicago, Boston, and New Jersey and then expanded nationally. According to their announcement about the plan, drivers could use their Uber app to "open a Betterment IRA (individual retirement account) or Roth IRA for free the first year. Uber drivers can get started without a minimum account balance." This move was rather surprising because Uber claimed several times that its drivers were independent contractors—not company employees—who had to provide their own benefits.[5]

Knowledge Is Priceless but Education Is Costly

Millennials face increasing education costs with less certainty of a positive return on education investments. This is a major shift. Economists in the field of human capital have extensively studied the effects of education on income. Although researchers have recognized heterogeneity in the effects, few studies have looked at the effects of education on income inequality. As an exception, Harvard economists Claudia Goldin and Lawrence F. Katz have found evidence of a correlation between mass education, economic growth, and inequality. In *The Race between Education and Technology* (2010), they argued that mass education allowed the United States to build wealth and reduce income inequality for most of the twentieth century.[6]

The United States took an early lead in education. By the mid-1800s, the clear majority of (white) children in many states received a free grade-school education, while only 2 percent of British fourteen-year-olds were enrolled in school in 1870. By the 1930s most US households had a child attending high school, whereas only 9 percent of British seventeen-year-olds were enrolled in school in 1957. The United States was far ahead of the rest of the world. President Roosevelt pushed for mass college education, and by 1970 half of America's students attended a university.[7]

Later in the 1970s the US education system began to stagnate, with high-school graduation rates of just 75 percent. This period was also associated with rising US income inequality. Around the same time, the rest of the developed world started investing massively in education. These nations caught up with, and in some cases surpassed, the United States.

As mentioned earlier, US postsecondary education fees since the 1980s have increased significantly. Average tuition and fees have risen 157 percent at private colleges, 194 percent for a public out-of-state education, and 237 percent for a public in-state education between 1987 and 2018.[8]

According to Mark Kantrowitz's analysis of 2014 government data, the average US college graduate has accumulated $33,000 in school debt. After adjusting for inflation, this is more than double the debt of the 1994 class. The average cost of higher education could reach a record level when considering the cost of an MBA. Such a degree can lead students to incur a debt of $100,000 to $200,000 (including tuition, rent, books, overseas trips) over a two-year period.[9]

As previously mentioned, jobs are evolving at a fast pace. The market requires professionals to perpetually develop new, relevant skills. In this challenging context, more people will need to pursue additional education to remain competitive. But what might prevent people from earning a college degree or advanced degree later in their careers? Initial costs could be a deterrent, especially if the returns from education diminish. That outcome is more likely for those who pursue additional degrees later in life because the payoff phase is shortened.

Saving Like an Ant or a Cricket?

Because they have inherited a dynamic economy with less job stability, millennials should be saving more. The concept of income smoothing implies that people should save money to cover the costs of job loss, health issues, down payments for a house, vacations, luxury items, a new car or car repairs, home improvements, education (including for children), and retirement income.

Savings is also important at a macroeconomic, or aggregate, level. Economies need to maintain a reasonable level of private saving because financial institutions match one person's saving to another person's investment. The latter is a key determinant of capital, productivity, technology, and eventually long-term economic growth.[10]

Different saving behaviors are influenced by the institutional, demographic, economic, and social characteristics of each country. Nevertheless, we can differentiate savers in two groups of high-income countries: (a) English-speaking nations, such as Australia, Ireland, the United Kingdom, and the United States; and (b) continental European nations, such as France, Germany, Luxembourg, Sweden, and Switzerland.[11]

First, the Anglo-Saxon countries tend, in general, to record a lower level of private saving. Anglo-Saxon countries are usually more indebted and less risk averse. A 2015 study of household debt in Europe and the United States shows that US households have access to large mortgage loans with a relatively low collateral value. Consequently, US households face significant debt-servicing costs.[12]

By contrast, countries in continental Europe generally have a higher level of private savings. According to a 2018 report by Bank of America, which surveyed 1,500 respondents, ages eighteen to seventy-one, millennials display distinct patterns of saving and spending.[13]

Millennials invest less of their money on goods with intrinsic value, such as cars or houses, and spend more on experiences and services. Moreover, millennials tend to prioritize personal interests over work (60 percent) and their salaries (24 percent). This relative disinterest in salary has led some to believe that millennials do not care as much about money or, more specifically, savings. Millennials are perceived, and see themselves, as a generation that does not save well: 75 percent of Americans millennials feel that their generation has overspent.

However, millennials are in fact a generation that has been keen to save money. Over the last two years, the portion of US millennials who have saved $15,000 or more has increased from 33 percent to 48 percent, which leads many to believe that the post-2008 financial crisis economic rebound enabled millennials to realize their saving aspirations.

A few theories may explain the rationale behind millennials' savings: (a) It is a generation that experienced a financial crisis early in their careers; (b) millennials expect little from companies—more than one-fourth have already been laid off; (c) millennials realize that it will be more difficult in an unstable working environment to plan for retirement, leading them to save more than their parents have; and (d) home prices have increased significantly over the last decades, which makes home investment a less attainable objective.[14]

The Era of Robo-Advisors

We have seen that many young people will spend years paying off educational debt. Technology, such as AI and robotics (among other changes), will make the job market more dynamic and less stable. And, as in any era, investment markets can crash and recessions can be severe. All of these factors—and more—will influence the ability of people to save and invest. Nevertheless, the fintech revolution will open new doors for wealth management strategies.

The Algorithmic Asset Manager

As the baby boomer generation moves into retirement, they will sell stocks and purchase bonds to stabilize returns and protect savings. And so, shifting demographics have encouraged millennials to look for alternative investment opportunities.

Unsurprisingly, many people lack basic financial literacy, which makes it difficult for them to manage investments and makes them more prone to make poor financial decisions. In that context, the safest bet is to let professional advisors manage the money.[15]

Millennials, however, embrace digital solutions, including new fintech advisory and investment options, such as exchange-traded funds (ETFs). These innovations are starting to make it simpler and cheaper for people to invest without hiring an asset manager.

What is an ETF? An exchange-traded fund is a security that tracks an index, a bond, a commodity, or a basket of assets. It automatically creates a basket of stocks or securities to match the underlying index or market performance. So, an ETF investor can invest in the average performance of the US stock market, or in small European companies, or in the technology sector. The first successful ETFs date back to 1993. In 2020, the assets managed by ETFs globally amounted to approximately $7.74 trillion USD.[16]

Active funds, in which asset managers select investments, are increasingly challenged by ETFs. In the 1960s, active fund managers mainly competed with amateur individual investors or conservative mutual funds holding blue-chip securities. As a result, active fund managers regularly beat the market by an average of 200 to 300 basis points each year between 1960 and 1980. Stock markets rose steadily between 1980 and 2000. Clients of active fund managers enjoyed large capital gains. Yet the performance of active fund managers was merely aligned with the index, after deducting fees and costs.

Between 2000 and 2010, active fund managers did not sufficiently outperform the index to finance operating costs and fees. Investors became increasingly interested in ETFs, although they remembered the good performance by active fund managers in earlier years.

From 2010 to the present, a large proportion of active managers have underperformed their benchmarks. According to a study conducted between 2012 and 2017, "84.23 percent of large-cap managers, 85.06 percent of mid-cap managers, and 91.17 percent of small-cap managers lagged behind their respective benchmarks." This underperformance is regularly explained by higher competition, widely shared information, and the emergence of related technologies.[17]

According to Morningstar, the relative underperformance of active funds (considering related fees) has opened a new avenue for ETFs. As of this writing, ETFs have grown four times faster than active funds since 2007.

The next generation of ETFs will use artificial intelligence to analyze a wide range of information on stocks, to track an index, and to make active investment decisions. Information about stocks can include the stock's related news, social media publications, as well as conventional financial information.

ETFs can, to some extent, replace an asset manager for a lower fee. They can also track specific indexes or follow defined investment strategies. However, several questions remain for the individual investor: What investment strategy would best fit my own needs and objectives? Where should I invest to preserve my capital or to make larger gains?

Harder, Faster, Better, Stronger: The Benefits of Robo-Advisors

The 2001 Daft Punk song "Harder, Better, Faster, Stronger" is an apt description of robo-advisors, which offer many advantages. Robo-advisors are not actually robots; they are online services that use computer algorithms to provide financial advice and manage customers' investment portfolios. In other complex domains of artificial intelligence, computer programs can beat chess masters. Can they now beat traders and asset managers?

The first robo-advisors, Wealthfront and Betterment, began providing financial advice to public investors in 2010. Wealthfront began as a mutual fund company called KaChing that originally used human advisors. Wealthfront's founders, Andy Rachleff and Dan Carroll, wanted to expand on this model by providing financial advice to the tech community. They quickly shifted focus by identifying the potential for lower-cost investment advice, which made services accessible to a larger number of people.

Robo-advisors combine several innovations to provide comprehensive financial advice to clients over the internet without human contact. The clients typically fill out a questionnaire that asks about their attitude toward risk, their age and expected retirement date, and perhaps about their other investments. Robo-advisors use quantifiable factors, such as wealth, income, tax situation, investment goals, and risk tolerance to analyze a client's financial status and to provide portfolio recommendations that are tailored to each client's needs. Typically, these programs do not provide advice relating to decumulation, which is the withdrawal of money from the pension account during retirement.

Robo-advice comes in different forms. It may be part of a program that manages other financial market assets of the participant, or it may be focused solely on pension plan investments. It may be part of a program that considers other financial goals, such as savings for college, or it may be focused on assisting in making pension investments. It may be part of a program that addresses issues of financial wellness, including issues of debt and insurance, or it may be more narrowly focused. It may be a stand-alone program, or it may also involve the participation of an investment adviser. It may directly interact with the pension participant, or it may be used by a financial adviser to assist the advisor in providing advice to the client.[18]

Fintech clearly impacts the financial advice service sector. Robo-advisors allow savers to receive less costly and more professional advice related to the management of their savings. Prior to the introduction of robo-advisors, such advice was unaffordable for many individuals. Thomas Philippon argued that robo-advising will likely democratize access to financial services and that Big Data is likely to reduce the impact of negative prejudice in the credit markets. According to Bartlett et al., algorithms improve financial inclusion because they are less discriminating than face-to-face lenders. Erel and Liebersohn found evidence that borrowers were more likely to get a fintech-enabled Paycheck Protection Program (PPP) loan if they were located in ZIP codes where local banks were unlikely to originate PPP loans. Carlin et al. showed that millennials incur lower financial costs when they use fintech to manage their finances.[19]

Robo-advice is generally cheaper and more accessible than human advice. This means it could be especially useful for defined contribution plans because members face numerous financial choices and relatively small accumulated savings. According to the UK's government chief scientific adviser, fintech companies can increase the availability of financial advice to previously underserved populations, thanks to "lower cost structures, greater customer reach, or superior ability to monitor or score risk." Robo-advisors were estimated to be managing $440 billion in assets as of June 30, 2019.[20]

A robo-advisor that has received little attention to date uses online advice programs provided to pension participants through their 401(k) plans. According to TIAA Institute research, in 2012 and 2013, 6.5 percent of TIAA participants in the sample sought asset allocation advice using an online tool made available to them. The demand for advice increased fourfold with the introduction of online advice tools.[21]

As an added benefit, the advice provided by robo-advisors is more transparent than that of human financial advisors. It is nearly impossible to monitor private conversations between human advisors and clients, but it is possible to evaluate the advice provided by computer models. Greater transparency may lead robo-advisors to adhere more closely to regulatory requirements than human advisors.[22]

Finally, robo-advisors are convenient. They are always available from any location. For some customers, accessing information from a website platform is more convenient than filling out paper documents or meeting with a human advisor. These robo-advisor features may be particularly appealing to young generations because they are so comfortable with technology and prefer handling their affairs at a convenient time and location.

The assets managed by robo-advisors have grown exponentially. At the end of 2014, Corporate Insight reported $19 billion in US robo-advisor managed assets. By 2016 that number had grown to $126 billion. The amount should grow even more because young people are more likely than older people to use robo-advisors. A survey of people with non-pension-plan investments found that 38 percent of individuals age eighteen to thirty-four have used a robo-advisor, compared to 4 percent of individuals age fifty-five and older.

Another advantage of robo-advisors is that they are more accessible to less wealthy people. Human advisors typically have a minimum asset requirement of $500,000, which makes them inaccessible to low- and middle-income customers. By contrast, robo-advisors offer far lower minimum account balance requirements. Wealthfront, for example, requires a minimum balance of only $500, and Betterment does not require *any* minimum balance. These lower minimums make robo-advisors well suited for young people who are just starting to save. As a result, the current user-base of fintech products is skewed toward the younger population (age twenty-five to thirty-four), who are technologically literate and in need of financial services.[23]

Historically, human financial advisors have charged fees ranging from 1 to 2 percent of assets under management. They have tended to charge lower fees for larger portfolios. In the United States, robo-advisors have typically charged fees that are substantially lower, ranging from no fees to fifty basis points (Table 3.1).[24]

Computer technology and algorithms, which are less expensive than humans, make these lower fees possible. Robo-advisors also have the advantage of economies of scale, meaning that one computer algorithm can advise numerous clients. These already low fees are expected to fall even further as robo-advisors acquire more clients and their clients accumulate more assets.

In addition to advisory fees, clients must pay expense-ratio fees for underlying investments. Most robo-advisors allocate their portfolios among passive index fund strategies, whereas traditional financial advisors are incentivized (and therefore more likely) to recommend active asset management options with higher fees. Thus, robo-advisors offer less expensive advisory fees and mutual

TABLE 3.1   Selected top US robo-advisor by assets under management, first quarter 2018

Robo-advisor	Assets under management ($billion)	Advisory fee as a percent of assets under management (excludes fee for investment in funds)	Minimum assets
Vanguard Personal Advisor Services	$101	0.30%	$50,000
Charles Schwab	$27	0 (fees for Schwab ETFs)	$5,000
Betterment	$13	Digital—0.25%/year	$0
Wealthfront	$10	Premium—0.40%/year 0.25% (free for accounts of $10,000 or less)	$500

Data source: Jill Fisch, Marion Laboure, and John Turner, "The Emergence of the Robo-Advisor," in *The Disruptive Impact of Fintech on Retirement Systems,* ed. Julie Agnew and Olivia S. Mitchell (Oxford: Oxford University Press, 2019), 13–37.

fund fees. They also cost less to trade. For example, Betterment's fees on investment options range from nine to twelve basis points.[25]

So, robo-advisors are more accessible and less expensive. But do they perform just as well? The first criterion for successful wealth management is the advisor's choice of asset allocation. Historically, equity investments have generally outperformed fixed income. This has been particularly true over the past five to ten years, when interest rates have been extremely low. An advisor's performance is therefore heavily influenced by the degree to which that advisor's recommended portfolio is concentrated in equities. For example, Cerulli compared the advice of seven robo-advisors for a hypothetical person age twenty-seven. Cerulli found that portfolio allocation of equities varied from 90 percent to 51 percent.

Market competition may lead robo-advisors to overconcentrate in equities in order to generate higher returns, a strategy that may operate to the customers' detriment in a market downturn. However, in 2019 the rates of return earned by the robo-advisors for Personal Capital (19.68 percent) and Betterment (18.97 percent) outperformed a weighted average return of a benchmark made of 60 percent equity and 40 percent fixed income (Figure 3.1).[26]

What about risk management? Kitces (2017) has criticized certain robo-advisor approaches, particularly those attempting to match people to portfolios using questionnaires. He notes that an individual with a high net worth and a high capacity to *bear* risk, but with a low *tolerance* for risk, could be placed in a moderately risky portfolio because of his or her wealth. The underlying reason is that the robo-advisor might set risk-bearing capacity and risk-tolerance scores

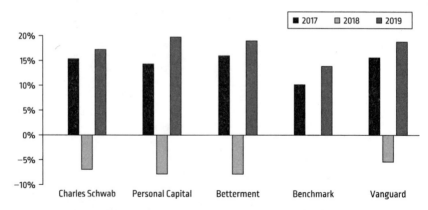

Data source: Jill Fisch, Marion Laboure, and John Turner, "The Emergence of the Robo-Advisor," in *The Disruptive Impact of Fintech on Retirement Systems,* ed. Julie Agnew and Olivia S. Mitchell (Oxford: Oxford University Press, 2019), 13–37.

Note: Benchmark is calculated based on a 60 percent fixed income index (US ten-year bond yield) and 40 percent equity (S&P 500) weighted average return.

FIGURE 3.1   Returns of selected robo-advisors vs. benchmark

to an overly conservative, or incorrect, risk/reward default. For example, an individual with high capacity to bear risk but low tolerance for risk should be put in a low-risk portfolio.[27]

In comparison to target-date funds, in which a person's pension fund portfolio is based solely on the year in which he or she plans to retire, robo-advisors provide more personalized advice concerning portfolios. In theory, the more relevant information a robo-advisor can gather about the client, the more it can provide personalized guidance. So, many robo-advisors are attempting to do a better job in determining the risk tolerances of clients. Robo-advisors already have an advantage over target-date funds because the former can help clients pick investments appropriate for their risk tolerances, not just their ages. Breen (2019) speculates that eventually robo-advisors could largely replace target-date funds.[28] However, these funds are often the default for people automatically enrolled in a 401(k) plan, whereas advisor-managed funds are not the default fund.

A future development may be that funds managed by robo-advisors will be offered to pension participants as default funds. Although target-date funds usually have fees of around fifty basis points, one financial service provider has started offering funds managed by robo-advisors that are designed for 401(k) plans with fees of twenty basis points.

Robo-Advisors in Europe

Robo-advisors began relatively recently in the United States, and the concept has spread rapidly to other countries. The number of robo-advisors in Europe has increased significantly since 2014, and the amount of money they manage has also grown rapidly. Robo-advisors now operate worldwide. Nevertheless, most robo-advisors are based in the United States.

Although it is difficult to generalize the European market, European robo-advisors (e.g., Nutmeg, Quirion, Marie Quantier) tend to charge higher fees than US robo-advisors—from forty to one hundred basis points more. The higher fees may be due, in part, to the fact that robo-advisors are a relatively new phenomenon in Europe and do not yet have the scale found in the United States. In addition, European financial and banking legislation is national and therefore differs across countries. This means that there are many national markets for robo-advisors rather than a centralized European market. Also, Europeans are usually more risk-averse than Americans, resulting in more saving and safer investments. These factors may have led European robo-advisors to grow slowly, thereby reducing their ability to benefit from economies of scale.

Learning Sympathy

Artificial intelligence and advances in computer science have recently generated humanized algorithms with a capacity to sympathize with people. Robo-advisors do not just *use* algorithms; they *create* algorithms that can adapt to and comprehend different environments. This is called "machine learning." The algorithms of robo-advisors can learn from a vast amount of data, just as human beings can learn from innumerable perceptions and experiences.

Researchers are already working to give the algorithms the ability to recognize human emotions based on voice intonations, thereby capturing not only the note, but the "color," tempo, and speed of enunciation. To accomplish this, up to 2,500 features must be individually programmed.

Innovative studies of neural networks have dramatically accelerated "deep learning," which enables robots to mimic the human brain's functions. This eliminates the step-by-step nature of robots. With auditory intelligence and facial recognition, robots can already recognize micro-expressions.

So, the future of robo-advisors is bright. They offer increasingly relevant and human services to clients. However, little is known about the wider socioeconomic implications of digital wealth management solutions. Can robo-advisors democratize finance and decrease wealth inequality?

The Future of Savings

Over the course of the twentieth century, finance has become a leading driver of inequality. Atkinson et al. (2011) showed that very wealthy individuals have access to investment products with significantly higher financial returns than the mainstream products accessible to most. In his book, *Capital in the Twenty-First Century*, Piketty outlined the evolution of wealth inequality over the last three centuries. He found that the rate of return on capital has been significantly greater than the economic growth rate and, as such, has been greater than income from labor activity.[29]

According to the IMF, the per capita real income of the top 1 percent of advanced economies grew by 282 percent between 1980 and 2012, whereas per capita real income of the remaining 99 percent grew by only 144 percent during the same period. When annualized, the difference per year appears less pronounced, but it is still significant. The income of the wealthiest has grown by 3.3 percent per year on average, compared to 1.1 percent for the rest of the population. This represents the difference between investments in low-yield, fixed-income assets and high-yield equity.[30]

Wealthy individuals have access to a wide range of investment opportunities, including investments in alternative asset management plans (such as hedge funds), whereas small investors typically hold "vanilla" investments (such as bank deposits and government bonds).

Figure 3.2 shows the annual rate of stock returns, Treasury bills (short-term bonds) and ten-year Treasury bonds (long-term bonds) from 1928 to 2020. This chart shows an investment of $100 in 1927.

On average, stocks have outperformed short- and long-term bonds during most periods over the last century. Clearly, long-term dormant savings can add up to a lot of money. We also see that small differences in investment returns make a big difference over the long term (compounding effect). And regular savings, even in moderate amounts, can accumulate significant wealth. These facts apply to pension planning and complementary retirement investments. Even small differences in investment fees can make a big difference over time.

The Importance of Fees

With the rise of the gig economy, many workers won't have access to steady employment with good retirement pensions, employer savings plans, or other benefits. This means that they need to do more on their own to prepare for the future.

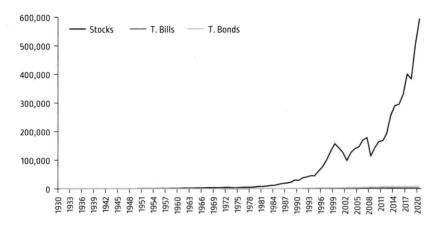

Data source: The raw data for Treasury bond and bill returns was obtained from the Federal Reserve database in St. Louis.

Note: The return on stocks includes both price appreciation and dividends. The Treasury bill rate is a three-month rate and the Treasury bond is the constant maturity ten-year bond, but the treasury bond return includes coupon and price appreciation. The graph is based on a compounded value of $100.

FIGURE 3.2   Annual rate of returns on stocks, T-bonds, and T-bills from 1928 to 2020

Older workers also have had to adapt in recent years. With the growth of 401(k) plans and Individual Retirement Accounts (IRAs), employees increasingly have had to take responsibility for investment decisions about pension accounts. While only 13.8 percent of US households directly held stocks in 2013, 49.2 percent of households held retirement accounts, primarily IRAs and 401(k) plans.[31]

Not everyone, however, is well positioned to take advantage of their own retirement investments. Choi, Laibson, and Madrian (2010) found that lack of knowledge about index funds led some people to experiment with high-fee index funds because those funds also had relatively high rates of return, due to the timing of the funds' inception. Similarly, Hastings, Mitchell, and Chyn (2011) showed that people who had greater financial knowledge paid lower fees for mutual funds.[32]

It is well established that people suffer from exponential growth bias, underestimating the effect of compounding over time: however, that bias affects both interest compounding and the effect of fees.[33]

Investors with smaller asset amounts usually pay higher investment advisor fees, as a percentage of assets. For example, most investment advisors have asset-based fees and a minimum fee. Therefore, the minimum fees paid by investors with low levels of assets are a higher percentage of assets than the percentage paid by wealthier investors.

Kitces (2018) reported that advisory fees have come down because financial advisors have been using robo-advisor assistance. This has allowed advisors to manage more clients and lower fees without reducing their income. Lower financial advisor fees may reduce the inequality of fees charged.[34]

A study by Munnell, Aubrey, and Crawford (2015) found that IRAs tend to receive net rates of return that are about 1 percentage point less than the rates of return for employer-provided contribution plans, such as 401(k) plans.[35] This was largely due to a difference in fees, but it was also due to differences in asset allocation. Based on this research, a higher percentage of assets in IRAs is often invested in money market funds, which would seem to be a poor investment choice for retirement savings.

An example from the US Department of Labor (2016) revealed the importance of fees on investment outcomes. "Assume that you are an employee with thirty-five years until retirement and a current 401(k) account balance of $25,000. If returns on investments in your account over the next thirty-five years average 7 percent, and if fees and expenses reduce your average returns by 0.5 percent, your account balance will grow to $227,000 at retirement, even if there are no further contributions to your account. If fees and expenses are 1.5 percent, however, your account balance will grow to only $163,000. The 1 percent difference in fees and expenses would reduce your account balance at retirement by 28 percent." If fintech innovations can reduce or remove these fees, the benefits for investors will be significant.[36]

The Digital Wealth Management Revolution

Younger generations are open to new fintech solutions, so we should expect to see rapid changes in digital wealth management. Due to increased use of robo-advisors and improved financial education, we could see a democratization of finance and decreased wealth inequality for low- and middle-income persons.[37]

As we previously saw, inequality is often exacerbated when the rate of return on capital surpasses economic growth and income from labor activity. Many people lack access to wealth management and therefore earn lower returns. This has fed growing inequality over the last decade. The recent emergence of robo-advisors could dramatically change the rules of the game, making wealth management accessible to most.

Digital wealth management solutions democratize finance by making investments accessible to millennials and the middle class. They provide tailored investment solutions and access to highly sophisticated asset classes. They virtually facilitate access to wealth management. It is very easy to set up automatic monthly savings directed to a robo-advisor that automatically invests it and reinvests the dividends and realized capital gains. Robo-advisors charge low fees and have no (or low) minimum asset requirements. As a result, many more people could see investments produce rates of return like those received by wealthy individuals.[38]

Financial literacy is an essential key for helping people think about investing and long-term financial planning (retirement, children's education, and so on). More people need to become acquainted with finance and investment, including its risks and benefits. The solution will probably come from the private sector (by simplifying the process, reducing fees, and lowering the initial capital required) and from governments (by educating people about financial principles).

As of 2017, US robo-advisors managed a combined total of less than $100 billion in assets. Since 2019, robo-advisors have risen 30 percent to reach $460 billion assets under management in 2020. Experts expect the robo-advisor industry's growth to be substantial, reaching $1.2 trillion by 2024.[39]

Of course, many economic variables (such as interest rates and debt levels) can negatively or positively impact the returns on savings rates and wealth accumulation. For the purposes of this discussion, we cannot address every variable. However, digital wealth management could become up to eighty times larger in the next three or four years. Retirement planning and pension management could be a promising catalyst for robo-advisors, especially in countries that lack universal access to retirement plans, such as the United States. Educated millennials could also be a promising customer segment for digital wealth management solutions because they are financially literate and comfortable with technology.

This level of growth could lead larger players to scale up their advertising and education efforts, possibly leading to a virtuous cycle that fulfills disruption promises. Thus, greater access to financial investments could become a critical tool in bridging the wealth inequality gap by providing low-cost financial services to relatively low-income people.

CHAPTER FOUR

The Digitalization of Public Services

This chapter analyzes the external forces that could impact government services, such as the development of the freelancing economy and the automation of economy's core functions. We also discuss the opportunity for governments to adopt fintech to improve public services. When a great deal of information must be processed and shared between several parties, blockchain can help to decentralize and automate processes. Thus, governments could use digital and blockchain technologies to increase the efficiency of core functions, such as providing social benefits, tax collection, and administrative documentation.

Digital Transformations for Governments

The world is moving fast. We are in the midst of fundamental changes to global financial structures, such as the emergence of tech giants and the explosion of peer-to-peer platforms. To continuously provide efficient services, governments need to adapt by moving toward digitization. But what does *digital government* mean? What does the future look like for government services?

Imagine Twenty-First-Century Public Services

Imagine that you want to renew your passport. If you were a citizen of a nation with a fully digital government, you could do this with a computer with an internet connection. You would log onto your account, fill in a few lines, and upload a few documents; all your personal data would be prefilled and stored. Your computer's camera, facial recognition and iris-scanning software, and microphone would be able to authenticate your identity. You would be able to press your fingers to a camera to record your fingerprints. Then you would receive a PDF file with an authentication number and a barcode, a "passport of the future." The whole process would take only ten minutes and would enable you to avoid lines and related travel expenses.

This is already happening in Dubai, where in 2018 the government launched the Dubai Paperless Strategy for visits to the Smart Dubai Office headquarters. From 2022 no employee or customer of the government will need to print any documents. For example, a police officer will have central access to driving licenses, passports, historical records, and such.

Imagine paying taxes with your smartphone by sending an SMS. We all pay various taxes (income, payroll, property, consumption), and fees and tolls. Instead of filing paperwork, writing checks, or sending wire transfers, we would only need to press the OK button on a smartphone or send an SMS. Wouldn't that make life easier?

This has already happened in many European countries. (In Sweden, such services have been available for more than a decade. In other countries, such as Romania, local taxes can be paid through mobile apps.) The Turkish economy relies on imports of raw materials and semi-finalized products, which involves a laborious and slow process of settling customs duties with customs brokers and banks. Since 2017, TEB, the Turkish retail bank of BNP Paribas Group, enabled companies to settle customs duties via SMS. The process involves three steps: Companies enter the phone numbers, send an SMS with a confirmation number, and make payments through the STP system. This has significantly shortened the time needed to pay taxes and has improved the cash management capabilities of many companies.

Imagine you live in a country where your welfare benefits are entirely digitized. All your personal information is registered and centralized in the government app, which removes the need for you to repeatedly fill out forms.

This already exists in India. India is using Aadhaar, the largest biometric identification program in the world, for digitizing government subsidy payments; financial services; recording employee attendance to reduce absenteeism; and issuance of passports, voter registration cards, and other forms of identification.

Imagine now that you create a new company, set up your company online, manage your business online, approve your prefilled taxes online, and access your banking and online payments from anywhere in the world. Amazingly, Estonia was the first country to offer e-Residency, a government-issued digital identity available to anyone in the world. "E-Residency offers the freedom to start and run a global business in a trusted EU environment." According to the government website, e-residents can (a) establish a company online from anywhere in the world, access business banking and online payment service providers like PayPal, and fully own their companies without a local director; (b) manage a company remotely (sign and authenticate documents, encrypt and send documents securely, and easily declare taxes); and (c) operate the company online while traveling, and even maintain the company after moving abroad.[1]

Estonia is a leader in terms of e-governance. The Estonian government applies data sharing among its agencies with consistent digital identification and signature protocols. It is also cooperating with private institutions so that Estonians can conduct government and business processes online or via mobile applications. Citizens can manage taxes with an e-tax board that allows them to review prefilled tax forms online and receive tax refunds in two days. On digital government platforms they can vote, register a new company or file annual reports, manage bank accounts, buy tickets, and enroll in schools. The Estonian government also founded a think tank and consulting organization called the e-Governance Academy to create and share best practices for e-governance, e-democracy, national cybersecurity, and the development of open-information societies.[2]

Governments Adapting to Technological Change

The demand for digital commerce drove the first wave of fintech changes within governments, a trend that continues. Until recently, a company's tax base was established according to the location of its headquarters. Now, in a globalized world, location is no longer as relevant.

Because global digital businesses present governments with new challenges, some countries and the European Union have begun to tax digital companies. Governments argue that taxation should be determined according to the consumer's location, not the location of a company's headquarters. This removes the arbitrage opportunities of e-commerce companies that locate their headquarters in low-tax or value-added-tax (VAT) countries, such as Luxembourg, while selling goods to citizens in high-tax or VAT countries, such as Italy and France. Today the United States is also looking at similar moves for e-commerce VAT by state of receivership.[3]

The second wave of change within governments relates to peer-to-peer platforms. Today's citizens are more mobile, and work is more decentralized. As a result, cross-border taxation issues continue to emerge. This socioeconomic trend will disrupt the overall economy and raise new taxation and social benefits challenges. The number of people using peer-to-peer platforms has consistently grown in recent years. The largest platforms (such as Alibaba, DiDi Chuxing, Amazon, and Airbnb) can reach tens of millions of people, opening the door to income opportunities for people working as taxi drivers, nannies, and software developers. They also enable people to earn passive income from, for example, renting a flat or a car while being excluded from normal taxation.

Clearly, governments need to understand the potential consequences of these changes and react swiftly. Tax erosion could be addressed by reforming social security rules and by "forcing" platforms to cooperate. However, systematic adaptation against smart and agile start-ups will require significant resources. Policymakers will need to rethink taxation, digitally savvy public servants will need to engage with new platforms, and IT infrastructures will need to adapt.

Cryptocurrencies are also causing a wave of change within governments. Over the past decade, since the introduction of Bitcoin, many other cryptocurrencies have emerged. The number of cryptocurrency users has grown significantly. In 2013 an estimated 300,000 to 1.3 million people used a cryptocurrency. In 2017 that number increased to between 2.9 million and 5.8 million.[4]

Cryptocurrencies bypass banks, which have traditionally served as intermediaries in the financial system. Without the banks, there is an increased risk of fraud. New cryptocurrencies could significantly affect today's currency exchanges, particularly in countries with high currency volatility.

Benefits of Digitization

Younger generations, such as millennials, are eager to do most government administrative tasks, such as paying taxes, online. Digitization can enable them to accomplish tasks with greater speed and efficiency, and it reduces government costs in the process.

Perhaps the greatest benefit of digital systems is the increased number of channels through which governments can reduce inequality. In the short term, digitization can make social transfers and tax collection more efficient, in the following ways.

First, digital payments can help improve the delivery of social welfare payments, by significantly reducing administrative costs for programs that aim to alleviate poverty. These improvements to social welfare programs can reduce inequality for individuals at the lower end of the income distribution.[5]

Second, digitization can increase tax compliance by allowing governments to process more taxpayer information, including income composition. This, in turn, can help identify tax evaders. Because tax evasion significantly impacts income distribution, by decreasing government revenues, systems that reduce evasion would decrease inequality and improve redistribution capacity.

Third, in the medium term, digitization can provide tools to reconfigure the tax system. It can help governments replace the proportional consumption tax system with a progressive consumption tax. Today's consumption tax is labeled as proportional, but many economists argue that it's a regressive system because lower-income households spend a larger proportion of disposable income on consumption. Using electronic transaction systems and biometric identification technology, the government could set lower consumption taxes for lower-income quintiles.

Finally, digitization could allow the government to implement a more progressive (yet complex) tax system based on individual and household income. By introducing a joint tax schedule across individual and household incomes, this tax system would generate fewer distortions, leading to greater accuracy and equality.

The E-Government

The continuous development of the welfare state, consumer society, and immediate digital service rewards have transformed what citizens expect from public administration. To meet these new requirements of speed, availability, and simplicity, administrations must rethink approaches to internal procedures and service delivery.

E-government, or e-administration, refers to the use of information and communication technologies (ICT) to improve public services and make them more accessible to users. Contrary to what one might think, electronic administration can be implemented through various mediums, not just internet web services. An e-government project can rely on any technology that improves the delivery of public services. These might include telematics, near-field communication, Bluetooth, or the Internet of Things.[6]

Governments can digitize numerous public services, but digitization is guided generally by two themes. The first theme includes dematerialization, centralization, and management of citizen data, whether for taxes, authentication, or social benefits.

The second theme focuses on simpler and smarter government interfaces that can offer fast responses to citizens and businesses without making people hop from one agency to another. This second theme includes automation, digitization, and simplification of back-office government processes.

The dematerialization and centralization of managing citizen data and administrative services is occurring in various countries. Governments are increasingly digitizing processes for passports, driving licenses, and other types of permits. Governments could eventually ask citizens to upload documents required for administrative services and only request in-person appearances for services that require fingerprints or on-site checks. For most documents, we could imagine public administrators sending PDFs with barcodes and authentication numbers rather than paper documents. Progress in authentication technology may also include smart cards, possibly combined with biometrics and / or RFID technology (electronic identity cards, biometric passports, and so on). We might see electronic voting procedures or video surveillances that converge with computers, databases, and biometric facial recognition processes. We can imagine a time when physical documents are no longer required. Airline and train tickets are now almost completely dematerialized.

An example of a dematerialized and centralized process is the French tax declaration. When submitting tax declarations, French citizens connect on an internet platform where everything has been prefilled in advance. They must verify and approve the accuracy of information. The full process takes no longer than five minutes. Obviously this necessitates integration with companies, banks, and other countries to make an automatic declaration.

In regard to the second theme—centralizing information at local, state, or national levels—government agencies that only provide information to citizens could be replaced by phone, digital services, algorithms, or robots.

Governments could also digitize the administrative services they provide to businesses. Companies could issue online requests for licenses, taxes, and benefits. They could initiate requests online and then receive the corresponding documents. Given the increasing complexity of business regulations, a centralized interface could be extremely beneficial to businesses, particularly when business leaders need information about tax, labor, and regulation issues.

The third theme relates to the automation, digitization, and simplification of government—the processes and services within sectors such as legal and police administration. These processes include such things as fines, criminal records, tolls, and parking lots. Some countries, such as the United States and South Africa, have already started digitizing these processes. For example, Pay By Plate MA in Boston provides customers electronic toll collection through video images of vehicle license plates.[7]

We can also identify four stages in which governments are dematerializing processes and transactions: (a) online information (ground zero of dematerialization); (b) downloadable forms (with no possibility of online filing); (c) forms to complete and validate online; and (d) online applications and declarations (with electronic form submissions).

A serious e-government project must make it possible to completely overhaul administrative procedures. The challenge is in knowing, not what proof must be transmitted by citizens to the administration, but *why* it should be transmitted, and whether the transmission is useful and effective. Therefore, beyond technical and informational issues, e-administration generally results in an in-depth reorganization of information systems and relationships with other organizations.

Although these changes are not easy, digitizing government processes will continue to improve accessibility and transparency. For users, many information services and online procedures can be completed seven days a week, twenty-four hours a day. This offers advantages for urban users who cannot leave their desks during the workday, and for anyone living in rural areas far from government offices. It can eliminate lines, provide accurate and sourced information, simplify procedures with fewer documents, and increase transparency by giving citizens status updates on their requests.

So, what prevents governments from adapting faster? First, in the short term it is expensive to transition away from legacy systems. Second, many of those who are called upon to manage such systems lack the relevant knowledge. Third, government leaders fear they will have to lay off civil servants. Imagine all the public servants with full-time administrative processing jobs who could be eliminated by automation or digitization. The digital transformation will create new types of jobs, but others will become obsolete. Thus, the challenge for governments is to successfully transition without causing citizens too much pain.

Follow the Digital Leaders

Advanced economies are most often the leaders in developing digital government functions. According to the 2020 E-Government Development Index (EGDI), published by the United Nations, Europe is the global leader. The Americas and Asia are almost equal in their transitions to digital governments, ranking in the high and middle EGDI levels. Africa, where many countries continue to struggle to improve their e-government standings, ranks last. At the national level, the top ten countries are Denmark, the Republic of Korea, Estonia, Finland, Australia, Sweden, the United Kingdom, New Zealand, the United States, and the Netherlands. Perhaps it is sometimes easier for smaller countries to reinvent themselves digitally. They have fewer jobs at risk, they can more easily coordinate constituencies, and some have stronger political systems.

The benefits of being a digital leader are significant. There is a strong correlation between a country's per capita GDP and its score on the 2020 EGDI. Is this causal? Which is the chicken and which is the egg?[8]

On the one hand, stronger economic growth allows countries to spend more to adopt digital public services, which increases a country's performance on the E-Government Development Index. And on the other hand, a high level of digitization contributes to economic growth, leading to higher GDP. A digital government can improve inclusion, reduce poverty, increase access to quality health care and education, and reduce CO_2 emissions.

Sometimes nations that lack a legacy system can have a competitive advantage. Two small countries, the UAE and Singapore, have become leaders in the next generation of digital government services.

The United Arab Emirates has quickly become one of today's leading digital countries. Dubai is now one of the world's biggest laboratories for interactive government applications, connecting every individual to the city in a seamless and efficient way. "We are marching ahead into the digital future," said Sheikh Hamdan. "Dubai will be set to embrace all sorts of smart and interactive applications."

In 2011, Dubai introduced e-payment cards for government services and e-voting. Two years later, in 2013, all government services became available through mobile devices and apps. Smart Dubai, a government project, facilitates collaboration among private-sector and government partners. The project was established to promote and improve experiences for residents and visitors by providing news about weather, traffic, entertainment, tourism, flights, dining, and emergency services. This information flows via fiber optic networks that facilitate high-speed internet access in main public areas. In 2014 the government launched the Happiness Index to measure the public's satisfaction with digital public services—with the goal of becoming the world's happiest city.

One thousand new digital initiatives were launched in Dubai in 2016 to embrace the Internet of Things. These included the world's first 3D-printed office block (with the vision of being a world leader in 3D printing technology). In 2017 Sheikh Mohammed directed the launch of the 10X initiative, encouraging "all government entities to embrace out-of-the-box, future oriented, exponential thinking with the aim of being ten years ahead of all other cities in embracing disruptive innovation." Dubai's leaders also decided to make 25 percent of all transportation in the city smart and driverless by 2030, and to use blockchain technologies for all government documents by 2020.[9]

The city-state of Singapore is also positioning itself as a leading global tech hub. Its geographical location at the crossroads of Asia and the West, its pro-business environment, and its stability make this island particularly attractive to companies around the world. Singapore benefits from government commitment to digitization through its Smart Nation program, which encompasses initiatives for mobility, environment, fintech, and public services.

Singapore can optimize data for public services. The government opened access to a central registry of seventy government e-services and thirty banking services, including applications for new apartments and school admissions. This registry is integrated with citizen information on MyInfo, which reduces the need to fill out forms and verify documents, and which reduces the time required to open a bank account.

The Land Transport Authority also uses data to improve commuter travel. This has reduced the number of overcrowded buses and the waiting times at some stations by 92 percent. Transportation data shared with the broader public includes bus arrival times, live traffic conditions, parking availability, and taxi-booking services. As a result there has emerged an ecosystem of third-party transportation applications (such as taxi and bicycle apps).[10]

Private companies share information about banking and financial markets with Singapore's Monetary Authority, which can be downloaded from the latter's website. This enables developers, for example, to automatically collect information on interest rates.

Information flow between these government services and the public is not one-way. The public uses an app to receive environmental updates and municipal information, and the government uses the same app to receive information about problems related to animals, pests, roads, cleanliness, greenery, construction, drains, and water. Feedback from citizens can be routed to the appropriate agency.

The "2016 Global Information Technology Report," published by the World Economic Forum and INSEAD, ranked Singapore first on the Networked Readiness Index, which measures a country's technological attractiveness and capabilities. The report lists Singapore and Dubai as being two of today's top digital government labs. As a result, they serve as models for what other nations could achieve in the next ten years.

As we write in early 2021, investment in digital technologies is also proving valuable as a means of containing pandemic issues. Although it is too early in this pandemic's spread for us to make research conclusions, Singapore was successful in eradicating the 2003 SARS epidemic within its borders, in only three months.

Singapore's containment strategies were centered around hospitals, other health care facilities, and community control. Government policy strictly enforced quarantine orders with fines, and all sectors were required to cooperate, including the Ministry of Health, clinicians who cared for SARS patients, and the laboratory experts who hunted for the virus and developed diagnostic tests.

Using its nationwide CCTV camera system, the government could quickly trace sources and contacts, enforce quarantines and meticulous social distancing, and deploy the armed services when needed. Virus detection was as systematic as possible. Health workers checked temperatures in schools, workplaces, communities, and the Changi Airport.

Blockchain and Government

Banks and governments share at least one thing in common: They both manage complex processes for data gathering and sharing across many divisions and entities. What can governments gain by adopting banking technologies such as blockchain?

Adopting Blockchain

Blockchain, which is basically a digital ledger, is increasingly used in financial services. It allows banks and insurance companies to better manage consumer data and to simplify interorganizational data exchanges and automation processes. Governments are the next horizon for the deployment of blockchain technologies because it can simplify tax collection, welfare spending, and other government services.[11]

Blockchain provides a powerful, decentralized way to safely aggregate, record, and share transactions via a cost-effective, transparent ledger. All sharing parties can see the data, personal information is kept confidential. For example, if bank A shares transactional data about its lending activity with client X, and bank B also loans and shares its data with the same client X, bank A cannot see the details of bank B's loans, and vice versa. This is meant to ensure that there can be no client poaching. However, both banks gain access to the client's aggregate indebtedness and can make decisions based on the client's potential lending risks.[12]

Within government sectors, blockchain technologies may lead to four key improvements: better data management between government agencies; reduced errors when handling citizens' data; automation of costly reconciliation processes and data handling; and safer and easier redistribution systems that track the aggregated wallet.

The first improvement deals with better data management between government agencies. The transparency of blockchain technologies can decrease skepticism about government mismanagement of money and provide better information about the flow of funds and the money supply. These improvements can apply to emerging economies, where currencies can be volatile. A common blockchain registry could reduce tax evasion and money laundering, which are prevalent in advanced and emerging economies, by facilitating cooperation between countries that need to track the same lawbreaker.

The second improvement is related to the reduction of errors in handling citizens' data. Because blockchain is defined by and implements predetermined rules, it offers a transparent framework that improves trust in digital processes and helps overcome data-synchronization issues.

Third, blockchain improves the automation of costly reconciliation processes and data handling. It acts as a cooperation tool between entities, while keeping data confidential. On the taxation side, blockchain can help tax authorities gather information from various entities, thereby helping them to collect taxes at a lower cost and possibly decrease the tax gap. For example, due to the emergence of P2P platforms and an increased number of small businesses, taxation could become complex and costly. Blockchain could help tax authorities reduce administrative burdens and lower the levying costs in a transparent, instantaneous, and secure manner.[13] Blockchain could also reduce the cost of administering government payments to citizens (that is, social welfare plans), thereby helping to address inequality.[14]

Fourth, blockchain offers a safer and easier redistribution system that tracks digital wallets. Blockchain can increase public-sector efficiency and transparency while decreasing transaction costs. The technology provides an alternative and potentially superior disbursement method by enabling end users to receive benefits directly into their digital wallets, which reduces the transaction costs paid by banks and local authorities. Blockchain can also increase the transparency related to public expenditures while reducing fraud and errors in the delivery of public benefits.

Several governments and governmental organizations, such as the UK Department of Work and Pensions (DWP), use blockchain to improve services. DWP has been working with the start-up Govcoin to develop a blockchain solution for welfare payments. Govcoin's objective is to virtually mimic the jam-jar method of budgeting (dividing money into separate pots for different expenses). Using a mobile phone app, Govcoin gives claimants instant access to benefits and payment processing. Claimants can download the app and then create virtual jam jars into which they can allocate pension money for expenditures such as rent or electricity.[15]

The Estonian government states that "since 2012, blockchain has been in operational use in Estonia's registries, such as national health, judicial, legislative, security and commercial code systems, with plans to extend its use to other spheres such as personal medicine, cybersecurity, and data embassies." The technology developed by Estonia has been used by many organizations, including NATO, the US Department of Defense, and the European Union information system for cybersecurity.

At the end of 2017 the Dubai government announced its willingness to become the world's first blockchain-powered government. Dubai's aim was to have all visa applications, bill payments, and license renewals transacted with blockchain. This accounts for over one hundred million documents each year. According to Smart Dubai, the strategy could save 25.1 million labor hours, or a $1.5 billion per year savings for Dubai, which is significant for a tiny country with about three million inhabitants. Much of this enhanced productivity will come from moving to a paperless government system.[16]

Plugging Blockchain into Peer-to-Peer Platforms

The emergence of P2P businesses is directly impacting the global economy. The trend is changing the workforce and creating new channels for commerce. To avoid tax erosion, governments need to react fast.

Tens of millions of people use P2P platforms such as Alibaba, DiDi Chuxing, Amazon, and Airbnb. A Pew Research study suggested that 72 percent of American adults have used at least one of eleven shared, on-demand services. Small businesses and individuals who otherwise have difficulty competing with large organizations increasingly use P2P platforms to reduce transaction costs. The platforms, as a result, have become intermediaries for millions of transactions worth billions of dollars. For example, in 2015, P2P platforms enabled transactions worth EUR 28 billion (USD 31 billion)—and the average transaction value was about $10.[17] These platforms have attracted so much capital and have earned such high valuations that they are encroaching on an increasing number of economic sectors.

However, the peer-to-peer economy is (so far) largely unregulated, which creates significant socioeconomic challenges, such as unfair competition and tax erosion. P2P workers often do not pay taxes on their income from the services they offer, giving them a price advantage over "regulated" workers. The downside for P2P workers is that they often lack social security, health care, and pension benefits that cover most regulated workers.

If P2P activities benefit from a lower tax rate, the shift toward a P2P economy would imply a reduction in government income. This will require governments to levy taxes from many small businesses. However, taxation in the P2P economy is much more complex, difficult, and limited, even in advanced economies, in part because the income sources of small firms are more dispersed. Misreporting is more common among small companies than among large corporations. Moreover, the status of participants within a P2P platform can impact the way taxes are computed. Some participants are classified as individual workers and some as small, registered businesses that leverage the platform to boost commercial activity (for example, many "professional" lenders or agents on Airbnb). The classifications of "self-employed" and "employee" can trigger different tax rates and change responsibilities for tax withholding and reporting. While a status "self-employed" is generally more advantageous for the P2P platform, it may imply lower social benefits and job stability.

In light of these challenges, levying taxes from small businesses with multisourced revenues needs to be achieved by simplifying tax policies and collecting digital records of transactions and income maintained by P2P platforms. Not surprisingly, tax authorities are tempted to request access to this information and, in certain cases, to require platforms to act as tax collectors that remit taxes to authorities. However, most platforms have not been eager to share information or participate in tax collection. Collaboration between a platform and a government may be negatively perceived by users, reducing the platform's attractiveness.

In most scenarios, governments will need to force tax cooperation, which could lead to legal disputes. That factor aside, governments will need talented individuals with a strong grasp of technology to: (a) understand the impact of tax rules on platforms, (b) write fair taxation policies, (c) develop the right approaches to enforcing the policies, and (d) implement policies transparently so as to build trust with the platforms and their users.

In that context, blockchain is a good tool. Governments can use it to gather data from platforms and aggregate the data for an individual without compromising privacy. Blockchain can improve collaboration between platforms and authorities, and therefore help to create an efficient tax collection system for individual transactions. The platforms could use blockchain to directly report and levy taxes.

The P2P economy is expected to grow and become more prominent. Thus, governments must find a solution. Adapting to the P2P economy will require significant resources. Policymakers will need to rethink tax policy while digitally savvy public servants adapt government platforms and IT infrastructures. The tax erosion problem could be overcome by forcing platforms to cooperate—over a blockchain system. The money saved by using blockchain could be used for social security, welfare, and pension benefits for freelance workers.

Collaboration against Fraud

In a globalized world, cooperation between governments and banks is essential to fight against fraud and to cope with the rise of cross-border taxation issues generated by worker mobility and the decentralization of work.

Wealthy individuals tend to pay lower taxes, on average, than low- and middle-income individuals. The Internal Revenue Service (IRS) of the United States computed the average income tax rates by income earner brackets. Interestingly, the tax distribution resembles an inverted U-curve. The top 1 percent of income earners paid more taxes than the top 50 percent of earners. The distribution's peak is the top 1 percent because the taxes paid by the top 0.001 percent of earners is lower than what is paid by the top 5 percent (Figure 4.1). High-net-worth individuals tend to pay taxes that are low as a percentage of total income, but relatively high as an absolute value, which justifies the use of tax advisors who can help them to optimize tax bills through loopholes and offshore tax structures.[18]

Tax evasion ranks high in government priorities around the world, as illustrated by the recent Panama Papers scandal. According to the World Bank, the wealth in tax havens has significantly risen since the 1970s and represents more

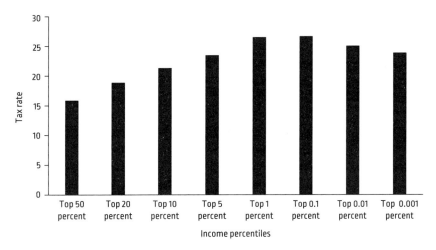

Data source: Internal Revenue Service, "Individual Income Tax Shares, Tax Year 2017," Statistics of Income, Summer 2020, https://www.irs.gov/pub/irs-soi/soi-a-ints-id2003.pdf.

Note: Average income tax rates, by income percentile in the United States.

FIGURE 4.1   More money but lower tax rates

than 10 percent of global GDP. In a low-growth, stagnate purchasing power environment, tax evasion erodes government revenue. As a result, it is an issue of social justice and credibility for governments that reduce social benefits to the poorest or increase taxes on the middle class.

Over the last few years, the taxation of the wealthiest has tended to increase. This temporary increase represents national efforts to rebuild economies after the 2007–2008 financial crisis. This rebuilding has occurred by increasing taxes on capital gains and wealth, and in some cases by taxing high-value residential properties, which is a model developed in China and the UK. In addition to increasing taxes on wealthy people, authorities have also done more to enforce tax regulations on those individuals. Authorities often justify the cost of enforcement (primarily by information exchange) by citing the large returns they gain from wealthy citizens. However, higher taxes and better enforcement comes with an increased risk of prosecution in cases of tax fraud or evasion.

Similarly, multinationals have typically paid lower tax rates on average than small and medium enterprises (SMEs). The European Commission's 2017 report "A Fair and Efficient Tax System in the European Union for the Digital Single Market" revealed that the effective tax rate for digital businesses is about 50 percent less than the rate paid by traditional businesses in Europe. Specifically, traditional domestic business models pay an effective rate of 22 percent compared to 8 percent for their digital counterparts (Figure 4.2).

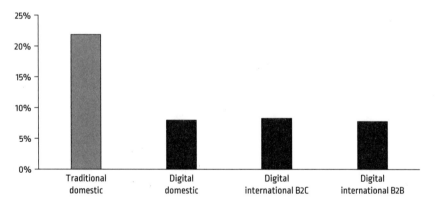

Data source: PWC, "Steuerliche Standordattraktivitat digitaler Geschaftsmodelle," 2018, https://www.pwc.de /de/steuern/pwc-studie-steuerlicher-digitalisierungsindex-2018.pdf.

FIGURE 4.2   Effective average tax rate in the European Union

By facilitating more intergovernmental cooperation, digitization and block-chain offer governments an opportunity to fight against underground econo-mies, illegal activities, tax evasion, fraud, money laundering, and terrorism. A global financial register, such as blockchain, that records and shares the owner-ship of assets and incomes would better enable governments to enforce regula-tions in the new economy.

Reconciling corporate revenues and taxation across countries is key. Better tax control will proceed hand in hand with financial transparency, international transmissions of bank information, global registry of financial assets, and global coordination of wealth taxation based on reliable data. These elements can be unified through digitization, thereby allowing governments to process more in-formation about taxpayers and to better identify tax evaders. This, in turn, can encourage tax compliance and deter attempts to optimize tax evasion, particu-larly among those in top income brackets.[19] In short, blockchain can be another tool to reduce inequalities caused by tax evasion and to increase funds allocated for social welfare programs.

Governments have already shared information with each other for security purposes. The International Criminal Police Organization has a long history of establishing strong relationships with a wide variety of international organ-izations, both governmental and nongovernmental. One of the oldest agreements, with the Council of Europe, dates to the 1960s. Since then, many agreements have been established with organizations, including the United Nations, the European Union, the Commonwealth of Independent States, the International Criminal Court, the African Union, the Organization of American States, and the Arab Interior Ministers' Council.[20]

Another example is the collaboration between the US government and foreign banks. The Foreign Account Tax Compliance Act (FATCA) gener-ally requires foreign financial and nonfinancial institutions to report assets held by their US account holders. FATCA can also subject them to with-holdings on some payments. The HIRE Act also contains legislation requiring US citizens to report some foreign financial accounts and assets, depending on the value.

International organizations have also initiated measures to optimize taxation. In 2012 the OECD/G20 launched the Base Erosion and Profit Shifting (BEPS) inclusive framework to overcome tax avoidance. The BEPS initiative addresses "tax avoidance strategies that exploit gaps and mismatches in tax rules to arti-ficially shift profits to low- or no-tax locations." In July 2021, 130 countries—representing over 90 percent of the world's economy—endorsed a global min-imum tax rate of at least 15 percent.[21]

At the regional level, the European Union has implemented the electronic VAT directive, as of January 1, 2015. This directive taxes electronic service providers at the VAT rate applied in the country where their customer is established, not the country where the customer has cleverly chosen to register. This regulation has had a primary impact on small economies in the EU that are attractive to corporations with low business taxes. For example, Amazon, eBay, and Apple (iTunes) were all located in Luxembourg, where the VAT rate was the lowest in the European Union (15 percent). When the law came into force, most of Amazon, eBay, and Apple' European customers were not in fact based in Luxembourg, but in France, Germany, and the United Kingdom. Because these companies had to then pay the VAT rates where their clients were based, the incentive to set up their headquarters in Luxembourg or Dublin became much lower. As a result, Luxembourg lost a lot of revenue; the VAT revenue no longer originated from the Luxembourg government, and some corporations relocated their headquarters.[22]

To reinforce this type of cooperation against fraud, national tax authorities could use blockchain to create a global financial registry of assets and income. This would require significant cooperation between G7 or G20 governments and "force" smaller countries and tax havens to join the game.

Blockchain technology can also reinforce cooperation between banks and governments. Banks can use blockchain to syndicate loans together, as a safe way to share and exchange data without compromising their respective commercial interests. Increased international coordination between governments and corporations against tax evasion could be facilitated by digitizing taxes.

CHAPTER FIVE

A Macroeconomic View of Growth, Inequality, and Financial Exclusion

Over the last century, low-income countries have benefited from increased global trade, the spread of new technologies, and the mobility of labor. These trends in world economic output have improved living standards, health, and education. However, many low-income countries still suffer from financial exclusion. This chapter provides the macroeconomic context for a more specific analysis of fintech in subsequent chapters. We describe, in overarching terms, how globalization has impacted emerging economies—the ways it has changed inequality between nations and within each nation. We discuss how the remaining gaps in access to financial services can be tackled in order to help more people escape poverty.

Growth, Inequality, and Technology

Technology may not be a *primary* driver of inequality, but it seems to work in tandem with globalization. In the twentieth century there was a trend toward increased productivity via machines and automation. Today technology continues to shape the global labor market; the markets with the cheapest labor often assume a large share of the jobs.

Technology enables and accelerates change in the types of jobs that are in demand. The proportion of G7 countries that added value to the manufacturing sector (as a percentage of GDP) rose between 1820 and 1990 and then took a downward turn. In the United States the number of employees in the manufacturing sector rose after World War II, which in turn contributed to the expansion of the American middle class. During that time the United States established pro-labor policies and faced limited global competition. In the 1980s and 1990s this trend reversed, which may be explained by the rise of China, globalized free trade, and decreased costs for communications and transportation.

Then, fractured production processes led to the emergence of global supply chains. These factors resulted in the offshoring of thousands of American manufacturing facilities. Millions of manufacturing jobs were transferred to countries with lower wage structures.[1]

Technology has been a catalyst for accelerating globalization, leading to massive job outsourcing and greater workforce competition. People today often research and design products in countries with expensive labor markets and then assemble the products in countries with low-wage labor. This results in a worldwide supply chain.

Several emerging economies have become global economic contenders over the past century. The 2007–2008 global financial crisis gave these economies a momentary pause, but their upward trajectory has continued.

Globalization: One Billion People Out of Poverty

Shortly after World War II, many economists feared that famine would spread and that disparity gaps between the rich and the poor would widen. Many expected that increased inequality would lead to increasing social disorder and unrest.

However, while the world's population more than tripled, to 7.9 billion people, the proportion of people living below the poverty line rapidly declined (Figure 5.1).

In the aggregate, humanity has arguably just experienced its best quarter century. Since 1980, for example, more than a billion people have been lifted out of extreme poverty. According to the World Bank, the global poverty rate has dropped from 35 percent in 1990 to 11 percent in 2013. In other words, 1,083,000 people have climbed out of abject poverty toward a more stable and secure life. And infant mortality—a critical indicator—has been halved. These trends are even more remarkable when we realize that the world's population grew by almost 1.9 billion during this period. The world has never seen anything like this before.

Between 1981 and 2008, the number of people living on less than $1.25 a day dropped in East Asia and the Pacific, and more specifically in China. Meanwhile, in South Asia the proportion of people below the poverty line remained unchanged. Likewise, poverty rates across the Middle East and North Africa, Latin America, the Caribbean, eastern Europe, and Central Asia remained unchanged. Conversely, in the same period the number of people living on less than $1.25 a day in sub-Saharan Africa increased.

Between 1980 and 2016, economic conditions in emerging countries improved at a rapid pace, particularly in China. The proportion of the population living

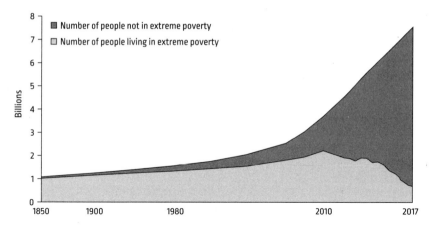

Data sources: The absolute number for the world population is taken from the Our World in Data world popula-tion data set: Max Roser, Hannah Ritchie, and Esteban Ortiz-Ospina, "World Population Growth," Our World in Data, May 2019, https://ourworldindata.org/world-population-growth. All poverty estimates from 1981 and later are taken from World Bank, PovcalNet, https://openknowledge.worldbank.org/bitstream /handle/10986/34496/9781464816024.pdf. All data from 1980 and earlier is taken from François Bourguignon and Christian Morrisson, "Inequality among World Citizens: 1820–1992," *American Economic Review* 92, no. 4 (2002): 727–748. These authors state that "the poverty lines were calibrated so that poverty and extreme poverty headcounts in 1992 coincided roughly with estimates from other sources"; here we rely on the midpoint. Ex-treme poverty refers to instances of people living on less than 1.90 PPP/day "international $." International $ are adjusted for price differences between countries and for price changes over time (inflation).

FIGURE 5.1   World population living in extreme poverty, 1820–2017

below the poverty line in China dropped from 50 percent in 1980 to less than 10 percent in the 2000s. In India the relative poverty rate was halved between 1993 and 2011.

However, the "China effect" may soon be over, for three reasons. Chinese economic growth has already begun inflecting. The nation's GDP growth rate has been below 10 percent since 2010. China's economy is still growing, albeit at a slower pace, which means that wages and exchange rates will likely rise. In response, Chinese supply chains are moving to less-developed coun-tries where labor is less expensive. This shift toward increased employment in lower-wage countries may result in Asia and Africa's ability to attract more supply chain opportunities. Furthermore, information technology innovations reduce transaction costs and therefore could facilitate rapid transitions in supply chains.

However, rapid growth in emerging economies, which has greatly reduced the number of people living in abject poverty, is often accompanied by an un-desirable outcome: widening inequality gaps within each nation, as we show below. It is important to recognize the difference between declining rates of poverty and rising within-country inequality. Both can occur simultaneously.

In the 1990s the Chinese and Indian governments took steps toward economic liberalization, but they played a direct role in fostering growth by making large-scale infrastructure investments. This produced a steep economic growth trajectory that lifted more than one billion people out of abject poverty in the 1990s. Nevertheless, intra-country inequalities also increased.

What happened in China and India has also happened in other parts of the world. In the last two decades, many emerging economies have undergone a complex transformation. One of the most remarkable features of this transformation has been the growing middle class. The most impoverished people have experienced improved living standards. Beginning in the 1990s, economic growth rates increased exponentially. China, India, Brazil, Russia, Mexico, Turkey, Indonesia, and South Africa all benefited from exponential growth and a growing middle class. In 2015 the world's top ten middle-class markets included Brazil, Russia, India, and China. Indonesia is expected to join this list in 2020, and both Mexico and Turkey are expected to enter the fold by 2030.[2]

Despite the absolute gains in wealth, roughly two-thirds of developing and emerging economies saw increased within-country income inequality between 1998 and 2011. Wealth generated in emerging markets was captured by a narrow slice of the population. Specifically, 82 percent of the wealth generated in 2017 went to the richest 1 percent of the global population. Meanwhile, the 3.7 billion people who make up the poorest half of the world saw no increase in their wealth, according to Oxfam.[3]

To illustrate the magnitude of the disparity, consider that in China the richest decile of the population earns thirteen times as much as the poorest decile, compared with a five-to-one ratio in the United States. In 2017, 73 percent of the wealth generated in India went to the richest 1 percent, while the bottom 50 percent saw their wealth increase by only 1—percent.[4]

These figures are concerning. When the income share of a population's top 20 percent increases, overall economic growth is expected to decline in the midterm. On the other hand, an increase in the income share of the lowest 20 percent is associated with increased GDP growth.[5]

Economic Growth and Inequality

One way to measure and compare income inequality within and between countries is by using the Gini coefficient. If a country had a Gini coefficient of one, it would mean one person received all the country's income. A coefficient of zero reflects perfect equality. Comparative data suggests that income inequality has risen in twelve out of thirty countries in Asia, including China, India, and Indonesia. Figure 5.2 suggests that in low-income countries, Gini coefficients tend to rise with increased economic growth. This provides evidence that emerging economies develop at the expense of rising inequality.[6]

One reason inequalities have increased in the past is related to shifting employment opportunities. Over the past four decades, increased global trade and financial sector expansion have precipitated exponential growth in the service sector; however, more traditional sectors have been left behind.

Many emerging economies still depend on agriculture as a primary source of employment. Worldwide, the agriculture sector employs more than 1.3 billion people, 97 percent of whom live in developing countries. The significant productivity gap between agriculture and service industries is positively correlated with income inequality. This helps explain why income inequality coincides with economic growth.[7]

Inequality is especially prominent in "dual beginner economies" where agriculture and non-agriculture sectors have diverging levels of productivity and average incomes (Figure 5.3). In such settings, a 1 percent increase in the intersectoral gap is associated with a 0.5 percent increase in income inequality.[8]

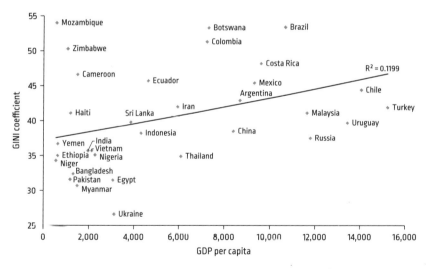

Data source: World Bank, GINI Index, https://data.worldbank.org/indicator/SI.POV.GINI; World Bank, GDP Per Capita, https://data.worldbank.org/indicator/NY.GDP.PCAP.KD.

Note: GDP per capita is 2020 for all countries, except Yemen (2018).

FIGURE 5.2   GINI coefficient and GDP per capita

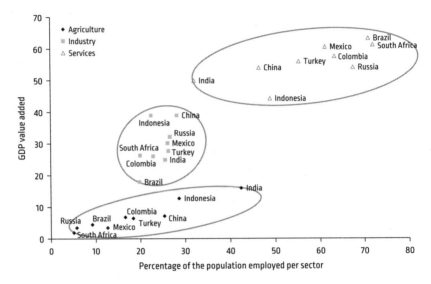

Data sources: World Bank, "Agriculture, Forestry, and Fishing, Value Added (% of GDP)," https://data .worldbank.org/indicator/NV.AGR.TOTL.ZS; World Bank, "Services, Value Added (% of GDP)," https:// data.worldbank.org/indicator/NV.SRV.TOTL.ZS; World Bank, "Industry (Including Construction), Value Added (% of GDP)," https://data.worldbank.org/indicator/NV.IND.TOTL.ZS; World Bank, "Employment in Services (% of Total Employment) (Modeled ILO Estimate)," https://data.worldbank.org/indicator/sl.srv .empl.zs; World Bank, "Employment in Agriculture (% of Total Employment) (Modeled ILO Estimate)," https://data.worldbank.org/indicator/SL.AGR.EMPL.ZS; World Bank, "Employment in Industry (% of Total Employment) (Modeled ILO Estimate)," https://data.worldbank.org/indicator/SL.IND.EMPL.ZS.

FIGURE 5.3 Comparison of GDP value-added vs. proportion of population working in agriculture, industry, and services (2019)

Studies indicate that non-agriculture employment growth can facilitate a movement from extreme to moderate poverty. In general, this mobility requires people to develop different skill sets and obtain higher levels of education. This in turn requires more investment in education and related skill-building services.[9]

Shifting from a predominantly agricultural economy to a more industrialized service economy can reduce poverty and inequality. However, countries must overcome three significant hurdles before they can successfully make the transition: They must develop infrastructure, education, and health care.

A lack of infrastructure presents a tremendous barrier to economic growth in developing countries that seek to transition from an agricultural society to an industrialized, service-oriented economy. A study in Nepal demonstrated that poor-quality roads made it more difficult for impoverished populations to travel to and connect with markets. This had an obvious impact on countrywide commercial activity. Researchers estimate that in developing countries, existing infrastructure (or the lack thereof) accounts for at least 40 percent of business productivity. For these reasons, the United Nations has emphasized infrastructure improvements as an essential sustainability goal.[10]

The World Bank has also suggested that increasing internet access by 10 percent could result in a 1.4 percent increase in a developing country's GDP. In these settings, smartphones are often the primary vehicle for gaining internet access and for connecting to digital financial services, health care, and higher-quality education. For example, M-Pesa's Vodafone mobile financial service helped lift 2 percent of all Kenyan households out of extreme poverty from 2008 to 2016.[11]

Unfortunately, infrastructure investments can cost from $1 billion to over $1 trillion, a price that many developing countries cannot afford. Existing infrastructure in many countries often requires major overhauls, as opposed to simple upgrades. This means that the governments of developing countries tend to rely on private-sector or direct foreign investments to modernize their economies.[12]

As developing countries struggle with inadequate infrastructure, they also face the challenges of insufficient education and health care services. In parts of Asia, the poorest students (in the lowest income quintile) are twenty times less likely to attend college than those in the wealthiest income quintile. Similarly, the chance of dying at birth for an infant born to a low-income household is about ten times higher than that of an infant born into a high-income household. Being born in a low-income household generally translates into less investment in education, health, and other essential forms of human development. These types of investments strongly impact one's future opportunities, living standards, aspirations, and self-perceptions.

Education is a highly productive investment in developing countries. At the country level, educational spending varies little across regions within low-income countries, ranging from 2 percent to 4 percent of GDP. Panel data of thirty-one low-income countries over the period 1970 to 2008 showed that a 1 percent increase in education spending (typically increasing spending by 0.02 to 4 percent of GDP) led to a 0.18 increase in overall GDP.[13]

The literature indicates that educational investment represents a trade-off between lost wages in the short term and higher wages over the long run. This is a trade-off that poor households must consider when deciding whether a teenager should work or attend school. Improvements in education rely, in part, on government ministries and nongovernmental organizations (NGOs) that clearly communicate the long-term value of education. For example, on average, an additional year of schooling is associated with a 10 percent increase in earnings.

Beyond individual and family benefits, developing stronger formal educational systems is a foundation for developing nations to transition away from agricultural economies. Moreover, improvements in education, health care, and infrastructure support economic growth and correlate with workforce transitions out of informal and into formal conditions.

Financial Technology and Reducing Inequality

Fortunately, there is a way to reduce income inequality in emerging economies that does not require dramatic overhauls of employment opportunities. When analyzing relationships between economic growth, inequality, and financial inclusion, scholars have found that fintech greatly reduces inequality. Clarke, Xu, and Zou indicate that *financial deepening*—a term used by economists to refer to increased access to financial service provisions—is associated with lower income inequality. When Thorsten and his colleagues assessed the impact of financial development on changes to low incomes and income distribution, they found that financial development was associated with a lower Gini coefficient growth rate and a higher income growth rate.[14]

Chakravarty suggests that economic development, as measured by a nation's per capita income, is positively associated with that state's level of financial inclusion. In addition, it is suggested that low rates of financial inclusion have direct negative impacts on health, education, and gender equality.[15]

The Asian Development Bank (ADB) researched financial exclusion's effects on women, and on micro, small, and medium enterprises. The bank estimated that addressing financial exclusion among these populations and business sectors could increase economic growth by 9 to 14 percent, even in relatively large economies such as those in Indonesia and the Philippines. Improving financial inclusion could have a tremendous impact particularly in smaller emerging markets such as Cambodia and Myanmar, where formal providers meet only a small percentage of current financial service needs.[16]

By improving access to financial services, fintech has the potential to boost productivity and income levels. It can thereby move low-income earners closer to the middle class. It could also help governments transition informal jobs into the formal, taxable economy and provide an efficient infrastructure for government redistribution efforts.

Hong and colleagues found in a 2020 study of Chinese inhabitants that fintech adoption improves risk-taking for all, but that individuals who are more risk-tolerant benefit more from fintech advancement. They found that cities with low financial-service coverage benefit the most from fintech penetration. Overall their results showed that by unshackling the traditional constraints, fintech improves risk-taking for individuals who need it the most.[17]

Another advantage of fintech innovations is that emerging economies can adopt them without disrupting existing infrastructures. Developing economies have an opportunity to become first adopters of new technologies, leapfrogging expensive infrastructure that wealthy countries built a century ago. A prime example of this can be found in South Africa's adoption of prepaid technologies.[18]

The following are some of the ways fintech can address inequality:

1. *Facilitating and increasing access to credit:* The smallest enterprises, even roadside vendors, can benefit greatly from credit; access to capital is one of the most recognized solutions for addressing poverty.

2. *Channeling small savings into the formal economy:* Small savers can benefit from access to savings and investment options provided by fintech, which can reduce the theft and fraud that cash and informal savings are prone to.

3. *Improving risk management:* Average low-income households or small businesses in an emerging economy can have risk profiles that are strikingly different from those in higher-income segments. Both low- and high-income segments require targeted and cost-efficient products and services that cater to their needs.

4. *Reducing information asymmetries:* Information about market pricing can reduce the influence of intermediaries who take a premium for providing better access to information. Fintech can help farmers, for instance, obtain current market prices for perishable produce, which enables them to immediately deliver their goods to the most profitable locations. This has the dual benefit of reducing storage costs and realizing more immediate profits.

5. *Reducing product and service costs:* E-commerce, including B2C, C2C, and G2C, offers greater convenience and higher value to underserved populations who previously lacked equal access. This also results in better economic and social outcomes for all.

6. *Reducing transaction costs:* Mobile money, for example, obviates the need to travel to a bank branch, enabling pensioners to access funds without transportation costs. Moreover, the costs of withdrawing social security payments, such as pensions, would be drastically reduced if cash did not have to be withdrawn from a distant bank branch (the losses include opportunity costs of lost wages while traveling).

Improving financial inclusion does more than advance the economic conditions of a population. It can also improve social and physical well-being. For instance, statistically significant mental health improvements have been recorded among those who received financial advice and services. This implies that financial inclusion has health-positive effects. Deprivation and inequality can have severe ramifications on an individual's life; thus, assessing the impact of financial inclusion should not be limited to the economic realm.[19]

Case Studies of Economic Growth, Inequalities, and Financial Inclusion

Various case studies demonstrate how fintech innovations can improve financial inclusion; however, these case studies also illustrate that (a) many nations struggle to implement new fintech, and (b) fintech does not solve all economic problems related to financial inclusion. In South Africa, better financial services have not led to greater inclusion. In China, which leads the way in transactional banking, credit services still lag. And in Colombia, despite the government's successful reduction of poverty through financial inclusion, economic inequality remains significant.

South Africa: A Vibrant Financial Sector with High Financial Exclusion

South Africa has a relatively well-developed economy, compared to other African countries. But it is a good example of the economic dichotomies within emerging markets. The country has one of the most sophisticated financial markets and macroeconomic management systems among emerging nations. Its finance, retail, and media industries are the most developed on the continent. Nevertheless, its inequality level—a GINI score of 0.6—is one of the highest in the world.[20]

Economic growth in South Africa is constrained by the oligopoly power of entrenched institutions, including the ruling party and its allied unions, and apartheid-era corporations that remain in power. Unions use their clout to give internal members pay raises well above the rate of growth in labor productivity. In 2009 and 2010 their average wage hike was more than 9 percent, well above the approximate inflation rate of 5.5 percent.[21]

A large proportion of South African corporate profits are earned outside the country. South Africa's sixty largest companies produce 56 percent of their earnings from other African countries and international sources. This is one of the highest shares of offshore income in the world. In other words, South African companies do not place much importance on local markets. This lack of within-country investment has resulted in declining productivity. In 2012, 33 percent of South Africans lived in rural areas and had little access to basic social and economic infrastructure, and 31 percent lived below the poverty line of $2 per day.[22]

In 2010, financial institutions in South Africa accounted for 39 percent of formal employment and contributed 15 percent of the total corporate taxes. This suggests that the South African financial sector was at that time large and vibrant. The same is true today; however, the banking sector, like other South African businesses, functions largely as an oligopoly: It is dominated by four banks that lack competition and charge high transaction fees. As a result, awareness and usage of *Mzansi* (low-cost) accounts is low.

In 2010 the combined assets of South Africa's long-term insurance sector and pension funds rivaled that of the nation's banks. South Africa should be fertile ground for long-term savings. However, South Africa's domestic savings rate of 15 percent lagged far behind that of other countries. By comparison, China's savings rate was 47 percent and India's rate was 31 percent for the period 2000–2010. Technology could help scale up and expand the banking sector, increase competition, lower transaction fees, and inform people about *Mzansi* accounts.

China: Advanced in Transactional Banking, Lagging in Credit

China's economic growth serves as a promising example of the merits of financial inclusion. As of 2011, 66 percent of Chinese adults held bank accounts at formal financial institutions, which is a much higher proportion of account holders relative to the other BRIC nations. By comparison, the percentage of adult account holders was 55 percent in Brazil, 44 percent in Russia, and 37 percent in India.[23]

Another distinctive feature of the Chinese economy is the high percentage of people who save at a formal institution. According to the 2012 World Bank Findex survey, 82 percent of the Chinese population saved at a formal financial institution. This too was significantly higher than in the other BRIC countries, where the corresponding indicators ranged from 50 percent to 72 percent. China's rate of those with savings accounts is also much higher than the world average of 22 percent.[24]

Even with China's high level of financial inclusion, almost 20 percent of the Chinese population, or 234 million people, remain unbanked. Some groups are more likely to be adversely impacted than others. Of China's unbanked population, 55 percent are women, 71 percent live in rural areas, and 80 percent have an elementary education or less.[25]

China has a significant urban–rural divide in personal income, economic growth, and financial market developments. Statistics show that 75 percent of urban households have access to formal banking services compared to less than 50 percent of rural households. Rural households also have less than 50 percent ownership of other financial products, including stocks, credit cards, and mutual funds. This can be partially explained by the rural populations' lack of income, education, and financial literacy. Another underlying constraint that prevents financial inclusion among rural populations is the shortage of local financial institutions. Fintech could help improve this situation.[26]

The proportion of people in China who can receive loans from financial institutions remains low, at about 9.5 percent. In rural areas the number is even lower (7.5 percent). With this in mind, China's former president Hu Jintao made "building a harmonious society" a top priority and promised to make credit more accessible for rural citizens. The government asked banks to promote social harmony and enhance social and economic inclusion by increasing access to financial services.[27]

Despite the government's strong emphasis on microfinance and increased lending rates, repayment rates remained low and programs rarely succeeded in reaching low-income households. The Chinese Banking Regulatory Commission took a conservative approach to granting legal status to credit providers, which suppressed the provision of credit. Households seeking formal credit had to meet a long, restrictive list of requirements, such as evidence of employment, educational attainment, income, urban residence, assets, and even proof of membership in the Communist Party.[28]

This environment provided fertile ground for increased informal lending and other financial services. It also raised the *ratio* of informal lending to total household assets. Overall, the constrained access to credit contributed to the growth of shadow banking systems, which often cause financial instability and multigenerational poverty.[29]

Despite some weaknesses, China has since become one of the fastest moving and most technologically innovative markets for financial institutions. In 2018 the World Bank acknowledged China as a global fintech leader.

For example, internet banking and e-commerce giants such as Alibaba and WeChat may have the potential to revolutionize the lending market. Digital loans in China have increased from $11 billion in 2013 to $284 billion in 2016. With the expansionary role of fintech in the financial sector, lending markets have also evolved. Fintech lending solutions have helped small- and medium-size businesses overcome barriers imposed by traditional financial institutions. The development of advanced data analytics tools has enabled companies, such as Alipay, to individualize loan products. Alibaba, the parent company of Alipay, monitors and analyzes online transactions to identify commercial opportunities and then offers loans to small businesses.[30] In China, and around the world, small- and medium-size businesses constitute a large part of developing economies. Thus, fintech lending solutions have had an immense effect on economic growth.[31]

As China's example shows, in environments where savings rates are low and domestic credit is high, fintech can help level borrowing and saving imbalances and create stronger domestic demand.

Colombia: Policy Focus on Poverty Reduction

Latin America is one of the most economically unequal regions of the world. Colombia's Gini coefficient is presently the seventh highest in the world, which is comparable to the Gini coefficients of Haiti, South Africa, and Honduras. In 2010 the richest 1 percent in Colombia held around 20 percent of the total national income.[32]

In the late 1990s, Colombia underwent a deep economic crisis driven by a reversal of capital inflows. The Colombian government responded with reforms aimed at overcoming the lasting effects of the crisis. In addition to its efforts to improve peace, security, and trade, the government scaled up its redistribution of wealth to low-income households. The share of household income that was redistributed to the lowest-income populations doubled between 2000 to 2010, reaching 20 percent. Average incomes and redistribution schemes rose, which improved the nation's low incomes.[33]

In 2003 Colombia's trade took a favorable turn. This enabled growth, reduced poverty rates, and dramatically improved per capita GDP. Between 2001 and 2015, incomes of the population's bottom 40 percent grew faster than the average income, and the poverty rate dropped to 13 percent, a decline of nearly 50 percent.

The Colombian government also focused on financial inclusion and introduced the nation's banking index, which helped banks and policymakers understand and track progress. The banking index is the ratio of legal-age adults holding one or more financial products to the total population of legal-age adults.

The coverage of banking facilities in rural areas increased by 85 percent between 2011 to 2013, totaling 4,724 bank access points. By 2013 only eight Colombian municipalities were without banking facilities. By 2015 all municipalities had at least one financial service provider. Through the monetary incentives offered by the Banca de las Oportunidades, 187 access points opened in Colombia's rural municipalities. By 2013 rural banking coverage had increased by 34 percent.

Digital technologies also helped the Colombian government increase its coverage and improve security for transactions and mobile banking. As a result, more Colombians chose to conduct banking transactions online because it was easier and saved time.

These factors have greatly improved Colombia's situation. According to one government indicator, financial inclusion in Colombia was 76.3 percent in 2015. The government aims to bring 84 percent of the population into formal banking by 2018.[34]

Building Infrastructure for Fintech in Emerging Markets

Fintech firms excel at reaching financially underserved populations who have a sufficient level of technological literacy. Developing countries have populations with high ratios of such profiles.[35]

However, countries must have the infrastructure that is necessary for fintech to function. For instance, telecom services are a necessary factor for wide-scale fintech deployment. In 2017 in the top ten emerging market countries, 39 to 89 percent of these populations owned a mobile phone. Researchers expect that those numbers will increase to 50 to 90 percent by 2025, bringing the enormous potential of fintech to emerging economies.[36]

Data: The Production Factor That Determines Market Power

Unlike traditional financial institutions, fintech businesses are built on bytes, not bricks. This gives them the power to quickly build services and rapidly meet consumer needs.

The ability to generate and access data in real time is a game changer that enables companies to customize products and services and to improve consumer experiences. Data generated from online banking transactions, digital sensors, and mobile devices can be captured and recorded at an incredible rate. Every day, 2.5 quintillion bytes of data are created. About 90 percent of all processed data was produced in the past two years. For this reason, large companies like

Google, Facebook, Apple, Samsung, PayPal, and Amazon have unique positions of power in their respective marketplaces.[37]

For example, Alipay, the Ant Financial/Alibaba spinoff, launched MyBank in 2015. This service, unlike all other banks, does not require debtor's collateral to grant loans. Instead, it analyzes the accumulated financial data related to purchased items across vendors and buyers on e-commerce sites, such as Taobao and Tmall. Applying for a loan on MyBank is much easier than at a bank because it has lower thresholds. As a result, it can improve credit access in rural areas.[38]

How Governments Can Use Data to Help Citizens: The Example of Aadhaar, the World's Largest Biometric System in India

Just as tech companies have found ways to monetize data, governments have also found ways to use data to improve the services they provide to citizens. India uses a twelve-digit citizen identification number called *Aadhaar* to grant citizens access to government services and social benefits.

Aadhaar's use of biometric data helps prevent service duplication, information leaks, fraud, and corruption. Recently the government of India made Aadhaar the primary form of identification when people open bank accounts. This improves synergy between government services and overall financial inclusion in the country.

Why was Aadhaar needed? Before the creation of Aadhaar, India did not have a unified, nationally accepted way to prove citizens' identity. To access government services or subsidies, people had to provide a myriad of documents. For example, ration cards were used for food subsidies and electricity bills, whereas a driving license was required to open a bank account. These documents were not available to 42 percent of the population. This meant that most citizens were either denied services or had to bribe officials for basic necessities, such as fuel, or access to pension accounts.

Fake or duplicate identities posed another issue for the Indian government; most citizens did not have school IDs or birth certificates. In 1969 the government made birth registration and death certificates mandatory by law. However, three decades later, in 2001, only 55 percent of births and 46 percent of deaths were registered. Children without a birth certificate faced difficulties receiving health care benefits and school admissions. Furthermore, a lack of paperwork often resulted in minors being tried as adults in court.

In a country with more than one billion people, only 50 million had passports, only 95.8 million had permanent account numbers (for tax purposes), and only 232.2 million had ration cards. As a result, the government decided that a single identity card would be the best way to prevent government leakages and to foster social and financial inclusion.

How was the data generated? Aadhaar's new technology was created with three main objectives: enrolling Indians on a very large scale, preventing fraud and duplication, and providing a trustworthy and secure authentication of residency and identification. The government decided that linking a unique twelve-digit number to a biometric system would address these three objectives. The biometric system included a photograph, records of all ten fingerprints, and iris scans. The individual's name, address, date of birth, and gender were also recorded.

Enrollment equipment consisted of a laptop with secured software, an iris scanner, a fingerprint scanner, a webcam, and a laser printer. All of this fit neatly into a briefcase and could be deployed at scale. The enrollment process took place in English and in the regional language, with translation taking place simultaneously to ensure data accuracy.

To enroll, one had to produce proof of identity, address, and date of birth. For those unable to verify date of birth, the date verbally given by the person was accepted. Data was then compared with existing IDs to prevent duplication. The accounts of children below age fifteen were linked to their parents' accounts; they had to re-register at age sixteen.[39]

Aadhaar was a revolutionary undertaking that helped the Indian government create an online database of 1.2 billion people. It was designed to enroll up to one million new people a day. By comparison, the FBI database has about 66 million criminal prints and 25 million civilian prints.

No other system in the world has performed as many transactions as Aadhaar. Visa, for example, processes 130 million transactions in a day. Aadhaar is designed to process up to 600 million transactions per day.

To prevent duplication, the system won't allow unique identity information to be used to log in with different ID numbers. In addition, the system must account for all other existing IDs a person might possess.

Communicating and registering the homeless, however, has proved to be difficult. Communicating about Aadhaar through traditional media is not helpful for this because many homeless people do not have access to televisions, newspapers, or computers.

Parallel to Aadhaar's deployment, in 2011 India passed its Information Technology Rules, which provided guidelines for the use of personal data. The Supreme Court upheld the constitutionality of these rules, security practices, and procedures for sensitive personal data.

Aadhaar's parent organization, the Unique Identification Authority of India (UIDAI), also created an ecosystem of government services around Aadhaar that subsidized education, public health, food, fuel, and rural jobs.

When India subsidized domestic cooking gas, or LPG, to protect citizens against fluctuating international prizes, people began taking advantage of price arbitrage by selling subsidized fuel in international markets. They did this by creating fake accounts and multiple identities. To prevent these abuses, the government linked Aadhaar to the distribution of LPG cylinders, thus mitigating the incidence of leakages and fake identities.

Before the advent of Aadhaar, banking policies for Know Your Customer (KYC) were overly complicated. The government used Aadhaar to ensure compliance with KYC banking norms and ran authentication pilot tests in Bangalore and Delhi. In 2012 banking regulators accepted Aadhaar as a proof of identity, which enabled people to open bank accounts or buy mutual funds.

Today, thirty-four banks across India use the electronic KYC to help customers open bank accounts. This has reduced by 50 percent the processing times and the related costs of granting banking products. By 2014, 3.8 million bank accounts had been opened, representing more than six million transactions. In 2014 the prime minister of India also released the Jan Dhan Yojana, a financial inclusion plan designed to provide bank accounts and life insurance policies to every household in India. This advancement resulted in people opening another 3.3 million bank accounts.

When Aadhaar's progress was presented to parliament, the prime minister, the finance minister, and the president of India agreed that Aadhaar had helped reduce leakages and improve the delivery of services to low-income households.

The Importance of Government Investment

It is important to recognize that fintech is just one element within a larger array of strategies to reduce inequality. This fact is particularly important when considering efforts to resolve the widening gap between rural and urban economies, and when studying efforts to improve living standards in emerging markets.

Currently it is more challenging for microfinance institutions to sustain efforts in rural areas than in urban centers. As a result, a lower share of rural borrowers benefit from direct microfinance institutions. Additionally, microfinance institutions with a higher share of rural borrowers may be less able to exploit economies of scale or to increase productivity. This makes it more difficult to achieve sustainable financial inclusion in rural areas than in urban areas.[40] This finding is relevant for policymakers trying to enable fintech innovations for poverty-stricken rural areas. Ibrahim has argued that for financial inclusion to alleviate welfare inequality and to ensure income convergence, rural financial markets must be redesigned to allow wider access to credit, specifically for low-income and vulnerable households.[41]

Another barrier is related to the dependency of fintech on the internet. Access to the internet through mobile devices or other means is a prerequisite for fintech access; however, in developing nations the internet is not evenly distributed. Therefore, the impacts of fintech on inequality will naturally follow the distribution of internet access and effective usage across a population.

In summary, technology can reach its full potential only when nations build robust infrastructures. This usually requires government investments. Reaching rural populations with fintech by increasing internet access should be part of a broader effort to provide access to roads, telecom services, and education. Without infrastructure investment, fintech deployment will not reach its full potential, for the following reasons.

1. Telecom access enables people to access digital services (e-commerce, fintech) and free sharing of information.
2. Road development allows for better commerce exchanges and shipment of goods purchased elsewhere in the country, including those purchased over the internet.
3. Education, including knowledge about technology, is a prerequisite for a population to benefit from fintech.
4. A country's existing financial sector and KYC form an important backbone for fintech providers to deploy new access and services; it's often possible to "plug in" new technologies to existing banking infrastructures.

As we can see, finance and technology evolve together in an ongoing process. There are numerous incremental and disruptive innovations, such as internet banking, mobile payments, crowdfunding, peer-to-peer lending, robo-advisory services, and online identification. As digital technology evolves and offers greater e-commerce inclusion for rural areas, fintech can increase financial inclusion.[42]

CHAPTER SIX

Fintech, Financial Inclusion, and Economic Infrastructure

In Chapter 5 we provided a broad perspective on global economic trends and how financial inclusion is a vital stepping-stone in economic development. In this chapter we address the specific financial services that citizens in emerging markets need. The current lack of these services in many nations mirrors other systemic social problems, such as political exclusion or discrimination. So as not to understate the significant hardships that financial exclusion can create for individuals, we will review in this chapter the specific barriers people face when they try to save and borrow by means of formal and informal sectors, and we will examine how these factors diminish their capacity to escape poverty. We then explore how fintech companies such as Paytm, Jumia, and Lazada have managed to design new products and models to offer low-cost financial services even to people in the most remote rural areas.

Why Financial Inclusion Is Vital

The uneven distribution of resources, such as labor, capital, and technology, can limit economic growth. This is one reason financial inclusion is such an important precondition for realizing strong, long-term growth within an economy.[1]

Beyond the macroeconomic benefits, financial inclusion leads to significant social and personal benefits. Consider the basic benefits of having a bank account: It allows individuals to save, earn interest, balance household consumption, and raise productive investment. Moreover, a bank account can empower women and give them more economic equality.[2]

Although more people have gained access to bank accounts, there is still considerable work to be done. Between 2011 and 2017, the percentage of adults worldwide with a bank account increased from 51 percent to 69 percent. This is encouraging, but 1.7 billion adults were still unbanked in 2017 according to the

World Bank Global Findex. If we look deeper into that database, we find that nearly half the world's unbanked people lived in seven countries: Bangladesh, China, India, Indonesia, Mexico, Nigeria, and Pakistan. In the aggregate, in 2017 women constituted 56 percent of the unbanked; gender has clearly played a role in financial exclusion rates. In countries such as China, India, and Kenya, the gender gap has remained wide, with women constituting 60 percent or more of the unbanked. In addition to the struggles of women, the undereducated have been disproportionately excluded from formal banking. Globally, 62 percent of the unbanked have a fifth-grade education or less.[3]

For these people to make gains in financial inclusion, there must be a thriving demand, a cost-efficient supply of easy-to-access services, and appropriate regulation to incentivize and protect the underserved.

It is also important to recognize that people need more than a bank account. The financial needs of individuals and families evolve along a life cycle, as shown in Figure 6.1.

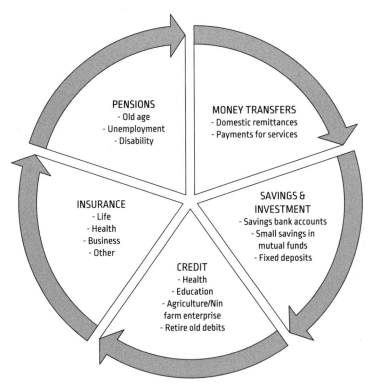

FIGURE 6.1   Essential life cycle of financial needs of low-income people

Figure 6.1 shows that the life cycle of financial needs starts with the basic need for money transfers.

1. *Money transfers:* Receiving and sending payments electronically saves time, which helps people stay at work (an income-producing activity). Electronic transfers are also more secure and efficient than high-cost transfers via intermediaries.

2. *Savings and investment:* Electronic savings, as opposed to physically storing cash, is a first step toward financial inclusion for low-income people. This facilitates the ability to save and invest on a regular, or irregular, basis. Increased savings enables low-income people to survive when economic shocks impact their households.

3. *Credit:* Accessing formal sources of credit mitigates poverty and helps low-income households escape abject poverty. Loans can be used to finance human and material capital, such as businesses, agricultural investments, education, and health care. Formal credit can also replace high-cost debt obtained through usurious informal financial channels.

4. *Insurance:* Subsistence farmers, rural citizens, and low-income individuals often face financial risks because they lack basic forms of insurance. Loss of life, serious illness, flooding, fires, drought, livestock diseases, and theft are common examples of risks that low-income populations often face without insurance.

5. *Pensions:* Public subsidies and pensions can reduce inequalities. Without pension redistribution, elderly people can become an additional financial burden on a family, with working-age family members having to carry the cost of raising children and taking care of the elderly. This also often forces children to work at younger ages to increase family income.

When households have access to these types of formal financial products and services, they tend to enter an upward cycle toward increased wealth and well-being. By contrast, the absence of these basic financial services can derail low-income households and push them into debilitating debt cycles and downwardly spiraling poverty traps.

Common Negative Outcomes of Financial Exclusion

An investigation into the causes of financial exclusion should include an analysis of why some people opt out of formal accounts even when such services are available. The World Bank Global Findex survey includes seven possible reasons for such behavior. Three reasons are related to cultural or family factors, such as religious beliefs or preference for sharing one family account. These voluntary reasons can be addressed via incentive policies, information campaigns, and social welfare.[4]

The four remaining reasons are related to practical obstacles: distance to banking services, high cost, lack of documentation, and lack of trust in formal institutions. Whatever the cause, an individual's choice to avoid formal financial institutions leads to direct negative outcomes—including reduced savings, reduced access to credit, lack of insurance, and particularly difficult circumstances for persons with disabilities, the elderly, women, and migrants.

Reduced Savings

In developing economies, a common alternative to saving at a financial institution is semi-formal or informal savings, such as a "savings club" or a moneylender. One common type of savings club is a rotating savings and credit association. These associations generally pool weekly deposits from all members and then disburse the amount to a different member once the savings target is met (typically in weekly disbursements).

In 2017, 25 percent of savers in developing economies reported that they saved this way. Within the unbanked population, the share of informal saving is even higher. About 28 percent of the unbanked reported saving; of those, 83 percent saved in informal or semi-informal ways. In total, about 150 million unbanked adults in developing economies save semi-formally. In sub-Saharan Africa, up to 65 million unbanked adults save semi-formally, including 35 million women.

Although formal bank account ownership has increased steadily across most developing markets, the accumulation of formal savings has stagnated. Globally the share of adults with an account rose from 51 percent in 2011 to 69 percent in 2017. However, the share of adults worldwide who saved formally only increased from 23 percent to 27 percent during the same period. In China and Malaysia, only 43 percent of account owners reported having saved formally in 2017. The share was about 30 percent in Kenya, South Africa, and Turkey—and as low as 20 percent in Brazil and India.[5]

Reduced Access to Credit

The microfinance movement around the world has been a response to restricted access to credit from formal financial institutions. Local moneylenders have notoriously filled this space with usurious practices, exorbitant interest rates and mortgage packages, and coercive recovery tactics. These problems are widespread. According to the World Bank in 2018, almost half of all borrowers in the world sought credit from family and friends. In 2017, 79 percent reported having borrowed only from family, friends, or other nonformal sources.[6]

In developing economies (globally), 7 percent of adults reported borrowing to start, operate, or expand a business. On average, about half of them reported borrowing from a financial institution and half from family, friends, or other informal sources.

In developing countries, a large share of the GDP comes from small and medium companies, including subsistence farmers, traders, and shopkeepers. These businesses need different types of financial services. A street vendor or trader is likely to require short-term financing for the purchase of supplies. Small-scale producers may need long-term loans to buy equipment or to employ and pay employees. Subsistence farmers may need seasonal financing to help with planting, growing, and harvesting.

Although formal financing exists in all countries, many traditional banks refuse to lend to small and medium businesses because the amount borrowed is typically too small to cover transactional costs related to the bankers' time and evaluation services. Many of these small and medium businesses are not registered with the government; most are not financially literate and therefore do not retain accounting records, such as a balance sheets or income statements. As a result, banks typically require borrowers to offer collateral against the loan. However, most small and medium businesses are financially constrained and lack collateral. Many of the people who own their land, homes, farms, or shops have no official proof of ownership. This renders their properties ineligible as forms of collateral. Weak regulations and laws also complicate matters. In some countries, women—including impoverished and middle-income women—face another notable constraint: They are often denied bank accounts unless a father or husband first approves it and the male "co-signer" presents proper documentation.

Thus, few small and medium businesses can gain credit assistance from formal financial institutions. Some of these businesses turn to moneylenders who offer short-term loans at very high interest rates. Similarly, an informal borrower might use a pawnbroker's services, which requires using expensive items as collateral. If the borrower has not repaid the debt when the repayment term has expired, the pawnbroker may sell the asset. In the case of seasonal agricultural loans, agents often provide credit to farmers, but only if the agent is allowed to sell the crops or take a percentage of the profits.

Lack of Insurance Increases Financial Vulnerability

Most literature on financial exclusion and/or inclusion focuses on credit, savings, and payments. Less attention has been given to insurance and risk coverage, which is a major negative outcome for those who lack access to formal financial accounts.

To better understand the need for formal insurance and risk coverage, consider what some agricultural workers in developing nations face. In 2017, four out of ten people in East Asia and South Asia reported living in a household where growing crops or raising livestock was a main source of household income. In sub-Saharan Africa, the ratio was five out of ten. About half of those people in both regions had experienced a bad harvest, significant livestock loss, or adverse weather patterns in the previous five years. In these cases, most bore the entire financial calamity without insurance or government assistance. Without access to insurance, agriculture becomes a high-risk enterprise for low-income households.

Those employed outside agriculture are also highly vulnerable because they operate within the informal labor sector without job security or benefits. People without insurance can be devastated by the death of a primary earner, fires, theft from small enterprises, floods, hailstorms, and other common issues. A lack of health insurance, for example, is a serious concern for many low-income families. If a major illness strikes the primary earner, a low-income household can become trapped in debt. Elderly persons and persons with disabilities who lack a pension can become destitute. The agriculture and capital of low-income rural populations often are ruined by natural disasters.[7]

The primary factor limiting access to insurance is cost. On the supply side, many insurance companies are unable to reach break-even levels of profit; they often operate at a loss. On the demand side, it is difficult to create affordable insurance products for low-income rural populations due to the risks and barriers describe above.[8]

Negative Outcomes for the Disabled, Elderly, Women, and Migrants

People in the lowest quintile of emerging economies are usually the most vulnerable and financially excluded segment of a population. In most economies, that population often includes the homeless, people with disabilities, the elderly, and religious minorities. They have a much lower likelihood of accessing formal financial services. In India, for example, the Dalits, or "untouchables," are considered low caste, which makes accessing formal financial services exceedingly more difficult for them than for persons of higher castes.

Globally, women are less likely than men to receive formal financial services. Findings suggest that in India women who lead households tend to face tougher credit restrictions than men due to low educational attainment and wage discrimination.[9]

As urbanization spreads in emerging economies, and as jobs migrate from rural areas to towns, cities, and international locations, the need for safe and effective remittance channels becomes even more essential. The bulk of household income for many rural families comes from money transfers sent by migrant workers. Without formal remittance services, these funds are often hand-delivered in cash by family and friends, which invites pilferage.

How Fintech Can Improve Financial Inclusion

Now that we have reviewed some of the negative impacts of financial *exclusion*, we turn to the benefits of financial *inclusion*—and the ways fintech can improve lives.

Financial inclusion benefits individuals in many ways. Because having a formal bank account enables people to invest, balance consumption, and better manage financial risks, financial inclusion helps people harness resources that promote specialization and innovation.

Financial inclusion also benefits national economies. It can boost economic growth and productivity by increasing access to capital, improving resource allocation and risk management, and reducing information asymmetries.[10]

However, it is important to remember that a large portion of people in developing countries work in traditional sectors, such as agriculture. Because innovation and productivity growth tend to take place within the nonfarming sectors of an economy, rural citizens are often excluded from the formal economy. This presents a strong need for technology that can enable higher productivity by improving the speed, reliability, transparency, and cost of information delivery.

Fintech innovations have the capacity to improve the transaction system, increase productivity, and help countries transition workforces from traditional to modern sectors—factors that improve economic growth.

Correlations of Financial Inclusion and Economic Growth

There is a growing body of literature regarding financial inclusion and economic growth. Most is built on Solow's theoretical growth model, according to which increased savings will raise the levels of capital and output per effective worker. However, there is a dearth of significant empirical evidence that links financial inclusion and macroeconomic growth.

Jose de Luna Martinez in 2017 studied the remarkably high level of financial inclusion in Malaysia, where 92 percent of the people have an active deposit account. Malaysia has achieved this due to twenty years of concerted effort by government and financial sector leaders. After the 1997 Asian financial crisis, Malaysia formulated two financial sector master plans that comprehensively diagnosed barriers to inclusion and prescribed policy actions that were executed under a robust monitoring system. Over time these factors have contributed to the sustained, stable growth of Malaysia's financial system.[11]

Sahay and his colleagues in 2015 examined global proxies, such as the number of ATMs, bank branches, and transaction accounts. These researchers reported a positive correlation between financial inclusion and economic growth. However, they found that the marginal benefits of financial inclusion decline at higher levels of development. They also pointed to the significant challenge of determining the direction of causality between inclusion and growth. Further research is needed to tease out whether growth drives inclusion, or whether inclusion drives growth.[12]

Lawrence Okoye and his fellow researchers in 2017 used thirty years of time-series data sourced from the Central Bank of Nigerian to examine the link between financial inclusion, economic growth, and poverty reduction. They found that financial inclusion—measured by financial deepening indicators and the loan-to-deposit ratio—supported poverty reduction but did not induce economic growth.[13]

Babajide and his colleagues in 2015 ran a similar study on Nigeria. They did find a statistically significant, positive association between financial inclusion (measured by the number of deposit account holders / number of bank branches) and economic growth per worker. The differing results likely reflect the challenges in accurately measuring financial inclusion.[14]

In India, Dipasha Sharma in 2015 found a positive association between economic growth and various measures of financial inclusion, including banking penetration in rural areas and the availability and usage of banking services. The author chose India as the country of interest due to its heavy reliance on banking institutions and because India mandated the building of bank branches in rural areas.[15]

We have conducted our own analysis of financial inclusion and growth by studying the empirical relationship between various indicators of financial inclusion and economic growth within seventy-four emerging economies. Following the theoretical framework of Sharma's work in 2015, our model incorporated two distinct dimensions of financial inclusion: penetration and accessibility. We defined penetration as the proportion of a population with account ownership and the total number of commercial bank depositors. Accessibility was defined as the number of branches and ATMs per one hundred thousand adults. These two categories of indicators were meant to demonstrate the pervasiveness and reach of financial services within the countries we studied.[16]

The overall results indicated a strong, positive association between measures of banking penetration / accessibility and gross domestic product per capita (Figure 6.2). Proving the causal relationship between financial inclusion and economic growth would require more work. However, we can say that providing affordable, low-fee services for the poor has a positive impact. By making significant investments in modernizing the national payment infrastructure and encouraging fintech innovation, financial services can become more accessible and sustainable for customers (financially and geographically) due to the lower cost of technological products.[17]

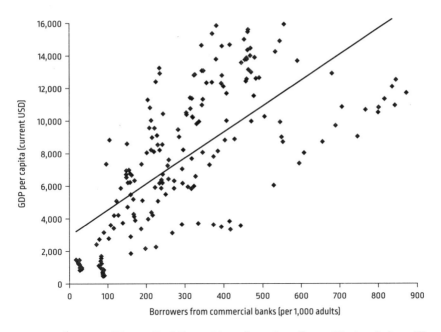

Data sources: International Monetary Fund, Financial Access Survey, https://data.worldbank.org/indicator/FB.CBK.BRWR.P3; World Bank, https://data.worldbank.org/indicator/ny.gdp.pcap.cd.

Note: The scatter includes the years 2004 to 2019 (depending on the countries) for the following countries: Argentina, Bangladesh, Brazil, Chile, China, Colombia, Hungary, Indonesia, Malaysia, Pakistan, Peru, Poland, Romania, Thailand, Turkey.

FIGURE 6.2   GDP per capita vs. borrowers from commercial banks (per 1,000 adults)

Fintech Deployment Meets Human Needs

In addition to improving economic growth, fintech has helped the underserved in specific ways that are related to their financial wants and needs. It offers reduced transaction costs and eliminates layers of intermediation, which could enable greater financial inclusion.

As an example, leveraging cellular networks to offer financial solutions has the potential to reduce costs by 80 to 90 percent relative to the cost of physical bank branches. Another added benefit is that mobile solutions can be rapidly deployed. In emerging markets, more adults had a cellular phone than a bank account and/or credit cards. According to a GSMA report, smartphone penetration is expected to reach 80 percent globally by 2025. Key countries contributing to the significant increase are India, Indonesia, Pakistan, Mexico, and Africa.[18]

Financial services, technology, and the real-world needs of people overlap. However, traditional financial services, such as physical bank branches, are more limited in their ability to meet needs when compared to mobile and internet banking. This highlights an immediate opportunity for fintech providers. When underserved segments of the population begin receiving services they value and trust, more people will subscribe to mobile phones and services, thus creating a virtuous cycle.

Fintech leads to greater inclusion by seamlessly offering financial products and services that meet the real-world needs of people. Fintech unbundles processes and then offers customized and rebundled services that meet customers' specific needs—in a cost-efficient manner. By contrast, mainstream financial institutions have found it challenging to offer services that meet the needs of the underserved.

Unbundling Financial Processes: Fintech has unbundled the core functions of financial intermediation, such as settling payments, assessing and sharing risks, and allocating capital. Unbundling enables new players—payment service providers, aggregators and robo-advisors, peer-to-peer lenders, and innovative trading platforms—to enter the market. The emergence of these new players increases the pressure on existing banking and financial institutions to adopt new technologies and to offer better services and pricing.

Processing Speed: Fintech increases the speed of processing transactions. This enables higher transaction frequency and opens the door for companies to offer a wider range of services and to scale up the acquisition of new customers. Lenders can improve the speed and veracity of credit decisions. By reducing the need for a physical presence in a bank branch, fintech makes financial services available all day and every day while substantially reducing transaction costs.

Multiplying the Scale and Scope of Logistics: By offering digital payment solutions, fintech enables e-commerce to reach the most remote populations and geographies. This is exemplified by the Chinese example of Alibaba's Alipay, which significantly reduced costs for both buyers and sellers.

From Cash to Digital

Most emerging economies are characterized by the high use of cash. Globally, in 2013 about 80 percent of consumer transactions were carried out in cash. In 2017 an estimated 300 million bank account owners worldwide worked in the private sector and received payments in cash. In India, 10 percent of account owners, or 90 million users, received private-sector wage payments in cash; that share is almost twice as large in Indonesia, Myanmar, and Nepal.[19]

Cash is also the prevalent payment mode for agricultural product sales. This impacts about 275 million individuals in developing economies, including 15 million in Bangladesh and 80 million in China. In fact, most vendors and retailers in India still do not accept digital money, which presents a significant engagement opportunity for fintech solutions.

Globally, in 2017 at least 145 million self-employed adults with an account received business payments exclusively in cash. These included about 15 million in Indonesia and nearly 12 million account owners in Brazil.

What explains the high usage of cash across various sectors and transaction types? In emerging economies, bank branches are rarely built in rural areas. This increases the time and distance required for customers to transact at banks, which reduces the time they can devote to productive purposes. Customers carrying cash across long distances (to reach the bank) face increased theft risks and high transportation costs.

Moving from cash to digital payments is a potentially easy and seamless entry point into the formal financial system, even for those without a bank account. This shift is likely to improve transaction efficiency. Cash stored under a mattress is vulnerable to theft, soiling, and spoilage—problems that digital money solves.

Digitizing the payments described above offers several benefits to all members of the ecosystem. Banks and finance providers can increase data collection, which could provide the information needed to extend and deepen access to new products and services for both retailers and customers. By digitizing payments, suppliers who distribute goods to retail stores and businesses can improve the efficiency of payment collection. Digital payment solutions remove the anonymity of peer-to-peer (P2P) transactions in cash, and they offer a transaction velocity and responsiveness that far outmatches cash.

If we compare the total number of bank accounts to the number of mobile phones held by consumers, we can reasonably conclude that cash will not retain its dominance for long, especially in emerging economies where few people have access to banking but nearly everyone has a mobile phone.

In order to transition away from cash, government must create the proper infrastructure to support digital payments and implement public policies and incentives that facilitate the digital transition. Incentives might include allowing citizens to receive social benefits with digital wallets.

India has made significant strides toward a cashless digital society. This transition started with the use of Aadhaar's biometric authentication system (which was described earlier) and then a movement toward demonetization. India's government has sought to promote broader financial inclusion and a more efficient financial services industry, and to tackle the corruption and fraud that cash payments allow.

In 2014 the Modi government launched the Pradhan Mantri Jan Dhan Yojana (PMJDY), a financial inclusion program designed to expand affordable access to financial services such as bank accounts, remittances, credit, insurance, and pensions.

People opened ten million bank accounts with the help of the Aadhaar-based verification system. By 2017, three hundred million bank accounts had been opened. Since then the PMJDY has included the option of an account from which depositors can withdraw money even with a zero balance. An insurance policy is also attached to this account type.[20]

Because Aadhaar can be verified online, mobile payments are now possible, including via zero-balance bank accounts. By linking mobile phones to Aadhaar and PMJDY, the government has successfully provided people with documented identities, bank accounts, and a means of transaction. This effort has significantly enhanced financial inclusion and has helped people save time and effort. It has also prevented leakages and has hindered corrupt bureaucrats from misusing power. This system of bundling financial services together has been dubbed the India Stack.

Implementing Aadhaar alone, however, did not put an end to the cash-based black-market economy, which citizens used to avoid paying taxes by using off-the-books cash transactions. So, on November 8, 2016, the Indian government removed all ₹500 and ₹1,000 banknotes of the Mahatma Gandhi series. Overnight, India eliminated vast amounts of wealth accumulated through tax evasion. Removing the value of cash currency essentially made India's black-market economy obsolete.

To compensate for the sudden cash shortage, the Indian government created a digital payment platform called BHIM, which was powered by Aadhaar. The new system was structured to be highly inclusive, enabling smartphone and non-smartphone users to make digital payments. In October 2016, one month before demonetization, the government payment system was processing an average of 100,000 digital interbank transactions daily. A year later the updated system was processing 76 million daily payments. According to the finance minister of India, by August 2017 the country had retired $45 billion in cash in favor of the new virtual transactions system.[21]

The government did not stop there. Leaders also decided to reform the tax system. India is a federally structured country, like the United States. The federal government and state governments collect taxes. India has twenty-eight states, each with its own tax laws and rules. This decentralized system results in an opaque and difficult-to-navigate system, with seventeen tax categories, including sales, value-added, and interstate transportation.

On July 1, 2017, India merged all seventeen categories into one transparent system—the GST—that simplified the tax structure for businesses. A month later, one million companies had registered with the new system. The GST has facilitated better taxation practices and has helped small and medium businesses save money and get loans.

The India Stack prevents intermediaries from pocketing the money and helps citizens receive their full entitlements, free of corruption and bribes. More people are receiving their pension benefits, and twenty-five million households now have gas subsidies directly deposited into their bank accounts. Banks have far greater liquidity. Small and medium businesses have an all-time-high lending rate.[22]

From Branch Banking to Banking on the Go

Physical bank branches require large, fixed costs, making them a difficult investment to justify in less-populated areas in developing countries. For rural populations, there is a two-way mismatch. First, bankers are reluctant to service customers who lack proper KYC documentation or loan collateral. Second, potential consumers are not willing or able to travel to faraway branches, and they often cannot meet minimum deposit requirements.[23] As a result, people in rural areas have been excluded from the formal system.

This exclusion fueled the formal microcredit movement, which was initiated by microfinance institutions (MFIs). Grameen Bank, founded in Bangladesh, treats low-income people as creditworthy and bankable despite lack of collateral. MFIs have offered credit, savings, and insurance solutions on a grand scale, bringing financial and social inclusion to millions of impoverished borrowers, most of whom were women. These MFIs have paved the way for the formal banking sector to follow suit, but there is still much to be done.

Quick deployment, competition, technological advancement, and reduced access costs have propelled the growth of mobile services in developing countries. In India, the first two mobile phone operation licenses were issued in 1995. In 2001 that number increased to at least four. As cell phone coverage expanded, the number of users grew. As of 2018, India had more than a billion mobile phone users, second only to China. Coverage for these two countries continues to grow.[24]

Mobile phone ownership is widespread among the unbanked. Globally in 2017 about 1.1 billion unbanked adults—representing two-thirds of the 1.7 billion unbanked adults in the world—had a mobile phone. In the seven economies where half the world's unbanked adults live, more than half of those adults have a mobile phone (the exception is in Pakistan). In China, the share of unbanked individuals who own mobile phones is as high as 82 percent.

This upward rate of global cell phone use has the potential to advance financial inclusion. In Indonesia, 33 percent of adults cited distance as a barrier to opening an account with a financial institution. Among those people, 69 percent reported having a mobile phone. In the Philippines, 41 percent cited distance as a barrier to opening a bank account and 71 percent of those people reported owning a mobile phone.

Technology has ensured that even basic devices can enable transactions, thereby reducing the need for branch banking. In sub-Saharan Africa, relatively simple, text-based mobile phones have powered the spread of mobile money accounts (for example, M-Pesa).

Fintech has achieved initial mass adoption levels in emerging countries. In 2017 the average fintech adoption rate was 46 percent. China and India had the world's highest fintech adoption rates, at 69 percent and 52 percent, respectively. In 2017, 84 percent of the population surveyed in Australia, Canada, Hong Kong, Singapore, the UK, and the United States were aware of local fintech services as opposed to 62 percent in 2015.[25]

Fintech's success in emerging markets comes not only by way of its ability to tap into a large tech-literate population but also by reaching those who had previously been financially excluded. South Africa, Mexico, and Singapore are likely to become significant fintech players, with borrowing and financial planning as the fastest growing fintech services. All of this indicates growing opportunities for the expansion of mobile banking.[26]

We can see there is fertile ground for mobile-based financial services. But for financial services to move out of the bank branch, providers need the following essential elements: physical infrastructure, such as electricity, mobile, and internet networks; technology solutions, such as mobile phone applications and sufficient security; financial institutions, such as banks and insurance companies that are willing to customize products and services for the underserved; and government regulation in the telecom, banking, and insurance sectors.

Growth Areas for Fintech in Emerging Economies

The demand for nontraditional financial services is spawning innovation and growth in numerous types of fintech services, with greater intensity in emerging markets. Low-income economies have historically been early fintech adopters.

There are two main explanations for this surge fintech demand within emerging economies (Figure 6.3). First, emerging markets usually have large, young populations who more readily adopt new technologies. In 2017, 48 percent

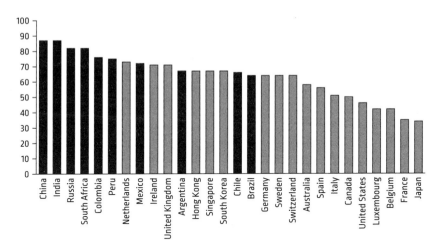

Data source: Ernst & Young, "Global FinTech Adoption Index 2019," https://www.ey.com/en_om/ey-global -fintech-adoption-index.

Note: The figure shows FinTech adopters as a percentage of the digitally active population. All averages are shown on an unweighted basis. Gray bars represent advanced economies while black bars represent emerging economies.

FIGURE 6.3   Fintech adoption rates across countries as a proportion of the digitally active population

of fintech users were age twenty-five to thirty-four, and 41 percent of fintech users were age thirty-five to forty-four. Moreover, 13 percent of users in both age groups have accessed five or more fintech services.

Second, most emerging markets are bypassing older technologies and jumping straight to fintech as governments crack down on cash circulation (as in India). The convenience of mobile technology also drives this trend. Advanced markets, such as the United States and Europe, have societies and infrastructures built around established credit card markets. Ironically, this contributes to slower fintech adoption rates in developed nations.

In terms of engagement (number of users), the most popular fintech applications help people make payments. But other notable services—insurance, lending, investment and savings, financial planning, and e-commerce—are also gaining prominence.[27]

Payments: At the Forefront of Customer Adoption

Fintech payment methods in emerging economies allow businesses and individuals to make or accept payments without merchant accounts. Mobile wallets are so popular that most traditional banks now offer a digital wallet application as a supplement to savings accounts. The popularity of these technologies started with international remittances.

In 2016 international remittances worldwide amounted to over $583 billion. According to the World Bank, Mexico in 2012 received $23 billion in remittances from the United States, followed by China ($13 billion), India ($11.9 billion), and the Philippines ($10.6 billion). With such volumes, it is not surprising that fintech innovators have considered investments in these payment channels to be low-hanging fruit.[28]

Western Union, which started as a telegram company in 1851, now has the largest reach of any remittance service. The company has 500,000 agents in more than 200 countries who support transactions in more than 130 currencies. Western Union's customers can transfer money online, through an app, or in person to a bank account or to a prepaid card. In 2016 Western Union completed 268 million transactions amounting to over $80 billion. The company controls around 25 percent of the market share with $5.4 billion in revenue.[29]

India issued payment licenses to several domestic players in the telecom sector and to some nonbank finance companies. The goal was to extend more financial services to the underserved in India. Similarly, apps for payments, such as Paytm, MobiKwik, and Freecharge have flourished in India. Given the size of India's market, other global players, such as Google Pay, Samsung Pay, and

Amazon Pay, are expected to follow MobiKwik's lead. WhatsApp, which has more than 200 million users in India, will soon pioneer payment facilitation. It is expected to drive large volumes of peer-to-peer (P2P) payments and become a popular platform for merchant payments.[30]

Because India had a predominantly cash-based economy, Paytm realized that if they launched a noncash payment service, they would have to keep costs low while increasing convenience. To pay for additional phone service using a credit card or internet banking platform, customers could use a Paytm mobile wallet linked to their names and mobile numbers. Because most Indians did not have high-end phones and because they faced frequent connection failures, Paytm created a simpler platform than the system offered by telecom companies.

Paytm was most successful among moderately affluent people age eighteen to forty-five because most of them owned mobile phones. Prepaid mobile phone users, who were 95 percent of mobile users, were also a large consumer base. With the advent of Paytm services, people no longer had to walk for miles in the heat to select mobile phone plans. Furthermore, Paytm offered them a wide range of services—at their fingertips.

Paytm profited and grew as digital payments were gaining popularity in India. To capitalize on this growth and to better position themselves against competitors, Paytm started to offer a wider array of services. They added a recharge feature for direct-to-home (DTH) television services. Seeing that online travel agencies were a $3 billion industry and that the sector was expected to grow by another 40 percent, they started offering bus tickets. They expanded next to utility bill payments. By 2013 they were processing six million utility bill transactions, primarily through mobile phones, which generated $11 billion in revenue. They expanded into school and college tuition payments, a $100 billion sector. Paytm began with ten schools and eight colleges. By 2017 their services had reached 25,000 campuses. They even worked with India's Nation Highway Authority to create radio frequency devices that allowed for cashless toll payments.

Paytm's first turning point came in 2014 when Uber introduced Paytm as a payment method. The partnership benefited both companies, as many users opened Paytm accounts just to use Uber. Paytm started with 200,000 Uber customers at the end of 2014. That number jumped to 5.3 million by 2016. Paytm then expanded its offerings by partnering with Meru Cabs, M-taxi, and Jugnoo. In 2015 Paytm opened a peer-to-peer service that offered a way to quickly transfer money without added costs. This was focused, not on remittance services, but instead on replacing cash.

The second turning point came when Alibaba and its subsidiary, Ant Financial, invested heavily in Paytm and introduced a new technology from China:

QR codes. Each retailer was assigned a QR code, which allowed customers to simply scan the QR code to process their payments. This model was so prevalent in China that customers even used it on chat apps.

As Paytm launched this business model in India, the company helped both customers and merchants. There was little or no fee charged for moving money around the Paytm platform. However, when a merchant or an individual transferred funds *into* their bank accounts, Paytm charged a 2 or 2.5 percent fee. By the end of 2016 Paytm was processing 5 million transactions through an offline network of 1.14 million merchants. In 2018 the average number of daily transactions was 5 million with an average of eighteen weekly transactions per user. More than 7 million merchants were registered. As of 2018 Paytm was accepted at 75 percent of India's retailers that accepted Visa and MasterCard.

In 2015 Paytm received a license to become a "payment bank," a new kind of banking entity designed to serve unbanked customers. The bank offered services such as savings accounts, current accounts, deposits up to 100,000 rupees, remittance services, third-party mutual funds, and insurance and pension products.

China has also seen explosive growth across online e-commerce and social networking platforms. The nation provides payment services that are almost universally accepted within China; they are used by low- and high-income, rural and urban households. These platforms include Alipay, developed by the Alibaba Group's affiliate Ant Financial, and Tencent's Tenpay, which operates the social media platforms WeChat and QQ.

Most banks and fintech companies have recognized that it is better to collaborate with traditional companies than to compete. But some service providers bypass the banking sector altogether. As previously noted, M-Pesa enables financial inclusion by providing money transfer services, local payments, and international remittance services with a basic mobile device.

All in all, investing in payments has been low-risk, and the efficiency and cost reductions of these innovations have been tremendous. There is a large and growing market for payments in emerging economies.

One of the largest success stories in the payments sector was M-Pesa in Kenya. Many Kenyan citizens are not able to open a bank account because they do not receive formal wages or income (most people are paid in cash). Bank transfers are prohibitively expensive, especially for smaller transactions. Transferring money to distant unbanked family members is expensive and challenging. It can also be risky. For example, many people ask the drivers of *matatus*—privately owned minibuses—or train conductors to transport money to distant relatives, only to see the money disappear.

Unlike banking, mobile technology is widespread and low cost. Kenya skipped the landline phase and jumped right to cellular technology. It is relatively inexpensive to get a device. Calls cost only two to four cents per minute and a text message costs only one cent. This means that even those in abject poverty can access a mobile phone. By 2000 most Kenyans had obtained a mobile phone.

Safaricom (Vodafone's Kenyan branch) wanted to create a financial service that could be conducted on a basic cellular phone (not a smartphone). "Originally, we worked on the idea of microfinance loans using mobile phones, and trialed a prototype service in Thika, north of Nairobi. What we found in practice was that people who received loans were sending the money to other people hundreds of miles away. In hindsight, we had inadvertently identified one of Kenya's biggest financial challenges. So, we took a chance and re-engineered the loan system to focus squarely on transmitting money from one phone to another."[31]

The Central Bank of Kenya cooperated with Safaricom to launch M-Pesa in 2007. Conscious that premature regulation could stifle innovation, the Central Bank of Kenya chose to closely monitor and learn from early M-Pesa trials and to formalize regulations later. This cooperation made it possible for Safaricom to start a financially viable service, which had a huge impact on financial inclusion and significantly alleviated poverty in the country. In return for the cooperation of the Central Bank of Kenya, Safaricom agreed to deposit the value of the M-Pesa accounts at commercial banks and set aside a percentage of these balances for a nonprofit trust fund.

Any citizen can open a M-Pesa account with a valid ID and a phone number. There are tens of thousands of kiosks operated by small businesses all over the country. People can deposit or withdraw money from their M-Pesa accounts through text messages, or they can complete transactions over their phones using the SIM-based M-Pesa menu. Consumers can also pay for goods and services directly from their mobile phones if the business has a M-Pesa business account.[32] There is no interest rate, and the relatively small fees are associated with sending and receiving money.[33]

Safaricom's target for the first year was 350,000 customers, but it reached 1.2 million. After only three years the company had nine million clients—40 percent of Kenya's adult population.[34] In 2017 there were "thirty million users in ten countries and a range of services including international transfers, loans, and health provisions. The system processed around six billion transactions in 2016 at a peak rate of 529 transactions per second."[35]

Several studies covering the social and economic impacts of M-Pesa have indicated positive effects on financial inclusion in Kenya. Eleven key advances in

2009 where identified in which M-Pesa had made community-level economic impact for both users and nonusers of the service. In order of impact, these were money circulation, transaction ease, money security, food security, human capital accumulation, business expansion, social capital accumulation, employment opportunities, financial capital accumulation, physical security, and quality control.[36] M-Pesa's influence is even more significant in rural areas than in cities because in rural areas alternative banking services (such as Western Union) are scarce. Many people in rural contexts who are defined as "bankable customers" are distant from the banks.

M-Pesa has made transactions safer and has helped people develop new financial skills, such as calculating a budget, maintaining a balance, building up savings, and so on. Moreover, mobile money services have helped an estimated 194,000 Kenyan households climb out of extreme poverty. They have also helped 185,000 women move from farming to business occupations.[37]

P2P Helps Small Savers and Borrowers Make Connections

In addition to helping people with payments, fintech is also improving the lives of people who lack access to credit. A primary barrier to providing lending services to the underserved is that banks classify these populations as high-risk borrowers. Low-income individuals are usually unable to provide collateral or guarantors. Even in China, where there has been enormous fintech progress, extending credit to rural and low-income populations continues to be an issue.

Traditional banks are risk-adverse and typically focus on the lowest-risk borrower profiles. This partially explains the existence of "loan sharks" who overcharge people who lack alternative lending options.

Fintech promises to change credit assessment paradigms for underserved customers. Technology can assess creditworthiness using alternative sources of data, such as payment transactions and telecom usage data, as well as online behavior analytics. These analytics can paint a more complete picture of creditworthiness and credit risk. As an increasing number of digital transactions take place, more data is recorded. This data can be used to build multifactor credit profiles and enable a faster and more equitable credit approval process for people rejected by banks. As fintech companies construct more savvy learning curves and data collection strategies, credit scoring will become increasingly robust.

Once credit risk can be assessed for a broader range of people, fintech can offer ways to match alternative lenders with borrowers. Peer-to-peer (P2P) lending models focus on creating new channels for intermediating savings and loans. They mobilize savings from individuals and route them directly to borrowers. Like banks, P2P platforms aggregate small deposits. That enables lending. The platforms play an intermediating role: gathering information about borrowers, assessing risk profiles, and bundling borrowers into various risk pools. Then the risk is directly assumed by the lender.

On the supply side, P2P platforms can reduce operations costs. There are no bank branches, credit assessments are automatized, and cash collection is digitized. These cost-saving processes open the door for providers to offer smaller loan transactions than banks could process. If the risk is priced appropriately, the incentives to lenders will be aligned with the risks, and the lenders will understand the risks.[38]

What about the demand side? Because lower-income people and those living in remote areas are often unable to save money at formal financial institutions, they are forced to find other ways to save. However, alternative savings propositions—investing in livestock, for example—tend to be risky. The added risk encourages more consumption and less saving. Thus, peer-to-peer lending can be very attractive to the unbanked. Even the wealthiest people who seek a higher yield, and thus are prepared to assume more risk, may find P2P lending attractive.

However, peer-to-peer lending platforms require a solid transactional system and platform. The example below describes how the Paytm in India managed to transition from a cash-based to a digital payments system. It also shows how new services are being built to create a full platform infrastructure for unbanked people.

As a result of building a large payments platform, Paytm in India now offers competitive interest rates to borrowers with savings accounts. Customers who want to earn higher returns can opt to move balances greater than 100,000 rupees into a linked deposit or money market mutual fund. This contrasts with the offerings of traditional banks, which have a minimum balance requirement for savings accounts and where customers must give specific instructions for making a deposit or investment.

Importantly, in India demonetization is under way. When 90 percent of India's physical money circulation was temporarily halted, Paytm became the default payment method. As a result, Paytm's user base grew to 300 million people in 2018, including 80 million active users.

When a fintech platform gains that many customers, it can use advanced data collection to match lenders with borrowers, thereby becoming a peer-to-peer loan marketplace. That could be Paytm's next big move.

E-Commerce: Inclusion by Buying and Selling

Another crucial area where fintech is helping people in practical ways is in connecting buyers and sellers through e-commerce. Jack Ma, founder of Alibaba, Ant Financial, and Alipay, has been a vocal supporter of financial inclusion for rural customers. Alipay and WeChat Pay bring the rural population of China into the fintech fold in part by offering them mobile wallets to use when buying goods and services provided by Alibaba and Tencent.

E-commerce can be particularly helpful for small businesses, for it enables local shops to sell products far beyond the store's physical reach. Merchants can avoid paying high fixed costs associated with building new stores (rent, staffing, and so on). Instead, for a relatively low cost small-business owners can utilize search engines, social media traffic, and online reviews to drive sales at a relatively low cost.

People in Chinese villages help each other learn how to sell traditional items or fresh produce online. In slightly larger villages, people set up small factories to produce goods to sell on Alibaba's e-commerce platform. Alibaba wants to keep this momentum going. They plan to invest $1.6 billion dollars in 2019 to build 1,000 county-level and 100,000 village-level service centers. In 2017 alone, the number of village service centers doubled to more than 30,000 villages.

Alibaba's competitor WeChat has also introduced new technology to rural populations, enabling small businesses to set up app-based business accounts to market and sell goods and services. Users share products and services with groups or friendship circles through the app. The seller needs only a picture, a product description, and a QR code linked to the seller's bank account.

There are benefits of e-commerce to consumers as well. E-commerce gives people access to a wider range of products and service providers at more competitive prices, and it levels out information asymmetries. For example, people in rural India use internet kiosks to find information on prices, buy insurance, purchase fertilizers and seeds, and consult with agronomists. Corporations such as ITC provide kiosks and purchase the harvest directly from farmers. These types of agribusinesses have led economic and social transformation for farmers in rural and remote areas.[39]

E-commerce and digital business can encourage rural populations to shift to mobile wallets. Digital payment methods are paving the way for business opportunities and improving financial inclusion.[40] The next horizon for these services is Africa. An informative case study is Jumia, which had to build a logistics infrastructure and innovative payment mechanism to enable larger-scale e-commerce.

In 2015 Nigerians made 98 percent of all retail purchases through informal markets, such as open-air markets and street stalls. The number of modern retail outlets remained small due to high real estate costs, difficulties in securing land titles, and poor infrastructure. Most upper-middle-class individuals imported products from outside the country. However, with the weakening naira (Nigeria's currency), importing was expensive and impractical for businesses. At that time Nigeria was also a logistically difficult place to navigate. Roads were congested and small towns were hard to access. The nation was also plagued with crime and fraud, causing distrust among consumers. Many Nigerians preferred to deal with businesspeople directly rather than remotely through phone or internet, and when they ordered goods online, they would only pay for them upon delivery.

In this complicated context, Jumia built its own e-commerce logistics team with trucks, delivery vans, and motorbikes. The company hired more than 1,500 employees. Workers sorted and packaged in the main warehouse, and then shipped products to a pickup station (a free delivery option for consumers). By the end of 2015 Jumia had a five-day service delivery option in rural areas, next-day delivery in city centers, and one hundred pickup stations.

Jumia also created a group of agents who traveled door to door, tablets in hand, to encourage households to buy products from Jumia's website. For these efforts, agents were offered a 20 percent commission. J-Force helped Jumia build stronger relationships, increase brand recognition, and understand customer needs and behavior.

Within four years Jumia had become the leading e-commerce business in Africa. In 2015 Jumia delivered over 1.6 million orders in twelve countries and employed 1,800 people. This exceptional growth has attracted some of the biggest investors in the world. The company raised $300 million from Goldman Sachs, AXA, and Rocket Internet. It is the only company in Africa to be valued at more than $1 billion. By 2016 the company had operations in fourteen African countries and three million customers.

However, Jumia did not find a profitable business model and suffered from very high investment in inventory combined with the high fixed costs of its delivery operations. The board looked to Alibaba's successful e-commerce approach as a model to emulate: If Alibaba could work in a country as vast as China, Jumia could work in Nigeria. Jumia executives decided to become an open marketplace. Jumia would open its platform to third-party sellers, who would be responsible for their own inventory. Jumia would focus on billing and logistics, such as pickup and item delivery. By shifting to an open marketplace, it was easier to scale up without exponentially increasing inventory.

But as Jumia continues to search for the winning e-commerce formula, it is increasingly turning its sights to fintech—specifically, Jumia Pay, its in-house payments solution. The company's goal is to expand its payment service across the continent. Jumia's fintech plans also include building a lending marketplace to allow customers and sellers to access loans and insurance. The Jumia Lending service supplies third-party financial institutions with data to determine the credit worthiness of its merchants and to offer them working capital loans.

Jumia is still an unfinished business, but it illustrates the fact that in emerging markets there are multiple interdependencies between e-commerce platforms, payment solutions, physical infrastructure, and logistics. Financial inclusion in rural areas goes hand in hand with the development of commerce.

Bringing It All Together: A Case Study on Alibaba

Alibaba's story illustrates how synergies between Big Data analytics, mobile technology, and fintech can lead to greater banking inclusion, particularly for underserved and difficult-to-reach populations. It is probably the most advanced and broadest ecosystem that a single company can bring together.

Alibaba used its logistics expertise and a strategy to reach rural populations. This strategy relied on the sale of local produce. The first initiative provided villagers with broader access to information, goods, and services. The company set up rural service centers at local grocery stores, installing computers and internet access. They trained local youth to work on behalf of Taobao Marketplace, which facilitates consumer-to-consumer (C2C) retail sales by providing a platform for small businesses and individual entrepreneurs to open online stores in Chinese-speaking regions. These centers became a valuable channel for rural communities to enter the mainstream economy and gain access to a wide variety of goods and services at much lower costs.

The second effort related to the sale of local produce. Using its extensive network of rural partners, Taobao began to route agricultural and other products directly to consumers. This helped local sellers secure a better price for their produce. With the middlemen removed from the equation, incomes for producers and sellers rose. This business opportunity encouraged village youth to avoid migrating, because they had new livelihood options at home.

Alipay—a third-party mobile and online payment platform established in 2004 by the Alibaba Group—helped build trust between Alibaba's online buyers and sellers by creating a digital escrow system that replaced cash on delivery. As the organization expanded into global logistics and infrastructure, Alipay utilized its technology, internet-based financial services, and Big Data analytics to generate credit scores, gauge customer creditworthiness, better understand expenditure patterns, and provide small loans to borrowers.

By 2018 Alipay's products served the needs of all customer segments:

1. *Payments:* Alipay boasts the world's leading third-party payment platform, with 300 million registered users, over 200 partner financial institutions, and 80 million transactions per day.
2. *Mobile wallets:* Alipay offers shopping payments, credit card repayments, money transfers, and bill payments to 190 million annual users.
3. *Asset management:* Alipay runs the largest money market fund in China, with 125 million users, and $84 billion in assets under management.
4. *Investments and financial products:* Alipay offers internet finance services to individuals, and to micro, small, and medium enterprises.
5. *Credit:* The company offers online microloans to microenterprises and individual entrepreneurs.
6. *MYBank:* Ant Financial now has a banking license, allowing it to serve individuals, small businesses, and microenterprises.

Alipay's effort to reach China's underserved population was motivated by the high rates of migration away from rural areas. This urbanization left only 46 percent of China's population in villages, which contributed to unlivable conditions in villages and left rural populations without basic financial services. Alibaba's ventures, which expanded access to internet and mobile phones, helped increase farmers' incomes and contributed to the growth of local economies. Alipay's initiatives redefined consumption and income paradigms for rural areas.

One of the most striking outcomes of the Alipay effort is that western China's relatively underdeveloped areas have higher use of the Alipay digital payment system than do developed areas. Financial inclusion gaps between Shanghai (ranked number one) and Tibet (ranked lowest) dropped from 4.9 times to 1.5 times between 2011 and 2015.

Following its massive success in China, Alibaba is beginning to duplicate its services in adjacent Asian markets. In 2016 the company acquired Lazada, an e-commerce marketplace in six Southeast Asian countries. This created synergies for Southeast Asian merchants to build relationships with successful counterpart sellers in China. Alibaba also introduced new technology and ideas to strengthen Lazada's position. The first was payment gateways. Southeast Asian customers preferred paying through ATM deposits or cash on delivery. Only 2 percent to 11 percent of consumers used online payment systems, and 70 percent to 80 percent of Southeast Asians did not have bank accounts. To help loosen these constraints, Lazada introduced HelloPay, a secure online platform that enabled non-cardholders to make payments.

In anticipation of Amazon's entry into the region, Lazada partnered with Netflix and Uber to form Live-up, a platform that competed against Amazon Prime by offering discounts for Netflix, Uber, Uber eats, and Taobao. This partnership helped Lazada tackle logistical issues while also giving customers access to products, content, and shipping alternatives—essentially strengthening Lazada's ecosystem.

The Lazada expansion highlights how the platform can patch together various services: transport (with Uber), entertainment (Netflix), payments (HelloPay), and digital platforms to develop commerce in rural areas of emerging markets.

CHAPTER SEVEN

The Interplay of Fintech and Government

Public services—such as electricity, water, roads, health facilities, and pensions—are designed to improve citizens' quality of life, welfare, and security while reducing economic inequalities. However, delivery of social services to vulnerable households, where support is most needed, is often ineffective. This shortcoming is most pronounced in developing economies. We will first look at the symbiotic relationship between government, development, and economic growth. Then we will explore the digital infrastructure required and the potential ways that governments can use fintech, to foster stronger economic development.

The Synergistic Growth of Governments and Economies

In emerging countries that are on a path of economic growth, governments can make various efforts to foster development.

The Growing Role of Government in Emerging Markets

Ideally, as a nation's economy develops, the objectives of its government should shift and advance. Maslow's hierarchy of needs, which offers a framework for understanding our personal lives, can apply to the role of governments. Governments often move from fulfilling basic survival needs, to providing goods and services, and then to ensuring the overall well-being of citizens. As economic growth occurs, government spending normally responds to evolving demographic transitions, such as improving health conditions and aging populations.[1] To better understand the changing role of government, it is helpful to focus on the stages described next.

The first stage of government growth is the *minimal state*. In this stage, governments tend to limit their responsibility to protecting citizens from coercion, fraud, and theft. They yield victim compensations and defend the country from foreign danger. Their role is primarily limited to sovereign functions (*regalienne* functions), such as internal security (police and justice), external security (military), and currency management. This is a common model in low-income countries. At this initial stage, the government budget is typically below 17 percent of GDP, reflecting minimal institutional involvement.[2]

The second stage is the *developmental state*. Governments implement a state-led macroeconomic planning system and take a more pronounced responsibility for economic development, with expenditures aimed at fostering production and economic output. As the economy progressively develops, governments may reduce their involvement by allowing for privatization, thus enabling market forces to shape the economy. The developmental state has been adopted by several East Asian countries, including China, Japan, South Korea, and Singapore, during their phases of expansion.

The third stage is the *welfare state*. Governments take responsibility for the welfare and well-being of citizens with programs that support physical, material, and social needs. Here the government's main objective is to design and promote an egalitarian society that minimizes income inequalities. Government responsibilities shift toward education, housing, health care, insurance, sick leave, supplemental income, and equal wages. Most advanced countries have adopted this model, including France, Denmark, and Sweden. However, there is still a wide spectrum of support services offered by each country. Among welfare states, there are three core submodels: conservative, liberal, and social democratic.[3]

Government-led transitions between these three stages of economic development lead to ever progressing public expenditures. Wagner's law of 1883 predicted this would occur as nations progressed toward industrialized economies. A nation's industrialization would be accompanied by citizens voting for ever-increasing social services, a movement from free-market capitalism toward the welfare state. He cited three main reasons for increased public expenditures: the state's social activities, administrative and protective actions, and welfare functions.[4]

In addition, endogenous growth models are useful for understanding links between government spending and growth. Robert Barro holds that economic growth is primarily the result of endogenous forces. He adds that public financial inputs, such as fiscal policy (taxation and spending), influence long-term growth rates. For instance, subsidies for research and development or education can drive growth rates by increasing the incentive to innovate.[5]

A certain level of economic development and revenue is required to divert limited resources from productive use (investment) to welfare. Interestingly, a

2018 study found a positive association between public spending and the economic growth rates of low-income countries, whereas they found negative associations across higher-income countries.[6]

The total expenditure-to-GDP ratio rises during economic development, a finding that supports Wagner's law. As countries transition from a minimal state to a welfare state, an increasing tax potential enables public expenditures to increase faster than GDP. This trend follows a logarithmic curve, illustrating that government spending is highly correlated with economic development.

We can categorize countries according to three per capita income levels. Within the first category—low-income countries with a GDP of less than $1,000 per capita—government spending accelerates faster than GDP (averaging 17 percent of GDP). The second category corresponds to middle-income countries with a GDP per capita between $1,000 and $12,000. In these cases, government spending averages 24 percent of GDP. The third category corresponds to high-income countries with a GDP per capita greater than $12,000. Within this category, public expenditures tend to stabilize between 30 and 40 percent of GDP. Continental Europe's countries are typically at the high end of this range (around 40 percent). Anglo-Saxon countries, such as the United States, Canada, Australia, and the United Kingdom, are at the lower end of this range (around 30 percent).

These increases in government expenditures represent differential spending patterns for social activities, welfare provision, and administrative expenses.

All in all, economic growth and the role of government are correlated and likely to be intercausal. On one hand, governments can stimulate economic growth by investing more. On the other hand, development and high economic growth can generate greater tax revenues, leading to higher government investment. However, this virtuous cycle needs an initial impulse before it can begin.

Social Security Transfers and Inequality

Today 39 percent of the global population lacks access to adequate health care. Low-income countries suffer the most. They commonly reach a staggeringly high health care exclusion rate of 90 percent (Figure 7.1). Similarly, almost half of the pension-eligible population (age sixty-five or higher) do not receive a pension, leaving them highly dependent on their families and extremely vulnerable to poverty traps. The absence of comprehensive social security coverage is particularly damaging in low-income countries, where over 700 million workers labor within the informal economy, live in extreme poverty, and survive on $1.25 per day.[7]

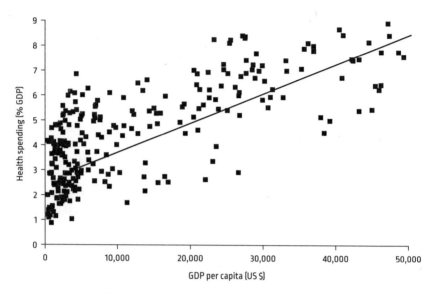

Data source: Laboure and Taugourdeau, "Does Government Expenditure Matter," 203–215.
Note: Countries weighted equally.

FIGURE 7.1   Health expenditures

Most emerging economies today have a larger elderly population than in previous generations. Labor contracts in these nations are often informal, and income and wealth inequality are high. For example, China's one-child-per-family policies introduced in 1979 (after a decade-long two-child policy) corresponded with a significant increase in longevity. China now faces a critical need to address service gaps faced by the elderly. China's coming demographic problems have led to a further relaxation in its child planning rules. In July 2021, authorities announced there will be no restriction on the number of children a family can have. The decision follows China's earlier announcement in May that a family can have three children. China's old-age dependency ratio (OADR) is expected to grow to an overwhelming 44 percent by 2050, a dramatic rise from 15 percent in 2017. For the same period, Russia's OADR is expected to increase from its former rate of 21 percent to 39 percent.[8]

As a nation's elderly population grows, pensions become increasingly important social buttresses against poverty traps. Pensions contribute to economic development through four channels. First, as a protective role, they guarantee income security and prevent poverty during retirement or old age (or when a primary earner becomes disabled or dies). Second, pensions have a productive role, by accumulating domestic savings (contributions) and stabilizing demand (benefits). Third, they have a redistributive role, by transferring risk and income between groups of insured people and across generations. Finally, they have a reproductive role, by reducing the financial and care burdens associated with aging. This improves gender equity and supports household efforts to maintain a healthy and educated family that sustains a functioning social fabric.[9]

In light of these important functions, shortfalls in pension systems in countries such as China and India are believed to increase inequalities because the majority of vulnerable groups—rural elders, informal sector workers, migrant workers, and low-income groups—have not been covered.[10]

Large emerging economies, such as China and India, have viewed employment and pension policies as being closely intertwined as part of a broader social welfare agenda. However, the advent of new pension policies has taken second priority to other economic issues. Rapid economic growth in these countries has been accompanied by large-scale migration from rural to urban areas. In China the number of rural migrants rose from 18 million in 1989 to 221 million in 2010, representing 16.5 percent of the national population and more than 33 percent of urban residents. Migrant workers participating in pension systems rose from 11 percent in 2006 to 21 percent in 2010. On the surface this seems like progress; however, workers often withdrew their contributions due to a lack of guaranteed accrued pension rights. And even if accrued pension rights had been established, the majority still lacked access to pensions, insurance, or health benefits.[11]

Several Latin American countries have introduced pension systems that reduce old-age poverty through social transfers (Table 7.1). These noncontributory social pensions have been celebrated as the most effective approach to reducing poverty, improving equity, and redistributing wealth with relatively low costs, but they are often weaker in terms of universal coverage and financial sustainability.[12]

Government Services Require Infrastructure

Another element in the synergistic relationship of government growth and economic growth is the need for financial infrastructure, without which governments will struggle to distribute social services.

According to the World Bank, Brazil's social insurance programs have reached about 12 percent of people in the lowest quintile, as compared to 30 percent across the overall population. China fares better on this account, covering 33 percent of people in the lowest quintile compared to 35 percent for the overall

TABLE 7.1   Social transfers and old-age poverty in Latin America (percentage)

	Poverty rate of adults aged sixty-five and older		
	Before transfers	After transfers	Reduction in poverty
Argentina	64.5	17.1	72.6
Brazil	67.8	16.9	75.1
Chile	52.8	15.0	71.6
Colombia	64.2	47.0	26.8
Costa Rica	52.7	28.7	45.5
Mexico	70.5	53.2	24.5
Uruguay	67.0	4.9	92.7
Average	62.8	26.1	58.4
Median	64.5	17.1	71.6

Data sources: UN Research Institute for Social Development, based on Victor E. Tokman, "Insercion Laboral, Mercados de Trabajo y Proteccion Social," *Serie Financiamiento del Desarrollo* 170 (2006), https://repositorio .cepal.org/bitstream/handle/11362/5143/S0600222_es.pdf?sequence=1&isAllowed=y; Andras Uthoff and N. Ruedi, "Diferencias en la Efectividad de la Politica Social para Atenuar la Incidencia de la Pobreza: Un Analisis a Partir de las Encuestas de Hogares" (paper presented at Politicas Hacia las Familias, Proteccion, e Inclusion Sociales, 2005).

population. In terms of Brazil's and China's expenditures, these programs translate to only 1 percent and 2 percent of their total public-sector social insurance expenditures, respectively (Figure 7.2).

The effectiveness of social welfare programs is more likely to improve when the programs are accompanied by improved state capacity: basic amenities, roads, electricity, water, primary and secondary education, basic health care, public health service inclusion, and internal security. These improvements facilitate productive consumption, which in turn improves the capacity of households and businesses to earn better incomes. As household incomes rise, governments need to manage expense priorities to improve fairness and decrease inequalities.

Factors such as low rates of formal identification of citizens can hinder wealth redistribution to lower-quintile households. Governments struggle to account for and redistribute funds to individuals who do not have official identification. In 2017, 19 percent of the world's 1.7 billion adults lacked the documentation needed to open financial accounts. Thus, many are left out of the system. Data collection and management are essential for countries to accurately plan, fund, and evaluate redistribution.[13]

Corruption is another major roadblock to redistribution. Economic losses caused by corruption far surpass potential welfare gains from redistribution. Corruption often forces governments to cancel welfare programs. It diverts funds away from the intended recipients, which means that those in need are denied

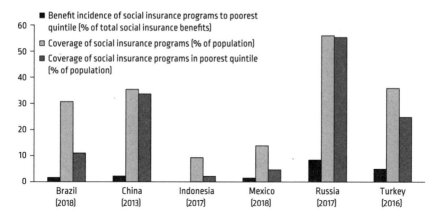

Data source: World Bank, "World Development Indicators," https://data.worldbank.org/indicator/per_si_allsi .cov_q1_tot?end=2019&start=1998&view=chart.

FIGURE 7.2   Social insurance programs in the lowest quintiles, and for the general population

access to benefits. Governments must address these issues if they are to provide meaningful redistributions to lower-quintile populations and, in turn, support economic development. Using fintech to make direct digital payments to citizens can solve these problems.[14]

Fintech and Types of Financial Services

Fintech can provide significant assistance to low-income populations in emerging economies. However, this requires the commitment of social actors with power and influence to direct technological designs toward the goal of improving financial inclusion in emerging economies. The Chinese and Indian governments, for example, have made financial inclusion and equality central aspects of their economic policies.

Paul DiMaggio and his colleagues have shown that the association between technological change and societal progress is not a unidirectional relationship. Technologies are often developed in response to the agenda of powerful social actors. Initially, innovators shape technologies to the contours of customary use, but eventually special interest groups seek to mold technologies to serve their goals.[15]

DiMaggio and his colleagues illustrated this point with examples such as the telephone, which was initially created to serve business communications but then evolved into an instrument of social interaction. They contended that the nature and forms of real-time internet communications were highly malleable. Today, as expected, technology specialists are eager to design and shape the internet to solve current problems.

DiMaggio's research can help us see how fintech innovations, such as blockchain, can encourage technological innovations that help governments benefit citizens.

Blockchains and Decentralized Trust

Within the long list of fintech technologies, blockchain is one of the most promising for emerging market deployment. Blockchain runs on distributed ledger technology (DLT), a system that creates "decentralized trust." DLT is powerful because it creates a contractual trust factor—the agreement, endorsement, promise to pay the bearer—without the need for a single, traditional intermediary. Thus, blockchain can fundamentally change the nature of transactions across sectors (financial, trade and commerce, legal spaces, and so on).[16]

At present, financial data are hosted within institutions that privately communicate through secured communication channels. Blockchain technology houses data within one or multiple global asset databases. This approach has the potential to be cheaper, safer, and easier for all transacting participants.[17]

Banks, financial institutions, and government entities are constrained by the inability to engage with a high volume of people, particularly those in low-income brackets who cannot prove identity. Know Your Customer (KYC)—the process of verifying the identity of a company's customers—resolves this issue, by forming a customer recognition system for financial institutions. However, this approach is not able to accommodate large-scale banking relationships or social redistribution. The vast, invisible legal framework that supports society is often not extended to low-income populations, which leaves them unable to benefit from government legal protections.[18]

Blockchain's decentralized trust, and its transformative, portable technology, could create irrevocable identities and bring the underserved into the fold of legal infrastructures. This can happen through a variety of channels.[19]

Legal identity. This is a core initial step for improving financial inclusion. Once a legal identity is generated, blockchain can make that identity a global identity, one that is not limited by the rules of any one nation. DLT, which enables blockchain encryption and validates information, can be used to create many forms of identity, such as passports.

Titles to asset ownership. The lack of clear and immutable property titles often cause conflict over asset ownership. In emerging economies, population growth puts pressure on land ownership systems. In places such as India, for example, land titles are often disputed. The weaker party is typically disadvantaged in the battle for ownership rights. Moving forward, blockchain could record immutable titles for newly acquired land, which would benefit low-income people the most.

Medical records. Medical records are practically nonexistent for underserved populations in emerging economies. With blockchain technology, medical records (once they are created) can be stored with a high level of privacy and data protection.

Smart contracts. Digital contracts use computer protocols intended to facilitate, verify, or enforce contracts. Smart contracts make it possible for people and / or businesses to perform credible, trackable, and irreversible transactions without intermediaries. This concept is not new, but blockchain technology better enables the execution of such transactions. Ownership titles, deeds, contracts, and notary verifications are examples of information that blockchain can permanently record. Furthermore, ownership can be transferred to subsequent owners without central authority permissions. This has the potential to fundamentally change the role of lawyers and the large government administrative machinery that presently endorses and updates contracts.

Payments. Real-time payments between two or more individuals can occur with blockchain, without requiring a bank account or clearing agency. The only requirement is smartphone-enabled internet access.

Policies can be more effectively monitored and implemented using blockchain's reliable data generation processes. Cisco estimates that the transactional processing capacity of this decentralized internet ledger will be available to over fifty billion devices by 2020.[20]

As a concrete example, the Building Blocks digital wallet is one of the first examples of a blockchain designed for humanitarian aid. It was rolled out in a refugee camp in Jordan in 2017. Each refugee scans his or her iris and the record is stored in a UN database. UN funds are deposited into each family's digital wallet account, which is kept on the World Food Program's Ethereum blockchain system. Then funds are deducted from the account after each transaction.

If governments deployed this type of technology, each citizen's digital wallet could contain a government ID, access keys to financial accounts, and transaction histories—all backed up on a blockchain identity system. This would allow more people to easily participate in the world economy, giving them a bank account for depositing paychecks, a viewable credit history, and a means of proving identity. Such a system could be modified to include documents and other valuable assets.

In the case of refugees who often lack official identity documentation, their critical personal data could be stored on a mobile phone and carried with them all the time. No matter their location, they would have the ability to prove identity, family relationships, educational credentials, and credit scores. Storing an encrypted identifier in a blockchain could separate the authentication system from personal data thereby protecting each person's privacy. This approach is easier to use, more secure than conventional records, and more able to survive disasters that sometimes wipe out centralized record-keeping systems.

In 2017 the United Nations World Food Programme (WFP) transferred more than $1.3 billion in Building Blocks benefits. With this technology, the WFP can now tally all refugee purchases and then directly settle the accumulated balances with participating stores, thereby removing the corruption of intermediaries (estimated to capture 30 percent of aid). The use of blockchain has also reduced bank fees involved in those transfers by 98 percent. This has saved the WFP millions of dollars that can now be used for higher purposes, such as expanding programs or offering more benefits to those in need.

Government-to-Person Fintech Applications

Fintech can facilitate direct links between government and individuals. Government-to-person (G2P) applications include wage and pension payments, health subsidies, unemployment allowances, and disability benefits. Digitizing these types of social transfers can help enroll large numbers of underserved persons in social programs while reducing costs, which might incentivize governments to promote G2P applications. For example, the South African government delivered social grants electronically at a 40 percent lower cost than for cash payments. Through this process the government also onboarded 60 percent of the previously unbanked population. Furthermore, consistent payment traffic has helped fintech providers expand payments to other services, such as retailers and utilities, or to introduce new services, such as loans.[21]

Digitizing government payments has the potential to increase bank account ownership. Among the adults worldwide who have an account, roughly eighty million people opened their first bank account to collect public-sector wages. Governments can enable even greater financial inclusion by digitally transferring funds, subsidies, and pensions.[22]

However, for digital government transfers to work, the technology ecosystem must be ready to use. Ideally, all citizens should be able to open and access accounts without hassle—and without usurious intermediaries who exploit the financial illiteracy of underserved people.

Over the next five years India's government-led e-KYC is projected to bring in over $1.5 billion in direct savings. Apart from substantial cost savings for banks and financial institutions, Aadhaar-enabled e-KYC is significantly more efficient than the current, paper-based KYC. Aadhaar is the mandatory platform for processing marriage certificates, school admissions, birth certificates, medical treatments, insurance, vehicle and property registration, bank accounts, e-wallets, and so on.[23]

Aadhaar's development in India, which we discussed in Chapter 5, is a case study on the importance of seamless cooperation between governments and banks. In its zeal to quickly digitize India's systems, the government made Aadhaar's unique identification system mandatory for pensions, which impacted a subscriber base of 5.4 million people. The sudden requirement caused a months-long stir among pensioners. Banks did not offer clear instructions on the matter and failed to honor pensioner requests in the stages just after the policy announcement. Authorities eventually clarified that participants did not need to use Aadhaar for withdrawals; however, the government did not permit withdrawals unless pensioners held an Aadhaar account linked to their pension accounts.[24]

So, when there is strong cooperation between governments and banks, digital G2P payments and remittance flows can create initial momentum for electronic payments, thereby supporting viable supply side businesses. The Indian government encouraged digitized transfers by sharing positive messaging about the system's ability to curb corruption and mitigate leakages. Equally important, the government sent a message to technology and fintech innovators: They could operate in a secure environment because the government was moving the economy swiftly toward digitization.

Fintech innovations have the potential to help low-income citizens who struggle to understand and properly value public services such as social welfare, pensions, and health care. Providing an online "pensions dashboard" could enable people to gain information and learn about their public and private pensions.[25]

As governments continue to digitize payments, citizens will be able to receive benefits with digital services, especially if service providers offer simple, user-friendly solutions that cater to customer needs. Globally, 2 percent of account owners—ninety million account-holding adults—receive government transfers, public-sector pensions, or wages in cash. The share is as high as 12 percent in Ethiopia and 14 percent in the Philippines.[26]

The Path Forward

If governments were to deliver social security payments—such as senior citizen pensions or unemployment allowances—digitally, it could encourage millions to enroll. We will discuss this further in Chapters 8–9. For now, we will look at the factors that are critical for developing government fintech initiatives.

Fintech Is Part of an Ecosystem

Private-sector initiatives in recent decades have expanded empirical knowledge about how fintech works. Governments can learn from these experiences. In this section we examine one of the largest fintech services in the world: WeChat. This popular messaging service had over 1.2 billion monthly active users in 2020, a number greater than the entire population of Europe. WeChat today is like Facebook, Twitter, WhatsApp, Zynga, Instagram, and Apple Pay all rolled into one platform. As China's largest social app, it has helped create a single digital identity. The app serves as a central hub, giving people a single platform for instant messaging, food delivery, medical appointment bookings, P2P payments, bank transfers, and wealth management services. This breadth of services empowers WeChat to collect data on each user, which enables the company to use analytics to develop more services and increase its competitive advantage. More than half of WeChat's customers have linked their bank accounts to the app, allowing them to navigate multiple services without cash, credit, or debit.

The WeChat example shows how fintech can connect products and services across many industries. The company started by providing information technology, telecom, and financial services, but it has since entered medical services, insurance products, food, entertainment, and more. These services increase the app's consumer value and the circle of trust for financial service consumers. Also, this collective information provides well-rounded data points about customer consumption and expenditure patterns.

However, for fintech to achieve WeChat's high level of impact on people's lives, there must be a functional economic ecosystem. Developing that ecosystem has significant implications for government planning, policy, and spending. The criteria for that ecosystem are outlined below.

First, the ecosystem must have electricity, computers, and phones. Reliable electricity transmission for computers and phone networks is necessary. This is not something most emerging economies can take for granted, particularly in rural areas. In Africa the penetration of mobile devices has increased from zero to

900 million people in fifteen years, but 500 million users still lack regular access to electricity.[27]

Second, the ecosystem must enable fintech to work with other financial services. Typically, fintech solutions cannot serve as substitutes for banks, insurance, or wealth managers. Instead, fintech either facilitates distribution, bundles services, or bridges gaps in the ecosystem. As such, fintech thrives when it is part of a broader financial ecosystem that includes banking institutions, insurance companies, wealth management companies, credit bureaus, and others. Fintech works when it can leverage a wider infrastructure of data collection systems, data security and privacy platforms, and disclosure norms that work seamlessly across multiple products and services.

Third, fintech requires market demand to drive supply. Fintech needs an online retail market that consists of individuals and small businesses. In emerging economies, many people are typically excluded from formal financial services, and most developing countries are cash-based. These factors limit online retail markets. However, as China has illustrated, a mature marketplace can be created within the contexts of emerging countries. Alipay was initially established as a payment method for Alibaba's e-commerce company. Later, in 2013, the Yu'e Bao money market was integrated with the Alipay wallet. This provided investors with an interest rate and gave customers an opportunity to make small investments. Today Alipay is the largest money market in the world.

WeChat Pay started as a payment service within a messenger app that primarily focused on games and social media purchases. WeChat first allowed taxi payments through WeChat Pay. By 2018, according to a representative survey, almost 92 percent of Chinese citizens said they used WeChat's mobile-based payment system to pay retailers.[28]

Similarly, India's Paytm started by providing recharge services for prepaid SIM cards. It has since evolved into a marketplace with payment services for everything from shopping to satellite television to taxies. Paytm is now launching its own fintech bank to provide loans and other financial services to clientele.

Fourth, fintech requires an environment with smart regulation. Legal and regulatory infrastructure is needed for e-commerce consumer protection, dispute resolution, and contracts. Government and legal systems should provide regulatory frameworks that enable sustained fintech growth while also ensuring equal access to benefits.

Consider the example of the People's Bank of China (PBoC). Fintech grew rapidly in China, but it was improperly regulated. This led to leakages and scams involving fake QR codes. An increased number of Alipay and WeChat Pay users caught the attention of the PBoC, which then began regulating these services.

Since June 2018 mobile payment institutions have been required to channel all payments through the China Nets Union clearing corporation. This has given the PBoC greater control over the payments than it previously held. The PBoC has also raised reserve ratios, which will eventually increase to 100 percent (to better protect consumers). Lastly, the PBoC has been placing payment caps on QR codes to prevent fraud. Now, payment systems must get PBoC permission permits before using QR codes.

Central banks like the PBoC no longer limit interaction to banking supervision, but they are enabling innovation and introducing stronger regulation. The examples of Alipay and WeChat illustrate the importance of regulations on new and emerging fintech.[29]

Fifth, fintech requires a digitally and financially literate population. When consumers are digitally and financially literate, it is significantly easier for them to use fintech services. One factor behind fintech's success in emerging markets is the high proportion of young people living in each market. They have greater financial needs relative to older segments of the population, and they are more willing to embrace fintech. In addition, emerging countries typically have lower levels of internet privacy protections than industrialized countries. Fintech can often spread quickly because people in emerging economies give less attention to protecting against data breaches and privacy violations.[30]

Sixth, fintech benefits from government assistance. A government that proactively pursues innovation can build a powerful ecosystem. As was the case with Aadhaar in India, only government could insist on grand-scale digitization for identification and payments while providing citizens with a platform for additional fintech services.

Fintech and Regulation

As we have seen, fintech has the potential to deliver an unprecedented array of products to previously underserved populations and geographies. However, for these benefits to reach general populations, government and the private sector must cooperate to create trustworthy, inclusive financial systems.

Fintech can be used to manage, transfer, and store a significant amount of people's money; however, if start-up companies are financially fragile and prone to bankruptcy, the financial risks for individuals increases. This implies a need for government-led stability.

Based on an international sample of 2,635 banks in eighty-six countries between 2004 and 2012, M. Mostak Ahamed and Sushanta Mallik in 2017 suggested that a higher level of financial inclusion contributes to greater bank stability. The positive association was pronounced among banks with (a) higher shares of customer deposits; (b) lower marginal costs of banking services; and (c) a presence in countries with strong institutions. These results highlight why inclusive financial systems should be a policy priority for governments and banks, as it leads to systemic stability.[31]

Nevertheless, developing new financial technology can be a strong challenge for regulators. Fintech spans telecom and banking sectors and financial products, making it difficult to know how to design regulations. A plethora of technologies is involved, including artificial intelligence, Big Data, and distributed ledger technologies. These applications interact with payments, savings, credit, risk management, mobile investment advice, digital currencies, and so on.

The regulatory task of maintaining a safe, efficient financial system becomes more complex when alternative legal tender and clearing system options are introduced and when new technology manages to disintermediate traditional licensed banks, which are the backbone of the financial system and its regulation. History shows that many fintech ideas fail before eventually succeeding. In this context of high risk and failure, regulation can bring system stability and user protections.

In this challenging and complex environment, regulators must understand the changes and find ways to balance economic benefits, financial risks, and rapid innovation. Figure 7.3 highlights the broader ecosystem of fintech.

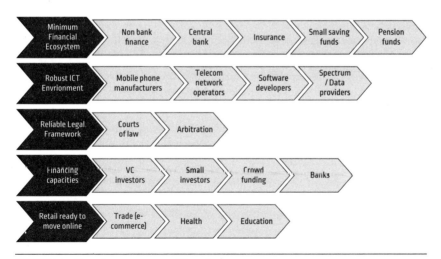

FIGURE 7.3   Broader ecosystem of fintech

As we can see, there is an interplay of innovation and regulation. Regulation can catalyze or hinder financial innovation, depending upon the degree of shared vision between a bank's innovation strategy and a government's policies. Performance pressure helps drive innovation, whereas organizational bureaucracy and rigidity are major barriers to innovation.[32] The following are some of the approaches used by central bankers to establish a good dynamic.

Test and learn. Regulators can pilot a framework and then learn about the related risks. This helps them determine how to solve problems on a small scale before implementing a plan more widely. The European Union has implemented this strategy when introducing crowdfunding and blockchain technologies. The governments of Kenya (M-Pesa), Indonesia, and the Philippines have each followed this practice.[33]

Wait and see. In this approach, governments can follow technological developments and then use the technology to implement a steady pace of internal change. A good example of this is Alipay in China.

Regulatory sandboxes. This involves a formal and transparent dialogue between a regulator and innovators during which each stakeholder learns from the others. Most of the fintech regulatory sandboxes today are launched in European and Asian countries. Australia, the UK, Singapore, China, India, Mexico, and Russia have experimented with this approach.[34]

Regardless of how regulators and innovators interact, banking and telecom regulators must address important ethical issues.

Ethical Parameters for Data Use and Debt

No system—government or private—will function long-term without the trust of individual users. Thus, government and private-sector leaders need to establish ethical parameters for the use of data, including data that could be used by lenders.

In regard to data use, it is reckless and irresponsible to use data collection and analytics for the wrong reasons. The same data analytics that enable product customization and outreach to underserved customers can also cross a line of ethical intrusion into customers' lives.

The data generated by digital footprints is increasing exponentially. Digital footprints can include, for example, who people call, what people write in texts, social media connections, records of purchases, and website visits. This raises a variety of governance issues relating to how data is accessed, used, stored, or shared to inform decisions. Low-income people are particularly vulnerable because they have limited access to information, they lack alternative options for accessing credit, and they have greater difficulty in voicing grievances.

Increased financial inclusion, and increased access to savings and credit, should enable more people to be steady consumers and establish household well-being. However, there are instances of data exploitation wherein individuals, or groups with similar profiles, had information used against them in credit assessments. In the process of assessing borrower credit risk, an individual's profession or education level can be correlated with one's ability to repay a loan.

As fintech platforms increase a general population's access to credit, there is an ethical need for governments and private entities to increase financial literacy. Consider what occurred in the Indian state of Andhra Pradesh, where the microfinance movement was pioneered in 2010. Over exposure to credit triggered a microfinance crisis. Lenders offered multiple loans to the same household, with lending rates often between 50 percent and 100 percent, leading to over-indebtedness. As customers became increasingly unable to repay on time, the lending institutions engaged in coercive recovery practices. These factors led to several suicides in the state. In response to those deaths, local politicians openly instructed people to not repay microfinance loans.[35]

Fintech start-ups will likely be exposed to the same risks, issues, and dilemmas that other financial institutions have faced. Many are concerned about data misuse and hacking, over-centralization, the rise of fintech monopolies, government control of personal data. Technology can enable fintech companies to assess risk profiles and then use that data to suppress or increase lending (depending on context). An improperly motivated company could, for example, use technology to incentivize people to accept a loan that they may not need. All of these problems are rooted in an absence of ethical concern.

CHAPTER EIGHT

Toward a Cashless Society

As a result of the proliferation of credit cards, there has been widespread speculation about the possibilities of a checkless, cashless society in the future.

—*Jack Lefler,* Las Cruces Sun-News, *July 24, 1968*

The one thing that's missing, but that will soon be developed, is a reliable e-cash, a method whereby on the Internet you can transfer funds from A to B without A knowing B or B knowing A.

—*Professor Milton Friedman, Nobel Prize winner, 1999*

If you wonder why physical cash still exists, you are not alone. Several countries have recently removed large notes worth $100 or more and have implemented policies to replace traditional payment customs with digital solutions. Yet the transition of usage and habits could take longer than previously expected. This chapter focuses on the digitization of money, including an analysis of twentieth-century innovations and the more recent rapid growth of global digital payment systems. For this chapter and Chapter 9, we did an exclusive survey of over 3,600 customers in China, France, Germany, Italy, the UK, and the United States. The goal of the survey was to assess attitudes about cash and digital alternatives across a range of cultural and economic variables.[1]

A Century of Innovative Disruptions

The transition from cash to digital currencies has occurred gradually, in phases. We will address these global trends and tensions in more detail in Chapter 9. First, we look at how currencies and transactions have developed since the early days and how change has accelerated in the last thirty years. A brief historical review can help us better understand current trends (Figure 8.1).

FIGURE 8.1   How currencies and transactions have developed

Commerce as Barter (from 6000 BCE)

The idea of people exchanging goods or services with no intermediary or base "market" price, by establishing a "double coincidence of wants," is one of the oldest forms of payment we know in human record. By most accounts, the history of bartering dates to circa 6000 BCE. The system was allegedly introduced by Mesopotamian tribes and further expanded by the Phoenicians through international trade. The Babylonian empire adopted this system with the concept of exchanging services and goods for items such as weapons, teas, spices, and slaves. The Romans went to great lengths to barter for items such as salt, which was a measure they used to pay soldiers in what we would call a *salary* today. This barter system became problematic in part because it limited dynamic economic activity, diversity, and growth. Around 1000 BCE the Chinese and others shifted away from exchanging weapons, and utilized lightweight bronze replicas of weapons as a form of payment.

The Evolution of Currency (from 1000 BCE)

The bronze and copper replicas described above could potentially be considered the earliest forms of metal currencies. This was just the start of metals used as a currency. Gold, silver, or a combination of both, such as the Lydia currency (circa sixth century BCE), became the dominant form of currency throughout Eurasia. The Lydia currency may be the earliest form of coinage. It was developed in the Mediterranean region and later copied and refined throughout the Western Hemisphere.

Beyond their visual value, precious metals gave people the ability to transport a durable, lightweight coin and thereby fostered a strong expansion of trade through the Middle Ages. Furthermore, coins enabled people to conveniently fix the prices of goods and services with a common metric unit based on the weights of coins. Additionally, coins facilitated the storing of value, which allowed for populations to buy, trade, and move resources all over the planet.

The Development of Bills (from the Seventeenth Century)

Paper money was implemented in Europe in the seventeenth century. This occurred in the context of a "price revolution" during which large amounts of gold and silver entered Europe (mostly brought by the Spanish from Latin America). With the influx of precious metals, banks handed out payable receipts to the bearers of documented resources.

By the first half of the nineteenth century, many towns in the United Kingdom (and the United States) had established local banks, and each issued local banknotes. Before national currencies and efficient clearing houses emerged, banknotes were only redeemable at face value by the issuing banks.

Paper currency, specifically the US dollar, only came to worldwide prominence after World War I. It has since played a major role in shaping global history. Inadvertently, paper currency, especially large notes, has also facilitated illegal transactions, underground economies, and money laundering.

The Credit Card (from the 1950s)

The concept of using a card for purchases was described in 1887 by Edward Bellamy in his utopian novel *Looking Backward*. In 1950 Ralph Schneider and Frank McNamara created the Diners Club card. Initially made of cardboard, this card was used to pay for entertainment and travel expenses.

Ten years later, Diners Club had around 10,000 New York City members, all elite business professionals. They could use the card for payment at twenty-eight restaurants and two hotels. The card promised its holder convenience and served as a status symbol. The company convinced merchants that its card would stimulate people to buy more.

Credit card demand dramatically increased once the US Internal Revenue Service began requiring detailed business expense records.

By 1958 American Express had launched the first plastic card. Bank of America released the first recognizable modern card with revolving credit, in California, which was first called the BankAmericard and later Visa. To compete with the BankAmericard, a group of banks joined to create the Interbank Card Association, which later evolved into MasterCard.

Visa and MasterCard created a system in which banks could join a network of Visa and MasterCard cards, with the ability to choose both cards for their offerings.

The Early Adoption of Mobile Payments (since the 2000s)

Mobile payments are transactions conducted with a mobile phone in combination with a credit card, an invoice, an electronic wallet, or a cash account.

As for emerging economies, mobile payments started in the early 2000s. Their deployment has facilitated and spread financial services to communities with "unbanked" or "underbanked" citizens—those without bank accounts. These payment networks have often been used for micropayments. Mobile payments started in emerging economies (Alipay started in 2004 in China). They are increasingly common nowadays, but they only started gaining traction in advanced economies recently. Apple Pay and Google Pay launched in 2014 and Samsung Pay a year later.

Meanwhile, in many parts of the world people are becoming more familiar with noncash payments such as paying with points accumulated through credit card spending and airline travel. Among US citizens, 45 percent are comfortable using an independent, nongovernment currency, as evidenced by an increasingly high number of companies that have points programs. The Starbucks Rewards app—one of the leaders in mobile payment apps—recorded 16.3 million US memberships in 2019. Thirty percent of payments at Starbucks stores occur with the company's points program.

The Early Adoption of Cryptocurrencies (since the 2010s)

We will discuss cryptocurrencies in more depth in Chapter 9. But for historical context, the concept of cryptocurrency started around thirty years ago when DigiCash Inc. created the first worldwide virtual currency. It went bankrupt in 1998, less than ten years after its creation.

The most famous cryptocurrency, Bitcoin, was created in 2009 by a developer using the pseudonym Satoshi Nakamoto. Since 2011, cryptocurrencies have gained momentum from investors and captured media attention. Bitcoin prices rose dramatically in 2013. Several new cryptocurrency companies were born, including Litecoin (2011), Ripple (2012), Ethereum (2015), and Bitcoin Cash (2017), to name a few.

Cryptocurrencies have passed the tipping point needed to become fashionable. In June 2019 Facebook announced its Libra (now rebranded as Diem) cryptocurrency. With about 2.8 billion users, or one-third of the world's population, Facebook's planned cryptocurrency has the potential to compete with traditional online payment platforms.

Moving Slowly toward a Cashless Society

For the last fifty years, various publications have predicted the end of cash. One of the first such articles was written by Jack Lefler in 1968. He envisioned the emergence of a cashless society that would use a single identification card for all transactions. In the late 1970s, a former Citibank leader presented a newspaper article titled "Cashless Society Is Predicted by Credit Card Use." In his 1981 book, *World of Tomorrow: School, Work and Play,* author Neil Ardley foresaw a cashless world by 2002. "The answer is simple: You do not carry any money on you and neither does anyone else. You pay for everything you buy with an identity card like a credit card. It has a magnetic strip containing your name and other personal information in the form of a magnetic code," he wrote. In February 2007 the cover title for the *Economist* was "The End of the Cash Era." The corresponding article projected that cash would be a dinosaur doomed to extinction.[2]

Are today's predictions about the demise of cash different? For now, people still want cash. The *Financial Times* revealed that wealthy investors had been holding ever-larger investable assets in cash. Two-thirds of the people surveyed said they had considered increasing cash holdings given the economic uncertainty around the US–China trade war, conflict in the Middle East, and the potential effects of Brexit.

But cash is losing ground as a payment method. Several countries have recently removed large notes worth $100 or more and implemented policies to replace traditional payment methods with digital solutions.

Governments, banks, and card providers share at least one common goal: the elimination of cash. Governments are more concerned with eliminating larges notes from circulation because those notes are mostly used for the underground economy, but banks and card providers have been finding ways to foster smaller payments with cards through technology innovations, such as contactless cards (cards that can be used without inserting or swiping them in a reader) and mobile payments.

Thus, the global campaign against paper money is lively, especially against large notes. One of the world's leading economists, Kenneth Rogoff, makes a persuasive case for getting rid of most paper money, and Larry Summers wrote an article in 2016 titled, "It's Time to Kill the $100 Bill."

Large denominations are mainly used for illegal activities such as tax evasion, drug trafficking, and terrorism. The increase of monetary circulation over the last twenty years is almost entirely due to large notes (the USD 100 note in the United States, the JPY 10,000 note in Japan, and EUR 50 note or higher in the Eurozone). It is also estimated that two-thirds of USD 100 notes are held outside the United States, which indicates they are not used for ordinary transactions.

Large notes are disappearing fast all around the world. In 2018 the European Central Bank decided to permanently cease new issuance of the EUR 500 note.

Nevertheless, cash is still widely used in many advanced countries, including Japan, western Europe, and the United States. According to our proprietary survey, one-third of people in developed countries considered cash to be their favorite payment method and more than half believed cash would always be around. This statement was true regardless of country, gender, and age.[3]

Indeed, our survey showed that nearly 60 percent of in-store purchases in Germany were paid in cash. Germans held EUR 52 in cash, on average, the highest rate among advanced economies, and the average German planned to use even more cash in the coming six months.

Americans, British, and Italians considered cash to be their second favorite payment method (approximately a third preferred cash). Interestingly, 11 percent of Americans planned to use even more cash in the next six months. People said they used cash as a store of value and as a means of payment. Specifically, 53 percent of Americans said they wanted to make sure they always had cash with them and about 70 percent of Americans still used cash every week. On average, each American held about $47 in cash (Figure 8.2).

Cash has properties that no other payment method has. It helps users remain anonymous and avoids cyberattacks. However, these benefits were not among the top five reasons the citizens we surveyed loved cash so much. Surprisingly, over 40 percent believed that cash enabled them to easily track spending and to make payments faster. They found cash to be convenient, accepted almost everywhere, and secure.

The key question is what happens in the world's two most populous countries—China and India. As the push to remove cash escalates, these governments are encouraging greater use of digital currencies.

In late October 2019, Chinese President Xi Jinping endorsed blockchain as "an important breakthrough for independent innovation of core technologies." He repeated the PBoC's intention to have cash replaced by a digital currency issued by the central bank.

In India, change is also coming. The government declared in 2016 that 1,000- and 500-rupee notes would no longer be valid, despite strong resistance to change and a temporary cash shortage. And recently a government economic panel pitched for the introduction of an official digital currency with the status of legal tender and regulated by the Reserve Bank of India.

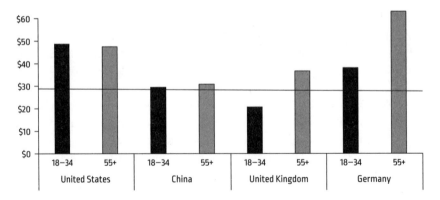

Source: Reformatted from Marion Laboure and Jim Reid, "The Future of Payments Part I. Cash: The Dinosaur Will Survive . . . for Now," Deutsche Bank Research, Corporate Bank Research, 2020, https://www.dbresearch .com/PROD/RPS_EN-PROD/PROD0000000000504353.pdf.

Note: Cash carried in France, Germany, and Italy is denominated in euros, in China in renminbi, in the United States in dollars, and in the UK in sterling.

FIGURE 8.2   Cash carried in 2019, by generations, on average

The Payments Transition

Fintech companies and smartphones have facilitated banking innovations that could inaugurate a new integrated and dematerialized ecosystem for payments.

On the business-to-consumer side, smartphones are making plastic cards obsolete. People in advanced countries are gradually adopting smartphone-based payments in the context of each country's infrastructure. Eager adoption by millennials and increased digitization of country infrastructures could diminish the use of plastic cards over the next decade—even as people continue to use humble notes and coins.

Most citizens we surveyed were not ready to abandon their beautiful leather wallets, but most of them also believed that digital wallets are more than a fad. Most planned to use a smartphone wallet more in the next six months, and most believed that digital wallets would eventually replace traditional wallets within the next five years.

This trend opens outstanding opportunities for brands, retailers, and, on a broader scale, any business selling directly to consumers. Digital wallets can allow businesses to better know, interact with, and personalize products for their customers. Personalization enables companies to stand out in the field and gain market share, especially because millennials tend to think that smaller, custom brands offer better-quality products. Looking forward to 2025, we expect

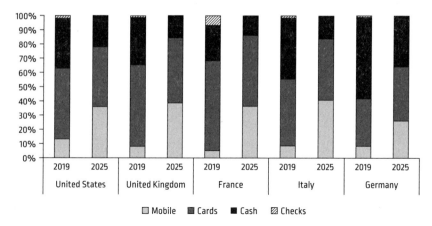

Data source: Marion Laboure and Jim Reid, "The Future of Payments Part II. Moving to Digital Wallets and the Extinction of Plastic Cards," Deutsche Bank Research, Corporate Bank Research, 2020, https://www .dbresearch.com/PROD/RPS_EN-PROD/PROD0000000000504508.pdf.

Note: We expect purchases with checks to be lower than 1 percent, and nearly all cards to be contactless, in 2025 in the United States, UK, France, Italy, and Germany.

FIGURE 8.3   Weekly in-store purchases per country, in 2019 and projected for 2025

e-wallets to be the second-most preferred method of payments after cards and the most preferred method among millennials (Figure 8.3).

A customer-centric mindset is critical in the business-to-business space. Yet B2B customer satisfaction indexes are lower than 50 percent. This ranks systematically lower than B2C companies, which typically score at 65 to 85 percent. Some of the biggest B2B problems are late payments, collection, and recovery. Payment time has increased by 10 percent over the last decade. The average has reached nearly seventy days. One reason for this long average delay relates to business clients who deliberately extend payment terms to maximize their working capital. But the primary reason for long delays is inefficient internal processes and methods for tracking receivables. This factor is usually overlooked because everyone has focused on shifting companies away from checks to electronic payments, a change that requires businesses to gather and manage all the data, such as data required to make timely payments and track deliveries.

Payments and Smartphones

In this section, we will focus on the key global fintech transitions related to payments—for both B2B and B2C. Understanding these changes will provide a framework for better understanding possible outcomes—the topic of Chapter 9.

To ask whether we will see the end of cash in the 2020s is a distraction. The right questions are these: Which new means of payments will emerge? Which existing means of payment will disappear soonest? What if plastic cards, a recent invention, disappear first?

The digital payment revolution is rooted in the 2008 global financial crisis. At that time, liquidity in the financial system was low, people struggled to borrow money, and distrust in the banking system grew.

Since the financial crisis, regulation over traditional banks has strengthened. Meanwhile, most fintech players have operated below the radar and benefited from weaker regulations. The number of deals and the amount of capital raised for payments innovation have strongly accelerated in recent years. Today about a third of fintech deals and capital raised is related to the payments industry.

This sector of the economy has been growing and experiencing profound technological changes. Global payments revenues have nearly doubled since 2010 to almost $2 trillion. Unsurprisingly, the Asia-Pacific region, due to its market size and mass adoption of new technologies, represents nearly half of worldwide payments revenues. When Apple released its first-generation iPhone in 2007, no one would have thought that smartphones would be so successful. Today in the United States, individuals spend on average three hours per day on their phones and check incoming messages nearly eighty times per day. Millennials, especially, are seduced by smartphone convenience and addicted to the flow of information (messages, email, social networks, app alerts, news, and so on).

The centralization of all these functions into a "one size fits all" device has, of course, greatly expanded the use of phones for making financial transactions. That, in turn, has spawned a plethora of payment services, such as Apple Pay and Google Pay (to name just two). These services have strengthened what is called the "retail payment value chain"—the interdependence of smartphones and payment services, which is essential for today's major fintech transitions.

The payment value chain is complex and highly intermediated. Let's split it into two successive phases: first the "consumer front office" and next the "operations back office" (Figure 8.4).

Within the consumer front-office framework, the consumer (or the sending side, broadly speaking) first initiates a payment using a device. The payment moves through different channels (internet, mobile payment platform, bank branch storefront, and so forth). Then the data are transferred to the payment receptors of the merchant's bank (the acquirer/processor). This first phase involves the highest *distribution* of sensitive data and might involve tens or even

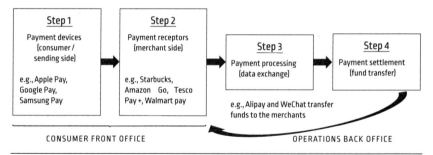

FIGURE 8.4   The retail payment value chain

hundreds of millions of consumers and merchants in short amounts of time. That data is subject to many points of vulnerability. Security measures to protect data vary greatly and are still in the early stages of development.

Consumer Front Office: Three Types of Mobile Payments Players

First, new players such as Apple Pay, Google Pay, and Samsung Pay have recently offered more convenience and speed to users. They enable users to store electronically, on a mobile phone, the personal and financial information that has traditionally been stored on plastic cards. Thus, the mobile phone replaces the traditional wallet and serves as a contactless payment tool. Importantly, this emerging system does not disintermediate the value chain; it creates, at least so far, *an additional* intermediary, which means increased fees for the merchant, but more convenience for customers.

The second type relates to retailers that set up payments through their own apps. This approach also does not remove (or add) intermediaries. But customers can avoid copying and pasting their card details into Apple Pay or Google Pay because they enter their cards details into the app.

The most popular and well-known app of this sort is the Starbucks Rewards app with 16.3 million US memberships in 2019. Thirty percent of payments at Starbucks stores occur with the company's points program. More recently, grocery stores have started offering mobile payments. For example, the British multinational grocery chain Tesco introduced Tesco Pay + and the American behemoth Walmart launched a Walmart Pay app. Both the Tesco and Walmart apps mimic the system Starbucks introduced in 2011.

The Starbucks mobile payment app initially allowed customers to make payments and to store their Starbucks gift cards within the app. Now customers

TABLE 8.1   Big tech retail payments

		Reach	
		Domestic	*Global*
Payments infrastructure	Overlay	Venmo	Apple Pay, Google Pay, PayPal, *Novi*
	Standalone	Alipay, M-Pesa, WeChat Pay, Swish	*Diem*

Data source: Bank for International Settlements (2019). Note: A standard font indicates a system or service in operation; an italic font indicates a proposal.

Notes: Venmo is a mobile US payments app owned by PayPal. M-Pesa is a mobile phone-based money transfer, financing and microfinancing service. Calibra is the mobile wallet that Facebook intends to run on top of the Libra network. Swish is a mobile Swedish payments app launched in 2012 by six large Swedish banks in cooperation with the Swedish central bank. "Overlay" systems build an innovative customer interface that improves the ease with which customers can instruct and receive payments. These systems then use existing payments infrastructure, such as correspondent banking, credit card, or retail payment systems, to process and settle payments. Standalone systems are "closed-loop" payment systems and do not interact with or depend on existing payments infrastructure. In these systems, payments are processed, cleared, and settled by the platform provider independently of any other system. "Domestic" platforms provide payment services within the jurisdiction or region of the platform provider. "Global" platforms provide payment services to users in several jurisdictions.

can also store their credit card information in the Starbucks app, enabling them to scan their smartphones at the register when they pay for their coffee. The coffee chain says that of the nine million weekly transactions conducted in their stores, 20 percent come from payments via smartphones.

Amazon Go stores implemented a system by which customers check in to the physical store, select the items they want from the shelves, and then walk out of the store without going through a checkout line with a cashier. Payment occurs automatically by the power of sophisticated in-store technology that includes overhead cameras, weight sensors, smartphone payments, and other innovations.

The third type of payment app provides features such as credit card payments, bank account management, P2P transfers, prepay mobile phone payments, bus and train ticket purchases, food orders, ride hailing services, insurance selections, and digital identification document storage. Examples of this type are the Chinese mobile players Alipay and WeChat (Table 8.1).

Back-Office Operations: Authenticating and Transferring Payments

The second step relates to the "operations back office." First, the merchant bank contacts the payment bank. Then the payment is processed though data exchange via the card platform (such as Visa, MasterCard). Finally, the payment is authenticated and the funds are transferred between the two accounts.

This second stage involves the highest *concentration* of organizations that gather sensitive data. Fewer than twenty organizations in the world process billions of transactions with few points of vulnerability. The strongest security measures are found in countries with mature government infrastructure.

This second phase could produce significant efficiency gains in sharing and exchanging data, and it might benefit from further optimization. Distributed ledger technologies (DLTs)—which are still in early days—promise to fundamentally improve international payments by providing a faster solution for cross-border payments, with reduced fees and increased transparency regarding delivery timing and the final payment amount. The most obvious applications of blockchain to the banking industry include clearings and settlements, payments, trade finance, identity, and syndicated loans.

In short, the trend is toward dematerializing payments and streamlining customer experience.

Data Is the New Gold: Monetizing Data in a Free Payment World

The dematerialization of payments also presents an advantage for sellers: data collection about customers. Most brands, retailers, and companies that sell directly to consumers have now developed a mobile app, for a variety of reasons related to consumer engagement. These reasons include building a stronger brand recognition; connecting better with customers; informing users of new products and offers; reaching out to younger populations; providing more value to customers; being visible to customers at all times; creating a direct marketing channel; improving customer engagement; standing out from the competition; and cultivating customer loyalty.

These mobile apps can contain a loyalty card or a prepaid card that users can load with funds for spending in a physical store or online. This approach is very popular with chain restaurants and coffee shops because users are confident that they will spend $15 to $25 each month. In addition, commerce companies that build apps or websites can take advantage of payment APIs from banks and vendors so that they can offer more options to consumers and seamlessly integrate with the means of payments. Some of these products, such as Appsflyer or Braze, can track users' behavior on a mobile device and offer them targeted advertisements and discounts. Rewards and discounts can be managed through mobile apps as well as through scannable mobile coupons or automated cashback options.

Some companies have avidly used apps to track personal data (such as age, gender, address, weight, height) so as to provide better and more personalized advice. Beauty apps use augmented reality that enables customers to explore clothing and hair styles by digitally overlaying products on a selfie. The same apps can be used to send regular notices, and to alert customers about new product launches. Athletic shoes retailers have developed apps for running that can track results (times, level, calories, and distance). Some insurance corporations have directly partnered with credit card providers, providing enhanced insurance services in innovative ways. Car corporations have developed apps to book maintenance, follow kids when they are driving, notify drivers of needed repairs, and file insurance claims.

Chinese citizens, who tend to be more advanced than people in more advanced economies, have realized the importance of in-app payments. Forty-two percent of the Chinese we surveyed said that e-wallets were just a fad and believed that in-app payments would be more widely used in the future.

Larger brands that have a strategic interest in selling direct to consumers must offer direct payments rather than rely on third parties (Figure 8.5). Mobile apps such as Apple Pay and Google Pay collect fees while collecting and analyzing customer data. For this reason, companies often insource their payment systems in a company app. Uber, Lyft, Starbucks, Tesco, and Walmart have made sure to safeguard customer relationships by offering loyalty programs, rewards, invi-

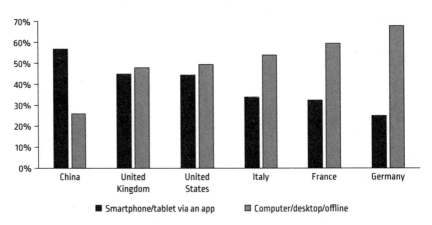

Data source: Marion Laboure and Jim Reid, "The Future of Payments Part II. Moving to Digital Wallets and the Extinction of Plastic Cards," Deutsche Bank Research, Corporate Bank Research, 2020, https://www.dbresearch.com/PROD/RPS_EN-PROD/PROD0000000000504508.pdf.

Note: The difference between the two columns accounts for indifferent between the two financial transactions channels.

FIGURE 8.5   Preferred channels for conducting financial transactions in 2020

tations, and special discounts, and other benefits. As a result, we expect payment fees to soon approach zero—while companies collect a record amount of data. Because data reveals customer patterns, it has become the new gold.

What Are the Benefits of Data for B2B Businesses?

The discussion above has been focused on two themes: The importance of knowing your consumer better by collecting data; and offering them an easy, personalized experience through suggestions, seamless payments, and rewards. This approach works well for companies dealing with many small consumers. However, it works less well for B2B companies dealing with a few large customers.

As indicated earlier, companies struggle to manage working capital and recover payments from bad payers. Quite often, large B2B corporations are organized as a myriad of SMEs that focus on a specific product or customer segment. To resolve these problems, each SME would need considerable financial staffing for billing, data collection, accounting, and payments; managing and tracking B2B payments is a highly manual process.

Digitization of B2B payments offers a remarkable opportunity for optimization. The transition of payments from checks (or even worse, cash) to wire transfers provides a far better tracking method. When trust is strong between supplier and consumer, then a direct debit mandate is even better. Indeed, digitizing payments is the first step toward automatization. Billing software is already widespread, but when combined with direct debit (or at least wire transfer) it allows companies to track and automate the whole back office. The software can automatically process direct debits, track payments made on time (or not), remind customers automatically, and confirm that payments were made.

Automation of back-office payments processes has a triple advantage: It reduces costs; it reduces complexity and coordination, which also lowers costs; and it can save time, thereby helping to conserve working capital and investments.

As changes in payment methods advance at a rapid pace, two technological advances could disrupt card providers: peer-to-peer payments and cryptocurrencies.

The main raison d'être of card platforms is to facilitate settlements between merchants and payers' bank accounts. The development of peer-to-peer payments and e-wallets to facilitate noncash transfers between individuals will disrupt card platforms. An app can connect directly to a bank account and ensure e-wallet settlements are finalized. If these platforms become widely used for merchant transactions, then they could also shortcut businesses that provide consumers with cards.

Cryptocurrencies could also undermine this arrangement because they are traded peer-to-peer without need for a commercial bank or card platform.

Dematerialization of Payments Gains Momentum

Cash is still widely used and probably won't disappear within the next decade. However, it is losing momentum to dematerialized payments. Over the last decade, contactless payments have gained momentum.

Dematerialization continues with the widespread use of contactless payments that include plastic cards (credit and debit cards) and other devices, such as smartphones and watches. In parallel to the contactless novelty, card providers have forged alliances with tech players (such as Apple Pay, Google Pay, Samsung Pay) to increase their reach and to incentivize people to pay via digital or plastic cards.

According to our survey, when people are comfortable with a payment technology, they tend to think even less about the amount they spend. This is particularly true for the Chinese, who are massive users of digital wallets and mobile apps.

Current trends show that most newly issued cards are contactless, meaning that they can be used without inserting or swiping them in a card reader. The next step will likely be the complete dematerialization of plastic cards as more people pay with a smartphone.

In emerging economies, digital wallets are replacing cash at light speed. That's because a large part of the unbanked population in emerging economies is transitioning straight from cash to smartphone payments, thereby skipping plastic cards completely. In India, cash payments declined from 59 percent in 2000 to 30 percent in 2016. In China, cash payments dropped from 63 percent of payments in 2000 to only 11 percent in 2016.

By contrast, cash and plastic cards are well ingrained in the cultures of advanced economies. Forty percent of citizens in developed nations reported that they prefer traditional payments over digital wallets. However, despite this slower adoption rate, most people in these nations believe that digital wallets will eventually replace traditional wallets within the next five years. China and Sweden offer two remarkable illustrations of what could resemble the payment industry in many other nations in the short to medium term.[4]

In western Europe, contactless technology has been around for a decade and is now commonly used. In Italy, France, and the UK, contactless payments are by far the preferred method. Over half of the people in these countries believe that contactless payments are convenient. They understand that cash is rarely needed because cards are accepted everywhere.

The United States: Leading in Innovation, Lagging in Adoption

Given that Silicon Valley gave birth to smartphone payment providers (Apple Pay, Google Pay), it is puzzling to see that only 13 percent of Americans use digital wallets on a weekly basis and nearly three-fifths of these started in 2019. The United States offers a stunning illustration of how physical payments—cash and plastic cards—are ingrained in the culture. On average, Americans hold a record number of plastic cards and an average of $47 in cash per person. Americans favor cash and cards because they are faster and convenient, and because most digital wallets offer no rewards and no cashback. So, even though the United States is the world's leading innovator, card innovations are just starting to take off.

With multiple firms involved in the process—banks, credit card companies, payment processors—the cost of transactions for US merchants increases as a result all the processing fees. Digital wallets and payments systems like PayPal, Apple Pay, and Google Pay are also connected to this system, but neither commands the market that Alipay and WeChat Pay do in China.

Although contactless cards became widely available in the United States later than in other advanced countries, usage is nonetheless growing. A fifth of Americans have received their first contactless card in 2018 and another fifth in 2019. As a result, just 16 percent of US citizens pay with a contactless card in 2019. By comparison, 38 percent in the UK use a contactless card in 2019.

In short, physical payments—normal cash and plastic cards—are still ingrained in the American culture. Americans also say they are not interested in having a digital wallet if it means no rewards or cashback offers, benefits that are common with cards.

Europe and Mobile Payments: The Beginning of a Promising Long Road

In Europe, mobile payments technology is just beginning. Apple Pay commenced in Europe in 2014 and Google Pay and Samsung Pay began in 2015. So far, only 7 percent of Europeans use smartphones to pay, and 70 percent started in 2018 and 2019, including 44 percent in 2019. However, these low rates are primed to take-off over the next five years, for two main reasons. Most Europeans surveyed believed that digital wallets were not just a fad. They agreed that digital wallets would replace traditional wallets within the next five years. This transition is already happening. Citizens who reported using active cards less than twelve months ago also mentioned using a digital wallet more frequently. Indeed, a third of Europeans planned to use mobile payments more in the next six months.

Consumers said they chose mobile payments for the convenience, speed, and absence of fees. Retailers are taking note. Many are installing a mobile payment app "to fit customer desire." The key benefit is reduced effort; with mobile payments, there is no need to type in a PIN or handle cash, which removes a psychological barrier.

Who Will Win the Payment War?

As the process of dematerialization speeds up, competition among companies seeking to digitally intermediate payments has been intensifying—with important regional variations. We first look at trends in China.

Digital Payment Solutions in China

As of the end of 2020, around 86 percent of internet users in China used online payment services, up from 18 percent in 2008. Credit card usage rates among the Chinese generally rank much lower than in developed countries. Why? First, the overall Chinese economy is not wealthy enough for widespread credit card use. Second, there is a low level of trust among Chinese citizens. Third, the Chinese government actively promotes its internet banking infrastructure.

China has seen explosive growth across online e-commerce and social networking platforms. It is a pioneer in digital payment solutions and adoption. Alipay was initially created as a payment solution for its B2C system called Taobao, which acted as an intermediary between consumers and merchants to improve trust. Taobao held the money paid by customers in an escrow account. If the customer was satisfied, Taobao would release the funds to the merchant. This improved consumers' trust and increased business for merchants. Taobao soon realized that it had a lot of capital in its deposit pool. To improve on its product, it offered to pay interest on the deposits in users' Alipay accounts. This money market account gave users a higher interest rate than the rates offered by traditional banks. As a result, more customers put money into their Alipay accounts; that is, they started using it like a traditional bank account.

WeChat was created as a messaging platform like WhatsApp. In 2013 it launched WeChat Pay for P2P transactions and purchases from online vendors.

WeChat Pay later introduced a money market account just like Alipay to create its own virtual banking system. Now small businesses can set up app-based business accounts to market and sell goods and services. Users share products and services with groups or friendship circles through the app. The seller only needs a picture, a product description, and a QR code linked to the seller's bank account.

Today, WeChat Pay and Alipay are the most popular payment methods in China. According to a Penguin intelligence study conducted in 2017, 92 percent of Chinese citizens in major cities claimed to use either WeChat Pay or Alipay. These services are used for everything from e-commerce to ride sharing, as well as for government transactions.[5]

As is evident, the big risk to cards comes from mobile payments. In 2004, mobile payments emerged in China with Alipay. Our survey showed that today Alipay is by far the favorite payment method. Chinese citizens paid 47 percent of their small, regular in-store purchases via mobile payments. Two-fifths were convinced that digital wallets would replace traditional wallets in the next five years.

Three main reasons explain the popularity of mobile payments in China. First, the Chinese government has been playing an active role in building a Chinese world-class infrastructure to support digitization—operating as an investor, developer, and consumer. The Chinese government has blocked foreign websites it considers suspicious. This action brought about widespread internet policing and censorship, practices known as the Great Firewall, leading the government to ban Google, Twitter, YouTube, and Facebook. A new line of look-alike apps that resemble their American counterparts have started to enter the market.

Against this backdrop, Chinese customers have quickly moved from cash to mobile payments. They considered mobile use to be secure, convenient, and reliable. Half of Chinese citizens also planned to use mobile payments more often in the next six months. Only a tenth mentioned the issue of privacy. This low concern for privacy is explained by the fact that privacy in China is viewed suspiciously, as a form of secrecy. It is assumed that an honest person should have nothing to hide from the public domain, so Chinese consumers are often happy to give up their data.

In turn, Chinese retailers have embraced mobile payments. In fact, some stores have begun to accept only mobile payments and have refused cash. This has led the Chinese central bank to issue a formal notice in 2018. It clarifies that renminbi cash is legal tender in China and should not be refused. Elsewhere in Asia, people have been skipping cards completely and moving directly from cash to mobile payments.

By 2013, China had more than 600 million internet users, more than any other country in the world. Of these users, 83 percent used smartphones and 81 percent accessed the internet via personal computer. The number of people using PCs to access the internet has steadily grown at a rate of 10 percent per year. Chinese youth have been spending more than half of their leisure time on the internet, making China the world's largest market for smartphones, e-commerce, and online games.

Can the United States and Europe Emulate China?

Major digital payment players like Apple, Google, and PayPal hope that Western countries will be able to emulate China's high use of fintech. However, it takes much longer to change ingrained habits of people in a legacy system than it does to start a new system from scratch. People in China, India, and the other Southeast Asian countries readily jump from a cash-based society into a digital-payment society. Because digital payment services are vastly more convenient than the cash-only market, the transition is natural. Moreover, China and Southeast Asian countries have significantly larger young populations than are found in Europe and the United States, and young populations tend to be more open to adopting new technologies.

People in legacy systems, such as in the United States and Europe, have a long history of using credit cards. This makes it harder for consumers to shift to digital payments. It's an uphill battle for digital payment methods to replace traditional consumer behavior. For this reason, the mobile US payments app Venmo, initially a digital wallet only, eventually introduced a Venmo debit card that deducts money from a person's Venmo balance. This is a compromise between digital and card payments.

If we look at the next five years in Germany, while keeping in mind that nation's current demographics and Germans' favorite payment methods and payment method intentions, we can expect cash to remain the most popular in-store payment method. Elsewhere we expect e-wallets to be the second most-preferred method of payment after cards and the first most-preferred method among millennials.

Who Will Win the Payments Competition?

In the late 1990s Google cemented itself as the search engine giant that it is today. In the following decade, a new technology contest broke out between smartphone manufacturers. Veteran companies such as Blackberry and Nokia fell to the rear, which opened the path for iOS and Android to become the operating systems of the future.

Now, a new battle over digital payments is brewing. The underlying technology for digital payments has been established. So, the companies that position themselves best for customers and merchants will end up winning.

On one front, there are smartphone providers like Apple and Google. Apple's iPhones come standard with Apple Pay. Its counterpart, Android Pay, is preinstalled on most Android devices. Samsung sells smartphones that come loaded with proprietary Samsung Pay. These services now use NFC technology with fingerprint and facial recognition for authorization.

Social media companies have also entered the fray. Facebook has implemented payment services on its popular Messenger and WhatsApp platforms, and Apple has introduced payment services on iMessage. Both companies focus primarily on P2P transactions. Apple Pay Cash costs the same as Square Cash and Venmo. It is free to send money using a debit card or in-app balance, and it costs 3 percent of the transfer amount if you use a credit card. By comparison, using a debit or credit card to send money with PayPal costs 2.9 percent of the total amount plus thirty cents for the users.

Other competitors include online payment systems such as PayPal, Square, and Stripe. PayPal subsidiary Venmo is extremely popular among millennials. Square, founded by Jack Dorsey, developed Square Cash to compete with Venmo, but it also provides financial solutions to merchants and vendors. Stripe integrates with e-commerce merchants, whereas PayPal and Square focus on e-wallet services that allow users to store and control their online shopping information and to purchase products from online retailers.

Finally, commercial banks are also competing in the payments arena. Most banks have partnered with Apple Pay and Android Pay to make their credit and debit cards easier for customers to use. Banks have also partnered with telecom providers. In this competition, banks have some advantages. They have preestablished financial networks, infrastructures, trusting customer bases, strong brand recognitions, and a history of regulatory compliance. One successful example of a bank's digital payment platform is Chase Pay.

Each of these companies caters to different aspects of the payment system. Before we can declare a winner in the payments competition, we need to understand what it takes to win.

The first thing any company needs to do is identify its customer value proposition. This marketing term refers to the reasons a customer would choose a payments service. According to a McKinsey study, customers' top priority is convenience. Apple Pay, Android Pay, and PayPal are more convenient than typing credit card information. Apple and Android have almost an equal market share in the United States. PayPal has long been a trusted online payment platform and has cross-platform adaptability. If PayPal can find a way to use Venmo as a payment method for online stores, then PayPal can tap into Venmo's large consumer base.[6]

However, mobile sales contribute to less than 50 percent of all online sales; most sales still take place on desktops. This reduces the advantage that mobile digital payment solutions currently enjoy. This may change as people increasingly transact with mobile phones. E-commerce giants such as Amazon and Walmart store credit card information on their platforms, which makes one-touch payments more convenient than third-party digital payment solutions such as Apple Pay or PayPal. Amazon manages 49 percent of all online retail in the United States

Online retail is growing at a rate of 15 percent per year compared to 4 percent a year for retail sales at brick-and-mortar venues. However, as of 2017, online stores made up only 10 percent of all retail purchases. A notable phenomenon of the Covid-19 pandemic was the accelerated digitalization of commerce, which implies future growth in the merchant payments market. That market appears to be large. For example, approximately 80 percent of small European retail businesses did not have any online shopping capabilities, and some did not even have a basic informative website. According to our proprietary analysis in western Europe, consumers spent on average between 30 percent and 60 percent more via online retail at the end of 2020 compared to March of the same year. The biggest e-commerce sales are in the United Kingdom, with 42 percent of the population buying online, and in the United States, where e-commerce rose to 36 percent in December 2020. Thus, the number of payments transactions conducted by cards surged. Because digital payment methods do not provide a distinct advantage at physical and online stores, especially in countries like the United States where card usage is very high. It's an uphill battle for digital payment methods to replace traditional consumer behavior. For this reason, Venmo introduced its own debit card that deducts money from a person's Venmo balance. This is a compromise solution between digital and card payments.

In order to compete in this part of the fintech revolution, companies will have to identify merchant value propositions. In other words, digital payment providers must convince merchants that it's worthwhile to accept digital payments. This is a tough task, as evidenced by the MCX consortium of the thirty-nine largest US retailers (led by Walmart). These companies each pledged to start their own digital payment systems rather than use a system designed by Apple or Google. One reason for that choice was to avoid paying a percentage of sales to an intermediary. This situation reveals that payments companies will have to offer services such as data analysis, reward programs, and higher conversion rates before they can convince merchants to use their digital payment methods.[7]

Apple has done a decent job of wooing merchants to its services by creating a buzz around Apple Pay. But without a long-term value proposition, it remains to be seen if Apple can retain those merchants. Google, Samsung, and Chase are far behind Apple in merchant partnerships. PayPal has established partnerships with companies in online markets, but it needs to find a way to leverage that advantage in onsite stores.

On the global stage, America and its Western counterparts must catch up with Chinese digital payments companies. As noted earlier, two companies dominate the Chinese market—Alibaba, with Alipay, and Tencent, with WeChat Pay.

Alipay has cooperated with banks to enable debit card payments, and it helped increase trust between buyers and sellers. As a result, Alipay contributed considerably to the prosperity of the Chinese online payment industry. As internet users migrate to smartphones, many believe that there is still considerable room for China's mobile payment industry to expand.

Who will be the real winner in this competition? The short answer is no one. Banks and card institutions like Visa and MasterCard cannot lose because all payment methods, including those operated by Apple Pay and PayPal, still need bank accounts and credit cards to function, at least for now. However, banks do not seem to have made a significant impact in digital payment methods. As for the mobile phone companies, they must propose an additional value proposition to consumers and merchants if they want to make headway. Messaging and social media platforms like Facebook and WhatsApp may yet become dominant players in this space. PayPal and Square seem to be the best situated players because they have built strong partnerships and have a sizeable active consumer base. If a situation like Alipay or WeChat Pay arises in the United States, then PayPal and Square will find themselves at the top.

CHAPTER NINE

Digital Currencies

The Ultimate Hard-Power Tool

> My personal conviction on the issue of stable coins is that we better be ahead of the curve. There is clearly demand out there that we have to respond to.
>
> —*Christine Lagarde, president of the European Central Bank,*
> *December 12, 2019, Governing Council meeting*

> I think the Internet is going to be one of the major forces for reducing the role of government. The one thing that's missing but that will soon be developed, is a reliable e-cash.
>
> —*Professor Milton Friedman, a Nobel Prize winner in economics*

The newest factor in the fintech revolution, and the one that gets a lot of attention today, is the emergence of cryptocurrencies. As cash and cards continue to lose their hold on consumer habits, government services, and business transactions, cryptocurrencies are increasingly seen as compelling alternatives. This chapter provides a detailed overview of digital currencies, including Bitcoin, Facebook's Libra (now rebranded as Diem), and sovereign digital currencies. It explores the factors that are moving these currencies into the mainstream and what is at stake for consumers, banks, and regulators in the next ten years.

From Globalization to Decoupling

In the not-so-distant past, currencies were tied to tangible commodities like gold. Today almost all national currencies are fiat currencies, which means they hold no intrinsic value and are legitimized only by government regulation. For example, the US Federal Reserve ensures the legitimacy of the dollar, but it does not hold the equivalency of circulating dollars in gold.

Digital currencies are also referred to as digital money, electronic money, or electronic currency. Examples include virtual currencies, cryptocurrencies, and central bank digital currencies (CBDCs). Digital money can be centralized, in which case there is a central point of control over the money supply. It can also be decentralized, in which case various sources control the money supply.[1]

At the end of 2019 the Chinese government, without a formal announcement, stated it would be launching a People's Bank of China (PBoC) digital currency. The plans were finalized and approved in October 2019. In April 2020 China began testing the e-RMB and is expected to be live at the venue for the 2022 Beijing Winter Olympics.

If this materializes as expected, China is likely to become the first major economy to use a digital currency. Because it has more than 1.4 billion inhabitants, China's CBDC could pressure other countries to follow suit and set up their own digital currencies. A government-issued digital currency could be a powerful political and economic tool for China.

To break into the global payment market, digital currencies must overcome some headwinds and forge alliances with key stakeholders. These might include mobile payment apps (Alipay, WeChat, Apple Pay, Google Pay), card providers, and worldwide retailers (Alibaba, Amazon, Walmart). Assuming that (a) governments back them, and (b) they become stable, and (c) consumers and merchants can get more value by using these new currencies, then increased adoption rates will more rapidly lead to mainstream use.

Our exclusive survey of 3,600 customers in China, France, Germany, Italy, the UK, and the United States found that millennials envisioned a purely digital currency. A large majority of millennials believed that cryptocurrencies would be good for the economy and said that they had already bought and sold a cryptocurrency. More than a third of millennials believed that cryptocurrencies could be already replacing cash.

The final section of this chapter focuses on factors that promote and hinder the adoption of cryptocurrencies. We present an overview of how private and government sectors are embracing (or not) this new technological reality. Finally, we consider what the global economy would look like if (or when) a digital currency emerges in China.

Current Adoption Rates of Cryptocurrencies: Age and Cultural Factors

Cryptocurrencies have been around for about a decade, but it was not until 2017, when Bitcoin's price surged to nearly $20,000, that they grabbed significant global attention. If we connect the dots between the dematerialization of payments and the rise of cryptocurrencies, we can envision a near future in which cryptocurrencies gain broad acceptance. This view is supported by trends among young generations, people who readily acceptance digital currencies and payments.

So far, relatively few people have bought and sold cryptocurrencies. They are largely seen as supplementary means of money storage rather than as necessary or advantageous substitutes for today's mainstream methods. They have not been widely accepted as a means of payments despite their well-known benefits: security, speed, minimal transaction fees, ease of storage, and relevance in the digital era.

Today's adoption rates could, and likely will, change. If the Chinese government, along with Google, Amazon, Facebook, or Apple (the so-called GAFA group), or a Chinese company like Tencent can create a stable cryptocurrency and launch it with immediate mass adoption on its platform, then cryptocurrencies could become more appealing. This would hasten their adoption and give them the potential to replace cash.

With those broad perspectives in mind, we can then look more closely at the adoption rates as affected by age and culture.

Comparing the Perspectives of Young and Old

The current adoption rates of cryptocurrencies are influenced by generational views, as shown in Figure 9.1.

Looking more closely at generational influences on adoption rates, our proprietary survey revealed three main barriers preventing a move from cash to cryptocurrencies. Each is related to age. Older people surveyed had more fears about cryptocurrencies, found them harder to understand, believed they create volatile financial bubbles (like the dotcom bust), and saw them as low-liquidity financial instruments. A third of those surveyed had no idea how cryptocurrencies work, and 40 percent only had a partial understanding. As you can see below, we found a stark contrast between older and younger people, with the latter expressing more positive views about cryptocurrencies.

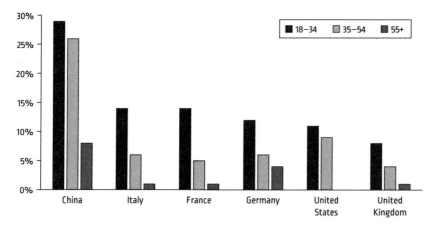

Data source: Marion Laboure, "The Future of Payments: Series 2, Part II. When Digital Currencies Become Mainstream," Deutsche Bank Research, February 2021, https://www.dbresearch.com/PROD/RPS_EN-PROD /PROD0000000000516270.pdf.

FIGURE 9.1   Citizens who have bought or sold cryptocurrencies, by age group

Privacy vs. Convenience: Cultural Perspectives and Adoption Rates

The adoption rates of cryptocurrencies are also influenced by cultural perspectives. The central cultural question surrounding cryptocurrencies is related to the tension between privacy and convenience.

Clearly banknotes and coins greatly reduce digital footprints. A cash transaction does not generate digital data. No third party, such as a payment provider, will automatically receive transaction data for a cash transaction, and therefore cash can protect individual privacy.

However, as shown in Chapter 8, consumers have a strong preference for digital payments, primarily for their greater convenience. Cards and smartphones, for example, eliminate the need for carrying cash and coins. Merchants do not need to use armored trucks to take cash to the bank each day.

Perspectives on these two poles—privacy vs. convenience—vary from culture to culture. Interestingly, citizens in advanced economies are more worried about privacy than are people in emerging economies. In the West, privacy is regarded as a personal right to one's own space and, by extension, to one's data. This conception of privacy is seen to be good for individuals and, arguably, for society.[2]

By contrast, the Chinese typically view privacy suspiciously, as a form of secrecy. It is assumed that an honest person should have nothing to hide from the public domain, so Chinese consumers are often happy to give up their data.[3]

Thus, Americans (22 percent), British (21 percent), French (29 percent), Germans (42 percent), and Italians (19 percent) reported concerns about anonymity and traceability, whereas only a tenth of Chinese reported similar concerns.

As the global population across all cultures becomes more knowledgeable about how cryptocurrencies and blockchain technologies work, the tension between privacy and convenience could diminish. That's because cryptocurrencies promise to enable financial transactions that are both digitally convenient and individually private.

Economic and Technological Factors

In addition to the age and cultural perspectives described above, technological and economic factors also play a major role in how widely digital currencies will be used around the world. In Chapter 7, we addressed the importance of government efforts to create an inclusive, trustworthy financial system. In this section, we look specifically at barriers that must be overcome if *digital currencies* are to be used as mainstream forms of financial transactions.

We will first look at some of the *technological and economic* factors that will influence (positively and negatively) widespread adoption of cryptocurrencies. Then we will address the *regulatory* factors, primarily by looking at how governments are responding to Facebook's effort to launch its global cryptocurrency, Diem.

Technology Limitations: Energy Consumption

One often overlooked factor that raises concerns about widespread use of cryptocurrencies is related to energy consumption. Although the liquidity of Bitcoin remains low and very few bitcoins are exchanged per day, mining bitcoins requires a tremendous amount of energy. As of early 2021, Bitcoin's annual electricity consumption nearly placed it among the top thirty nations that most consume energy. In one year, mining bitcoins uses about the same amount of electricity as the entire population of Pakistan (roughly 217 million people) and more than the Netherlands (approximately 17.5 million people).

Energy use increases proportionally with Bitcoin's market valuation (because it will make mining more profitable and as such attract more miners). As such, numerous alarms have been warning us about the environmental impact caused by cryptocurrency energy consumption. However, capital currently engaged in the cryptocurrency market could be used to develop green technological advancements. This is called a "positive externality"—a technological innovation in the financial sector that drives innovation in the energy sector.

Facebook's Diem is designed so that an algorithm issues cryptocurrency units in proportion to the size of a company's initial deposit into the system. Therefore, it does not have a "mining" operation but is still expected to consume as much energy as normal data centers, which is about 2 percent of total US energy usage. As with Diem, CBDCs would not require mining, and would therefore have a much smaller environmental impact that Bitcoin.

Economic Factor #1: Businesses Need an End-to-End Financial Infrastructure

An important factor that affects mainstream adoption rates of cryptocurrencies is the relatively small number of businesses that use and / or accept them. Today cryptocurrencies are not yet widely accepted by retailers, and buying cryptocurrencies with a debit or a credit card remains difficult. Therefore, in order for cryptocurrencies to achieve a global reach in the payment market, alliances must be forged with key mobile payment apps, card providers, and retailers. The Chinese digital currency could be used across major payment platforms, including WeChat, Alipay, and UnionPay. It is strategically positioned to become de facto global digital currency in emerging economies.

In late 2020, PayPal officially announced that the company would add cryptocurrency capability to its wallets. PayPal has seen strong early adoption of cryptocurrency payments within its digital wallet platforms, and there is a larger-than-anticipated waiting list in the United States, showing high demand. The company expanded the rollout of its crypto offer to the rest of its platform, including Venmo, in the first half of 2021. PayPal plans to allow users to complete transactions for goods and services with its digital currency in early 2021. This is a big development for cryptocurrency adoption, because PayPal is one of the biggest payment providers in the world. PayPal services are being used by over 300 million customers worldwide. Twenty-eight million stores now accept PayPal as a payment method.

Visa and MasterCard are also pivoting toward cryptocurrency. Visa CEO Alfred Kelly in May 2020 stated his view that digital currency backed by fiat will be an emerging payment technology. His statement came as Visa filed a patent for a "digital fiat currency." This filing points to a CBDC use case. Visa also partnered with Circle in December 2020 to let card issuers integrate USDC payment capability.

MasterCard also jumped on the bandwagon when the company announced a card deal with Wired, thereby expanding its cryptocurrency efforts. Wired's multicurrency MasterCard debit card will allow users to buy, hold, exchange, and sell up to eighteen traditional currencies and cryptocurrencies, while also allowing for free international ATM withdrawals up to a certain amount. MasterCard also launched a customizable CBDC testing platform in September 2020.

These private initiatives are beginning to see input from government agencies. A major development came from the US Office of the Comptroller of the Currency (OCC) when it said in July 2020 that national banks can provide custody solutions for cryptocurrencies. In September 2020 the OCC confirmed that banks can hold reserve deposits behind stablecoins. In December 2020, the Swiss Exchange also said that it will launch an "Institutional Digital Asset Gateway" to get banks into crypto. Meanwhile, various banks, including BBVA, CITI, Standard Chartered, PNC, and US Bank, have shown willingness to get into the cryptocurrency-related business.

Globally, and especially in the United States, China, and Russia, there are a number of venues through which people can purchase goods and services using Bitcoin. According to Coinmap.org, there are nearly 15,000 of these venues worldwide. Major businesses (such as Microsoft, Expedia, Wikimedia, NewEgg, AT&T, Virgin Mobile, Shopify) have started to accept cryptocurrencies. An increasing number of travel companies (Expedia.com, cheapair.com, ScubaOtter, and Alternativeairlines.com) and online shopping companies have recently entered the cryptocurrency market. Some major retailers (Overstock, Home Depot, Namecheap, Starbucks, KFC Canada, and Whole Foods) have also started to accept cryptocurrencies as payment. Additionally, there are services from companies like Coincards and Bitrefill that accept user Bitcoins and turn them into credit for use at a store of choice. Companies such as Purse.io allow consumers to spend bitcoins on their sites to buy from online retailers such as Amazon.

Economic Factor #2: Stability and Reliability

For investors, crypto assets have numerous advantages compared to traditional assets, which could lead more and more people to use cryptocurrencies. First, they could offer a low or negative correlation with financial assets, meaning that they might not be driven by interest rates. Second, they could decompose composite returns, thereby offering a more precise exposure to alpha return components; that is, they could enable people to trade a revenue stream that comprises a share price / ROE, somewhat like securitization. Third, a cryptocurrency could enable individual assets to be compiled into a composite asset for better return profiles, which would be like a "composable token" or SET protocol. Fourth, cryptocurrencies could fractionalize financial assets for accessible investments.

However, unless governments interfere, cryptocurrencies will likely lack price stability, making them risky to hold and invest in. The real gold price (in US dollars) was relatively stable between 1850 and 1970, but Bitcoin is highly volatile. Its value can change dramatically from one day to the next. It's not uncommon for Bitcoin to trade within a 10 percent spread over twenty-four hours. In May 2021, Bitcoin's price dropped by 30 percent in one day. For comparison, the price of the British pound sterling declined about 10 percent in its worst-ever one-day fall, which followed the Brexit decision—a once-in-a-lifetime event.

Such dramatic price fluctuations make it hard for Bitcoin to function as a stable store of value or as a means of exchange. It conjures memories of hyperinflation in Germany in 1920s and more recently in Argentina, Venezuela, and Zimbabwe. Imagine how hard it would be for e-retailers to set up a price for their goods in Bitcoin. A used car could have been worth 110 bitcoins in early 2015 and only 1 bitcoin in December 2017!

Currency is also a unit of account for debt. Bitcoin's large price fluctuations make it hard to even think about financing a house with a cryptocurrency mortgage. Just in 2017, a Bitcoin debt would have risen tenfold. However, because salaries are paid in dollars, euros, or other currencies, it would not have grown as rapidly. As a result, had Bitcoin been widely used, the last year might have been massively deflationary. (See Figure 9.2.)

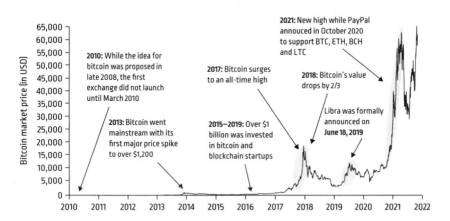

Data sources: https://www.blockchain.com/charts/market-price.

Note: Average USD market price across major Bitcoin exchanges.

FIGURE 9.2   Bitcoin is too volatile to be a reliable store of value (market price in USD)

People are working on ways to add more stability to privately developed cryptocurrencies with "stablecoins." Their value can be pegged to an existing asset, such as a commodity, or to a fiat currency for transaction and settlement processing on a DLT-powered business network with fewer legacy infrastructure expenses and operational costs. Since 2017 around 120 stablecoins have been created, including Tether, which is the largest stablecoin. But this represents only 2 percent of Bitcoin's market capitalization. For example, Diem could use stablecoins pegged to fiat currencies like the dollar, the euro, and the sterling.

When we did our survey we learned that corporate treasurers are unlikely to adopt cryptocurrencies in the near future. In 2022, only 5 percent of corporate treasurers are likely to receive cryptocurrencies, and approximately 80 percent of them are unlikely to use cryptocurrencies.[4]

One reason for this hesitancy is the lack of cryptocurrency regulation (a topic we address later in this chapter). That said, we expect 2022 to be a turning point for the regulation of cryptocurrencies globally. Clearly, regulators have cryptocurrency issues listed on their agendas. We can reasonably expect a number of regulations to be adopted between late 2022 and early 2023. The EU, following a comprehensive market consultation in early 2020, proposed a single regulation for all crypto assets not falling under existing regulations (such as MiFIDII). The so-called Markets in Crypto-Assets Regulation (MiCAR) is expected to come into effect between late 2022 and early 2023. In the United States, the government has issued numerous regulations since early 2019 (such as Framework for Digital Assets). The Biden administration is expected to establish a collaborative and unified strategy to adjust the existing comprehensive regulatory framework and establish new regulations as needed to provide legal certainty.[5]

If governments improve the regulatory frameworks for cryptocurrencies, then business leaders will likely think it is safer to use them for B2B and B2C transactions.

Regulatory Factors: How Will Governments Act?

When considering questions about widespread, global adoption of digital currencies, a major factor is how governments will act. In this section we present current trends in government regulation and then illustrate those trends by describing the interplay between the US government and Facebook's Diem.

Regulatory reviews by governments have identified numerous risks related to cryptocurrencies. Among the most prominent are liquidity, custody, anti–money laundering (AML), and security. Market manipulation (of price and volume) of cryptocurrencies is already known to occur.

In regard to security, private cryptocurrencies significantly increase the risk of financial crime (such as AML, KYC, bribery, sanctions, and tax evasion). An interesting 2019 study from Raphael Auer and Stijn Claessens showed that regulating cryptocurrencies could imply giving credibility to these new assets, even though they are often used for nefarious activity. In an empirical analysis, they show that news about regulation affects the prices of these assets, signaling that national regulators do have some power. A potential solution is to enforce a minimum amount of regulation along the lines of anti–money laundering activities.[6]

Another security complication is that people can cash out illegal gains made with a cryptocurrency very rapidly, even across borders, which presents law enforcement agencies with jurisdictional complications. People can transfer Bitcoin (BTC) to Zcash (ZEC) and then to Ether (ETH) and then trade using an ETH-to-dollar contract to cash out in a third jurisdiction. This approach is very portable even though the cryptocurrency is pseudo-anonymous.

For several years people believed that Bitcoin could facilitate anonymous transactions beyond government purview. However, blockchain does keep track of transactions; it just does not reveal them publicly. Governments can use other information to reconcile any transaction and obtain identities. This could be used to track terrorist and criminal activities.

In light of all these concerns, no cryptocurrency will ever emerge as a mainstream payment solution without approval from regulators. Governments have already started regulating cryptocurrencies around the globe, in both advanced and emerging economies. In the United States, the Internal Revenue Service has issued decisions on how Bitcoin earnings should be taxed. Bitcoin wallets must now comply with anti–money laundering rules.

But there are even bigger concerns. As we show next, governments are increasingly concerned that private cryptocurrencies could upend the global economy.

Government Response to Facebook's Diem: A Case Study

Perhaps the best illustration of rising tensions between governments and private cryptocurrencies is found in Facebook's effort to launch its digital currency, which used to be called Libra and is now called Diem. Facebook, with over 2.9 billion users (one-third of the world's population), has the potential to compete with traditional online payment platforms and advance digital currencies into the mainstream. Diem is part of a broader Facebook ecosystem—including the digital wallet, Calibra, which was rebranded as Novi—and was initially scheduled to be launched in early 2021.

The 2019 announcement of Libra (we will refer to it as Diem from here on) spooked the world's major central banks into swift action. Jerome Powell, the US Federal Reserve chairman, in congressional testimony less than a month after Diem's introduction, spoke extensively about this proposed currency, stating that it had raised "many serious concerns regarding privacy, money laundering, consumer protection, and financial stability." He stated the Fed's view that Diem could not be allowed to go forward. Other central banks followed suit, with Christine Lagarde, president of the European Central Bank (ECB), warning that cryptocurrencies are "shaking the system." This constant friction between fintech innovation and regulatory efforts is likely to be an ongoing concern. How the dust will settle remains to be seen.

Governments had two big concerns with Diem: (a) the creation of a competing global currency via pegging Diem to a basket and, as a result, (b) the risk that governments would lose control of the money supply and regulatory control.

Initially, when the Diem project was unveiled in June 2019, Facebook described it as a futuristic global money that could serve as the foundation for a new kind of financial system. But early 2020 Facebook scaled back the project and shifted to placing more emphasis on cheapening payments rather than on competing with governments on creating a parallel means of payments. The company has tweaked its plan for Diem by "offering single-currency stablecoins in addition to the multicurrency coin." Facebook plans to create an infrastructure for multiple Diem cryptocurrencies (Diem EUR, Diem GBP, and so on), the preponderance of which will be backed one-for-one by individual fiat currencies.[7]

Thus, the revised version of Diem is less audacious and less controversial than the original project presented in June 2019. Facebook clearly made a big shift in its strategy to address the main objections of regulators and central bankers and help Diem break through into mainstream use.

If large numbers of people use Diem to make payments and engage in other transactions, what might happen to the traditional banking systems that normally intermediate financial transactions? Diem could also stifle competitors. For example, Diem is about to set a standard for the digital euro and thus gain a competitive advantage that will be difficult to overcome. How much space for other digital euro providers will be left?

Moreover, Facebook's new approach will create a "clear path for seamlessly integrating central bank digital currencies (CBDCs) as they become available," according to the Diem Association new white paper. The paper also states that if a central bank were to develop a digital representation of one of the currencies already on the network, the Diem Association, which "is tasked with facilitating the operation of the Diem payment system in a safe and compliant manner," could simply replace the single-currency stablecoin with the CBDC.[8]

Diem is unlike typical private cryptocurrencies because it operates without a "permissionless" blockchain system; instead, Diem uses a network of central actors that can validate transactions. Diem will be a closed system in which only partners with the approval of the Diem Association can build Diem's infrastructure, such as the digital wallets used by consumers.

Compliance will take place in close cooperation with regulatory authorities. Facebook has worked closely with regulators and central banks to address governmental concerns, especially the potential for money laundering. Safeguards are added by establishing Diem reserve, an asset fund that can back each Diem unit. This reserve fund would function to protect Diem users during an economic stress scenario. Diem Reserve would hold assets with very short-term maturity, low credit exposure, and high liquidity to avoid losing too much value should there be a run on the currency or a liquidity crunch.

The Diem Association has continued to add new members. Recently joining the association are Shopify and the financial firm Tagomi, which joined in late February 2020. Recently installed members also include the nonprofit organization Heifer International and the British payments start-up Checkout.com (in late April of 2021). On April 16, 2020, the Swiss Financial Market Supervisory Authority (FINMA) acknowledged that they had received a payment license application for Diem. Although the license has not yet been granted, the application demonstrates the Diem Association's acceptance of regulation—after multiple conflicts with global financial authorities.

Diem and the Broader Financial Services Movement

With Diem, Facebook's goal is twofold: to increase advertising revenues (also capturing more FX and payment processing fees) and to provide payment solutions to those who are unbanked (representing 1.7 billion people worldwide).

Facebook's business model is entirely based on advertising through its social network and services ecosystem, including WhatsApp, Instagram, and Facebook Messenger. Facebook controls 8 percent of internet traffic and 86 percent of social media traffic. It has become one of the largest online targeted advertising companies in existence.

The company aims to diversify its revenue by offering a digital wallet to unbanked populations, starting most likely with India and then Africa. In April 2020, Facebook invested $5.7 billion in JiO, an Indian telecommunications company, which signals Facebook's intention to target India. Meanwhile, the Indian Supreme Court lifted a ban on trading in cryptocurrencies, which could pave the way for Diem there.

As global regulatory barriers fall, Facebook can expand as a financial payments platform. Facebook's digital wallet, Novi, is scheduled to be released with a planned rollout beginning late 2021 and going into 2022 but has not been released yet in September 2021, at the time we are finishing the manuscript. It supports multiple currencies, including Diem. Novi will be integrated with Facebook Messenger and WhatsApp, and with a standalone app. Like most payment apps, Novi will hold money securely for free, and allows P2P worldwide transfers for a fee. It will eventually be a platform for loans, credit, and money transfers. Considering that Facebook and WhatsApp have more than three billion monthly active users, Novi will be able to capture a huge share of worldwide payments.

Similar to Apple Pay and Google Pay, Novi could collect fees from these transactions while also collecting and analyzing customer data—and possibly monetize this data in exchange for nearly free payments. Data is the new gold!

Novi could also help large brands that sell directly to consumers. These companies must offer a platform for direct payments rather than relying on third parties. For this reason, companies often insource their payment systems. Uber, Lyft, Starbucks, Tesco, and Walmart have safeguarded customer relationships by offering loyalty programs, rewards, invitations, special discounts, and other benefits.

Facebook Could Become a Western WeChat

Facebook, with its own ecosystem, is on the way to become a Western WeChat super app. WeChat, the large, Chinese third-party mobile and online payment platform, was created as a messaging platform similar to WhatsApp. In 2013 it launched WeChat Pay for P2P transactions and purchases from online vendors.

To develop its own virtual banking system, WeChat Pay later added a money market account. Small businesses may now market and sell their products and services via an app-based business account. Through the app, users may exchange products and services with groups or friendship circles. A photo, a product description, and a QR code connected to the seller's bank account are all that's required.

These numerous forms of e-commerce and digital companies encourage people in rural areas to use mobile wallets. Digital payment systems are increasing financial inclusion and extending company options.

WeChat Pay (together with Alipay) are the most widely used payment options in China today. According to a study conducted by Penguin Intelligence in 2017, 92 percent of Chinese citizens in large cities claimed to use WeChat Pay or Alipay. These services are used for a variety of purposes, including e-commerce, ride-sharing, and government transactions.[9]

The Possibility of Sovereign Digital Currencies

It is important to remember that Diem and other cryptocurrencies are privately controlled. What if central banks become more daring and start creating cryptocurrencies? A central bank cryptocurrency would provide an official form of money backed by the government and the capacity to exchange peer-to-peer without intermediaries (commercial banks). Cryptocurrencies utilize distributed ledger technology (DLT) to allow remote peer-to-peer transfer of electronic value in the absence of trust between contracting parties.

The Wake-Up Call of Central Banks in Advanced Economies

Even during the outbreak of the Covid-19 pandemic, cash was still king in many societies (Chapter 8). However, the use of cash has been declining over the past decade. Central banks have investigated ideas to advance the development of digital cash. For example, Sweden, a country where cash in circulation now represents only 1 percent of GDP, revealed in February 2020 that it started piloting a digital krona project: the e-krona.[10]

These digital currencies would perform all the functions of banknotes and coins. They could be used by households and businesses to make payments and to save. Digital central bank currencies require infrastructure that can record in-person and online transactions, which means that governments will need private-sector cooperation.

Over the past three years, central banks and governments around the world have multiplied and sped up digital cash initiatives. A 2021 survey by the Bank of International Settlements revealed that 86 percent of central banks are developing a CBDC. The work goes far beyond research: 14 percent of central banks are already running pilot projects, and 60 percent are experimenting with proof of concept. Looking ahead, central banks representing about a fifth of the world's population are likely to issue a general-purpose CBDC in the next three years.[11]

The motivations to issue a general-purpose CBDC are numerous: financial stability, monetary policy implementation, financial inclusion, payments efficiency (domestic and cross-border), and payment security.

Terminology: Different Design Choices for Different Consumer Needs

The Bank for International Settlements characterized money by using four dimensions: wide vs. restricted accessibility; digital vs. physical; central bank vs. privately issued; peer-to-peer vs. transacted via banks. With these categories in mind, a CBDC would be widely accessible; digital; and issued by a central bank.

A CBDC could take two forms: (i) retail: a widely accessible and public electronic currency available for retail transactions; (ii) wholesale: a restricted electronic currency available only for large business transactions. The retail form of a CBDC would play the same role as any currency in circulation today, whereas the wholesale form would be like the reserves held by banks and other financial institutions (Table 9.1).[12]

Needless to say, consumer needs are driving choices about CBDC designs. Consumers primarily want digital currencies to have cashlike functionality (peer-to-peer) and to be secure and convenient for real-time payments. Design decisions will shape currency platform architectures.

The question is whether consumers will have a direct claim on the central bank and/or an indirect claim via payment intermediaries.

Second, consumers will demand strong cybersecurity (resilient operations) as it pertains to solvency, the technical glitches of intermediaries, and possible outages at the central banks. These demands will shape CBDC infrastructures and determine whether currency databases should be centrally controlled or decentralized, perhaps with digital ledger technology (DLT) such as blockchain.

Third, consumers will use a digital currency if it is simple and universally accessible. They are also likely to favor some form of privacy, which cash offers. In

TABLE 9.1   Key design features of central bank money

	Existing central bank money		Central bank digital currencies		
			General		
	Cash	Reserves and settlement balances	Token	Accounts	Wholesale
24/7 availability	✓	✗	✓	(✓)	(✓)
Anonymity vis-à-vis central bank	✓	✗	(✓)	✗	(✓)
Peer-to-peer transfer	✓	✗	(✓)	✗	(✓)
Interest-bearing	✗	(✓)	(✓)	(✓)	(✓)
Limits or caps	✗	✗	(✓)	(✓)	(✓)

Data source: CPMI, "Central Bank Digital Currencies," Markets Committee Papers no. 174, March 12, 2018, https://www.bis.org/cpmi/publ/d174.pdf.
Note: ✓ = existing or likely feature, (✓) = possible feature, ✗ = not typical or possible feature.

terms of setting up technology for privacy, there will be a trade-off between the identity system (account-based tokens) and on the need for an anonymous/ encrypted system (digital tokens).

Consumers will also need to make cross-border payments with CBDCs, which is feasible via technical connections at the wholesale level. This will improve and strengthen the wholesale and retail interlinkages.

Central bankers have started to consider digital currencies as a new tool. Why would a cryptocurrency be more desirable than the reserve system in place today? What are the advantages for end users and central bankers?[13]

Advantages for End Users

First, a CBDC would reduce the risk of identity theft, of being tracked by a dangerous counterparty or direct advertiser, and of being spammed. Today's intermediated digital payment systems allow too much private information to be revealed to third parties (such as commercial banks). DLT would alleviate the problem.

Second, a central bank cryptocurrency would increase the efficiency of securities settlements and postmarket activities. Today's security clearing and settlement process has a lag of several days. The DLT of a cryptocurrency promises immediate securities clearing and settlements. This would increase efficiency and reduce associated reconciliation costs.

Third, a cryptocurrency could also act as a more stable currency, especially for emerging economies, which usually experience higher currency volatility than advanced economies. Compared to the volatile nature of cash's purchasing power (caused by fluctuations in the price level), a cryptocurrency could be built in a way that maintains the real value of money. That would stabilize the holder's purchasing power. Under an indexation scheme, the nominal value of an individual's cryptocurrency holdings would increase temporarily during periods of above-target inflation.

Advantages for Central Bankers

Following the 2007–2008 financial crisis, the central banks of advanced economies cut interest rates. So far, only a few central banks have set negative interest rates. Introducing a fully digitalized currency (not necessarily a cryptocurrency) would eliminate the risk of cash hoarding, since cash would likely stop being used after the "full" introduction of a digital currency.[14]

Central banks could rely on the currency interest rate as its primary monetary policy tool and thereby avoid using controversial, unconventional tools such as quantitative easing. This would substantially improve a central bank's ability to stabilize business cycles.

Finally, interest-bearing digital currencies could enhance competitiveness in the banking sector. Currently the digital currency model favored by most central banks seems to be two-tier issuance. As with a traditional currency, transactions would be decentralized and supply would be centralized. But, technically, people could have the option to move bank deposits into interest-bearing digital currency accounts at the central bank. Allowing the public to hold digital currency accounts at central banks would resolve many problems caused by the current fractional reserve banking system. For example, the central bank would not be vulnerable to bank runs, and governments could stop providing deposit insurance and bailouts to institutions deemed "too big to fail." By doing so, moral hazard problems on the part of banks would be eliminated.

The use of DLT, however, has risks. In most instances, the risks associated with payments, clearing, and settlements are the same irrespective of whether the activity occurs on a central ledger or a synchronized distributed ledger. That said, DLT may pose new or different risks, including: (1) potential uncertainty about operational and security issues; (2) the lack of interoperability with existing processes and infrastructures; (3) ambiguity relating to settlement finality; (4) questions regarding the legality of DLT implementations; (5) the absence of an effective and robust governance framework; and (6) issues related to data integrity, immutability, and privacy. DLT is an evolving technology. It has not yet been proven to be sufficiently robust for wide-scale implementation.

Where Are We with Ongoing Retail CBDC Projects?

So far, very few central banks have completed CBDC projects. As of September 2021, only the Bahamas and the Eastern Caribbean Central Bank (ECCB) have launched their CBDCs, in 2020 and 2021, respectively. China is set to become the third country; the PBoC is prepared to trial the digital yuan with foreign visitors at the Beijing Winter Olympics in February 2022.

But research still goes on. Most central banks are exploring the possibility of retail CBDCs. Several have published statements regarding their motivations and architecture designs, and research about the risks and benefits of CBDCs.

Table 9.2 lists ongoing projects involving CBDCs. The chart does not cover wholesale CBDCs and cross-border payments projects without CBDCs.

In terms of design choices, many central banks are still exploring several designs. As a result, it is hard to classify them. In terms of architecture, five central banks focus on a direct CDBC. In terms of infrastructure, five focus on

TABLE 9.2 Ongoing retail CBDC projects

EUROPE	Project	Architecture	Infrastructure	Access	International	Status
Czech Republic	Digital koruna	?	?	?	?	Research
Denmark	"E-krone"	Direct	?	Tiering of account- and token-based	National	Research
Estonia	Digital euro	Direct/Hybrid/Intermediated	DLT	?	International	Research
Euro area (ECB)	Digital euro	Hybrid or Intermediated	DLT and conventional	Tiering of account- and token-based	International	Research
Finland	Digital euro	?	Conventional	?	International	Research
France	Digital euro	?	?	?	International	Research
Georgia	Digital Gel	D/H/I/S	?	?	International	Research
Iceland	Rafkróna	Direct	?	Tiering of account- and token-based	National	Research
Lithuania	Digital euro	?	?	?	International	Research
The Netherlands	Digital euro	Hybrid or Intermediated	Conventional	Account-based	International	Research
Norway	"E-krone"	Direct/Hybrid	DLT and conventional	?	International	Research
Russia	Digital rouble	Hybrid	DLT and conventional	Account-based	International	Research
Spain	Digital euro	?	?	?	International	Research
Sweden	E-krona	Hybrid or Intermediated	DLT	Tiering of account- and token-based	National	Pilot
Switzerland	E-franc	?	?	?	?	Research
Ukraine	E-hryvnia	?	DLT	?	National	Pilot
United Kingdom	"E-pound"	Hybrid or Intermediated	?	?	?	Research
AMERICAS	Project	Architecture	Infrastructure	Access	International	Status
The Bahamas	Sand dollar	Hybrid	DLT and conventional	Tiering of account- and token-based	National	LIVE
Brazil	Digital fiat currency	Hybrid or Intermediated	DLT	Token-based	International	Research
Canada	"E-dollar"	Hybrid or Intermediated	DLT and conventional	Tiering of account- and token-based	National	Research

(Continued)

TABLE 9.2 (Continued)

AMERICAS	Project	Architecture	Infrastructure	Access	International	Status
Curaçao and Sint Maarten	Digital Curaçao and Sint Maarten guilder	Intermediated	Conventional	Token-based	International	Research
Eastern Caribbean	DCash	Hybrid or Intermediated	DLT	Tiering of account- and token-based	International	LIVE
Ecuador	Dinero electrónico	?	Conventional	Account-based	National	Pilot
Haiti	Digital gourde	Hybrid or Intermediated	DLT and conventional	?	?	Research
Jamaica	Digital Jamaican dollar	Hybrid	Conventional	Account-based	National	Pilot
Uruguay	Billete digital	Hybrid	Conventional	Token-based	National	Pilot
United States	"Digital-dollar"	?	?	?	?	Research

ASIA and OCEANIA	Project	Architecture	Infrastructure	Access	International	Status
Australia	"E-AUD"	Direct/Hybrid/Intermediated	?	?	?	Research
Cambodia	Bakong	?	DLT	?	National	Pilot
China	e-CNY	Hybrid or Intermediated	DLT and conventional	Account-based	National	Pilot
Hong Kong SAR	e-HKD	?	?	?	International	Research
India	Digital rupee	?	?	?	?	Research
Indonesia	"E-rupiah"	?	?	?	National	Research
Islamic Republic of Iran	Digital rial	?	?	?	International	Research
Islamic Republic of Pakistan	Digital Pakistani rupee	?	?	?	?	Research
Israel	E-shekel	Hybrid or Intermediated	?	?	International	Pilot
Japan	"Digital-yen"	Hybrid or Intermediated	?	?	International	Pilot
Kazakhstan	Digital tenge	Hybrid or Intermediated	DLT and conventional	Token-based	International	Pilot
Korea (the Republic of)	"E-won"	Hybrid or Intermediated	DLT	?	National	Pilot

	Project	Architecture	Infrastructure	Access	International	Status
Kuwait	Digital dinar	?	?	?	?	Research
Malaysia	"E-ringgit"	?	?	?	National	Research
Morocco	Digital dirham	?	?	?	?	Research
Philippines (the)	Digital peso	?	?	?	?	Research
Thailand	Digital baht	Hybrid or Intermediated	DLT and conventional	Tiering of account- and token-based	National	Pilot
Turkey	E-lira	?	?	?	?	Research
New Zealand	CBDC series	?	?	?	National	Research
AFRICA	Project	Architecture	Infrastructure	Access	International	Status
Ghana	E-cedi	?	?	?	?	Research
Kenya	Digital Kenyan shilling	Direct/Hybrid/Intermediated	?	?	?	Research
Madagascar	eAriary	?	?	?	National	Research
Mauritius	Digital Mauritian rupee	?	?	?	?	Research
South Africa	Electronic legal tender	?	?	Token-based	National	Research
Swaziland	"E-lilangeni"	?	?	?	National	Research
Trinidad and Tobago	E-dollar	?	?	?	?	Research
Tunisia	"E-dinar"	?	?	?	?	Research

Data source: Marion Laboure, "CBDCs: Ideas Are Easy but … Execution Is Everything," Deutsche Bank Research, Future Payments, July 15, 2021.
Notes: ? = unspecified or multiple options under consideration.

DLTs. However, the Sveriges Riksbank, the National Bank of Ukraine, and ECCB note that DLTs would not bring any solutions due to inadequate performance, scalability, and possible electricity outages.

Regarding cross-border payments, no CBDC project has a specific focus beyond central bank jurisdiction.

Central Banks: Monetary Control and a New Payments Era

The Leaders: Bahamas, China, and Sweden

The Bahamas launched the nationwide CBDC (the sand dollar) in October 2020, after a successful pilot in 2019, to improve financial inclusion, reduce service delivery costs, and to increase transactional efficiency.

This CBDC is based on digital ledger technology (DLT) at its foundation with a hybrid wireless network at the top to connect mobile devices. The hybrid wireless network provides connectivity in exacting ecosystems, a critical feature where hurricanes can cause power outages on the islands in the archipelago. The sand dollar will be up for use 24/7/365 in disconnected settings and will bear very low transaction fees. The sand dollar will not pay interest and cannot be held nondomestically. It can be used for all domestic wholesale and retail transactions.

With the Bahamas having 90 percent penetration for mobile devices and one of the highest per capita incomes in the Americas, the adoption rate of the sand dollar is likely to be high and quick. Furthermore, the sand dollar is pegged to the USD; in effect, it can be seen as a pilot release of a digital US dollar by proxy. To support digital payments, an ecosystem of authorized financial institutions (AFIs)—money transmitter businesses, payment service providers, and commercial banks—was created to provide services to retail customers.

In Sweden, research on a CBDC started in 2017, in part because since 2007 there had been a decline of cash in circulation (1 percent of GDP in 2020). In February 2020 Sweden revealed that it had started the first trial of its digital-krona project: the e-krona. The government was expected to implement its digital currency throughout the country sometime in 2021.

Sweden has been developing alternatives to cash since 2012, beginning with the new mobile payment system called Swish. The rapid transition toward a cashless society has roots in the country's laws, technology, and culture. First, although the nation's central bank laws stipulate that cash is legal tender and should be accepted by those receiving payment, the commercial law states that two parties (a merchant and a consumer) can enter an agreement that supersedes central bank guidelines. Second, the country benefits from strong infrastructure—specifically, strong broadband coverage, even in remote areas. Third, cultural factors have moved Sweden toward a cashless society, including a small, tech-savvy population, and a generally strong trust in institutions and new technologies.

China started researching CBDC projects in 2014 and piloting them in April 2020. This will be developed in the next part.

The Followers: Eurozone, Japan, United Kingdom, and United States

The ECB Governing Council has not yet made a decision about whether to issue a digital euro. After a consultation process that ended in January 2021, the ECB Governing Council agreed to move to the two-year "investigation phase" of developing its CBDC in July 2021. Assuming all goes well, it will take another three years to issue the digital euro.

According to the ECB report, "A digital euro would be a central bank liability offered in digital form for use by citizens and businesses . . . and would complement the current offering of cash and wholesale central bank deposits." In other words, a CBDC would (i) be a third form of central bank money, existing next to cash and reserves; (ii) try to combine the advantages of world reserves, which are already digital but only available to banks, and cash, which is available to everyone, but physical; and (iii) be digital and available to everyone.

The digital euro would have cashlike functions. Offline payments would be possible, which is good because payments need to be available in rural areas and to people without internet access. Cash would remain legal tender. The ECB has emphasized that a digital euro might be essential in several scenarios: if cash were to decline significantly; if other electronic payments methods were to become unavailable, owing to extreme events; or if foreign digital money were to largely displace existing means of payments.

In the UK, the Bank of England (BoE) released a CBDC discussion paper in March 2020, but no decision has been made on whether to introduce a CBDC. The main arguments in favor of a CBDC are: the use of banknotes—the Bank's most accessible form of money—is declining; the use of privately issued money continues to increase with technological changes driving innovation; it will help maintain monetary and financial stability.

In the United States, Federal Reserve chairman Jerome Powell stated the need for further work and "extensive" public consultation with stakeholders before deciding to issue a CBDC. Fed Chair Powell has said that the central bank is not concerned with not being first in the CBDC race, while adding that the US dollar's status as the world reserve currency already gave it a "first-mover advantage."

The Fed announced in August 2020 that it was expanding experimentation with technologies related to digital currencies. The Boston Fed is currently working with researchers at MIT to build a hypothetical digital currency oriented for central bank use. The Fed has indicated that any code base developed through this effort will be offered as open-source software for experimentation. Meanwhile, the Fed has also constituted a team of application developers from the reserve banks in Cleveland, Dallas, and New York. They are working with a policy team at the Fed board in Washington to study "the implications of digital currencies on the payments ecosystem, monetary policy, financial stability, banking and finance, and consumer protection."

The Federal Reserve Board's Technology Lab has also expanded its experimentation to better understand and evaluate the risks and opportunities of technologies relevant to digital currency and related payment innovations.

The Bank of Japan (BoJ) has started CBDC trials in 2021. The government's aim is to explore the technical feasibility of a digital yen. The first-phase proof of concept is scheduled to end in March 2022. The BoJ has not yet decided whether to proceed with a CBDC. The reluctance of the BoJ to rush toward a digital currency stems from the fact that cash remains the dominant method for transactions in Japan. Nonetheless, the BoJ has put its chief economist in charge of researching digital currencies as the pandemic possibly accelerates the use of cashless payments.

Looking to the Future: China Leads the Way toward Digital Currency

In our view, for their populations to adopt digital currencies, advanced economies must overcome two barriers: lower interest rates and cultural privacy norms. Cash is regarded as a "store of value" and a "safe haven." In our survey, one-third of Americans and Europeans ranked cash as their favorite payment method, and more than half of the people in developed countries believed that cash would always be around. This statement pertained to survey participants regardless of their country, gender, or age.

Unsurprisingly, during the three months prior to May 2020 the number of banknotes in circulation in the Eurozone increased by EUR 75 billion. This was a new all-time high that exceeded the increase during the three months following the collapse of Lehman Brothers in late 2008.

Higher interest rates are necessary to bring the end of cash as a store of value (providing incentive to store in accounts). We have conducted an analysis of cash in circulation and interest rates within advanced economies. There is a strong negative association between the level of central bank interest rates and cash in circulation. Proving a causal relationship between cash in circulation and interest rates would require more work. However, we can say that low central bank interest rates certainly play a role in increasing cash in circulation.

The US Federal Reserve, the ECB, the BoE, and the BoJ have all lowered interest rates to near or below zero. Looking ahead, despite upside risk for inflation to increase, we expect central bank interest rates to remain near or below zero through the year 2023 in most advanced economies. In that context, consumers have little incentive to move cash from under the mattress into a bank account.

Cultural factors related to convenience, usage, and privacy will also influence adoption rates. Banknotes and coins greatly reduce digital footprints because a cash transaction does not generate digital data. By contrast, digital currency transactions are convenient but can be traced.

In China the rate of adopting the government's CBDC—influenced by existing consumer habits and demographics—will take off at a faster pace than in most other countries. The Covid-19 pandemic has accelerated an ongoing shift among younger populations away from cash and toward digital payments, particularly in Asia and specifically in China. At the end of 2020, around 86 percent of internet users in China used online payment services (up from 18 percent in 2008). According to the World Bank, 85 percent of Chinese adults who bought something online also paid for it online. This is significantly higher than in other emerging economies, where 53 percent of adults who made an internet purchase in the past twelve months paid for it by cash on delivery (COD).

China's Potential to Advance Digital Currencies into the Global Mainstream

The People's Bank of China (PBoC) started to conduct research on a government-backed cryptocurrency as early as 2014. Beyond replacing cash[15] and improving financial inclusion,[16] the long-term goal of the PBoC's digital currency was to improve the efficiency of transactions across the nation's financial system. The former president of the Bank of China, Li Lihui, argued that a digital currency's efficiency, cost-effectiveness, and convenience would make it especially desirable during an epidemic.

In April 2020 China began testing the e-RMB for payments in several major cities, including Shenzhen, Suzhou, Chengdu, and a new area south of Beijing called Xiong'an. The government is expected to launch it at the venue for the 2022 Beijing Winter Olympics. According to state media, the e-RMB has been formally adopted into the monetary systems of the cities mentioned above, with some government employees and public servants receiving part of their salaries in the digital currency in May. In December, JD.com, one of China's e-commerce giants, announced that it will accept digital yuan as payment for some products on its online mall.

In early December, the chief executive of the Hong Kong Monetary Authority (HKMA), Eddie Yue, said that the PBoC and HKMA are preparing to test the digital yuan for cross-border payments. On the same date, Suzhou municipal government announced that it would give away 100,000 digital red packets, each containing RMB 200 in digital yuan, to residents via a lottery. A similar trial was run in Shenzhen, where the city carried out a lottery in October to give away a total of RMB 10 million in digital yuan. Nearly two million people applied and 50,000 of them won.

According to new patents registered by the PBoC, official speeches and press releases, China's CBDC is not built on a blockchain, the digital ledger often used by Bitcoin and other private cryptocurrencies. In August 2018 the deputy director of the PBoC's payments department, Mu Changchun, suggested that a blockchain platform would not be able to deliver the throughput needed for retail. Therefore, it appears that the e-RMB will be centralized and issued first by the central bank to local commercial banks and then to users for circulation. So far China's four major state-run banks—China Construction Bank, Bank of China, Industrial and Commercial Bank of China, and Agricultural Bank of China—have started large-scale internal testing of the digital RMB wallet.

The digital currency plan will be fully backed by the central government and pegged one-to-one to the Chinese renminbi. To initiate a payment, consumers and businesses would download a digital wallet on a mobile phone and transfer e-RMB from a commercial bank account to the digital wallet, almost like going to an ATM. Users would be able to transfer the e-RMB seamlessly with their phones using NFC technology and the internet. Offline transactions—digital transactions that the central bank can't track in real time—are expected to be saved and processed once the digital wallet is back online. The reason for its offline feature is to make it appealing in areas with poor internet coverage or little access to commercial banks.[17] China's state media reported that UnionPay is working with China's CBDC trials to test online and offline payments—using existing infrastructure. According to PBoC deputy governor Yi Gang, more than RMB 2 billion had been spent using digital yuan in four million separate transactions in China. Residents used multiple payment methods, including bar code, facial recognition, and tap-to-go transactions.

The e-RMB would allow regulatory authorities to see and trace every transaction (unlike cash transactions). "The e-RMB will spot certain behavioral patterns using Big Data and identify the users" so the technology can "help the government crackdown on money laundering, tax evasion, and financing terrorist groups." The e-RMB will adopt the principle of "controllable anonymity," which means that when trading with the digital currency, both parties can be anonymous to protect the public's privacy, but when it comes to combating corruption, money laundering, tax evasion, and terrorist financing, the state banks can still track the trading information.

Dethroning the US Dollar?

The next question is what an e-RMB would mean for the renminbi's international standing. If we consider China's central bank digital currency in isolation, without considering China's role in world affairs, we might conclude that the e-RMB's impact would be minimal. However, looking at the broader context, we should keep in mind that the relationship between China and the world is changing. China has the world's second-largest economy. Its share of world consumer spending increased from 2 percent in 1980 to 12 percent in 2018 (in dollar terms). China is becoming one of the world's biggest consumer markets and it has been the world's largest exporter since 2009. China has been reducing its relative exposure to the world while the world has been increasing its exposure to China.

The Chinese government is still making tremendous efforts to internationalize the renminbi. From 2000 to 2015, the RMB's share as a settlement currency in China's trade has increased from 0 percent to 25 percent. As a settlement currency, the renminbi has surpassed the euro, which is now the second most used currency in global trade. However, in international financial transactions unrelated to trade, the renminbi lags far behind other major currencies. The US dollar largely dominates foreign exchange reserves and as the global payment currency.

China aims to become a world leader in science and innovation by 2050. China is the second-largest investor in artificial intelligence enterprises, after the United States, and it appears to be on track to have an "AI ecosystem" built by 2030. The nation's R&D expenditure has surged from about $9 billion in 2000 to $293 billion in 2018, which is the second-highest R&D figure in the world after the United States. China benefits from advanced payments systems (especially settlement technologies) that could attract more merchants and vendors to use this new, more efficient currency. China is also gaining a decisive advantage over financial applications that use digital ledger technology, such as blockchain. Whoever controls the first major government digital currency will control the banking and e-commerce sector within that nation (at least).

In the medium term, US dollar dominance should continue. The renminbi is unlikely to overtake the dollar anytime soon. For several reasons, China could use the e-RMB mostly for national trade, in which case it would not challenge the dollar as a currency for international financial transactions. China's controls over capital and its limits on foreign bond and equity holdings will likely restrain the renminbi from supplanting the dollar in the global economy.

In the long run, if the trade deficit between China and the United States widens far enough, we could see a situation in which the dollar, euro, and renminbi share the global reserve currency spotlight. In that case, the renminbi could eventually become a major currency for global trade. Moreover, a commitment from Chinese authorities to liberalize and develop local capital markets, and to innovate new convenient payment technologies like Alipay and WeChat Pay, could catalyze greater international use of the renminbi.

The critical question is: As more nations worldwide adopt CBDCs and real-time payments, will the world need a reserve currency (in the traditional sense)?

Could CBDCs Disintermediate Banks?

With bank accounts paying low interest rates, a CBDC has a high potential to disintermediate the banking system. People might choose to hold their money directly at the central bank. Obviously this would disrupt legacy bank franchises and impact financial stability. Credit card volumes, interchange fees, payment transaction fees, and deposit interest margins could be seriously affected. This would shake the current two-tier system and create additional responsibilities for central banks, such as: Know Your Customer (KYC) issues and disputes; monitoring transaction levels; preventing money laundering and terrorism financing; and tax compliance.

Several central banks, including the BoE, have warned that if significant deposit balances move from banks to CBDCs, the balance sheets of both central and commercial banks could be impacted. This could impact credit granted by commercial banks and financial stability.

Some degree of disintermediation is an inevitable consequence of a successful CBDC. Thus, commercial banks need to consider how to react to a prospective loss of deposit funding. Two possible solutions would be to pay a higher interest rate on deposits to limit further outflows to a CBDC, or to replace lost deposit funding with alternatives, such as longer-term deposits or wholesale funding. Overall, both options would raise the cost of funding. Assuming banks seek to maintain profit margins, this could lead banks to increase the cost of the credit they provide to the economy, resulting in a lower volume of lending by banks, all else being equal.

Currently the digital currency model favored by most central banks seems to be two-tier issuance. As with a traditional currency, transactions would be decentralized and supply would be centralized.

Conclusion

The advent of new technologies is profoundly changing the delivery and distribution of financial services. Periods of "disruptive innovation" have always transformed the inequality map. For example, following the Industrial Revolution, European countries saw their entire populations benefit from improved GDPs and increased living standards. However, economic inequalities widened in comparison to the rest of the world. By learning from the past, policymakers can spot early trends and ensure that this technological revolution will benefit most people rather than just a few winners.

In this Conclusion, we will first summarize the ways in which key trends are deeply disrupting financial services. Next, based on an outline of previous financial crises and economic revolutions, we will provide recommendations designed to help policymakers avoid future mistakes. Then, we will show that the global spread of Covid-19 might be the catalyst that finally brings digital payments more fully into the mainstream. Finally, we will argue that the new fintech revolution has the potential to significantly improve life for people in advanced and emerging economies.

Synthesis of Financial Services Disruptions in Six Key Trends

We here identify six key revolutions in modern financial services and present them in chronological order. These trends range from online brokerage services, a mature segment, to the recent rise of cryptocurrencies, which are challenging the core function of central banking.

Trend 1: Online Distribution of Financial Services, with Increased Transparency

The shift to online financial services was probably the first modern disruption. Online comparators and brokers allow individuals to compare financial products, banks, and insurance policies in a matter of seconds from home. This has made the old job of main-street brokerage nearly obsolete, except for very niche or complex products. This has increased product transparency and imposed downward price pressure—to the benefit of the end consumer.

Trend 2: Simplified and Automated Back-Office Functions for Banks and Insurance Companies

This second wave of the modern technological revolution mostly automated the input, storage, and analysis of data. Data management is a critical and central part of banking and insurance sectors, which employ thousands of people to handle middle- and back-office processes. McKinsey estimated that around 50 percent of current work activities in these sectors are technically automatable. They also estimate more than 30 percent of the activities in six out of ten occupations today could be automated.[1]

Blockchain offers the next generation of data management. A decentralized system of trust enables blockchain to avoid data duplication when services, transactions, and contracts are handled by several banks. Automation and other improvements in bank data management will continue to evolve and challenge current organizations.

Trend 3: Artificial Intelligence (AI) Upends Strategic Jobs within Banks and Insurance Firms

The first wave of automation mostly targeted back- and middle-office functions. Now, new algorithms and other forms of AI are replacing people in higher-paid, more sophisticated front-office jobs. For example:

- Traders are being replaced by optimized algorithms (as in high-frequency trading). In the US stock market and many other advanced financial markets, around 70 to 80 percent of overall trading volume is generated through algorithmic trading.[2]
- Financial advisors and wealth managers are being replaced by questionnaires and robo-advisors, which can offer similar or higher investment returns at a lower cost.
- Big Data is enabling companies to automatically identify consumers' needs, thereby replacing relationship-based branch managers and key account executives.

- Advanced portfolio screening and risk algorithms allow banks to detect risk, exposures, and loss potentials in asset portfolios and loans much faster than with traditional human-based risk management.
- Actuarial work in insurance companies is being increasingly supplemented and partially replaced by risk algorithms and systems.

In the long run, progress in software development and artificial intelligence will continue to replace parts of value chains and key roles within banks.

Trend 4: Financial Services Branch Activity Moves to Smartphones

A massive digitalization of basic banking services (such as account management, transactions, money transfers) is bringing increased convenience to consumers. To date, northern Europe appears to have the most advanced online banking industry. Nordic and Dutch banks have already cut their branch numbers by 50 percent. The larger and more traditional markets of western Europe and the United States are likely to follow, cutting 30 percent to 50 percent of existing branches within the next decade.

While traditional banks adapt their networks to the new reality, new banks like N26 have managed to offer fully digital processes without using any branch or physical interactions. This allows online banking platforms to rapidly gain market footholds across countries and regions. These innovations will continue to challenge the traditional banking model's core value-chain components.

Trend 5: A Revolution in Digital Payments Threatens Credit Cards

The coming decade will see a rapid increase in digital payments, leading to the death of the plastic credit card. Over the next five years, mobile payments are expected to constitute two-fifths of in-store purchases in the United States, which is quadruple the current level. A similar rate of growth in digital payments is expected to occur in other developed countries; however, the rate at which the use of cash and plastic cards declines will vary from country to country. Many customers in emerging markets are transitioning directly from cash to mobile payments without ever owning a plastic card.

As digital payment technologies become more widely used, people might consume more. Digital payment platforms will be able to gather increasing amounts of highly personal data from consumers. That data will become increasingly valuable, which in turn will allow these businesses to significantly reduce the fees they charge, perhaps to nearly zero. The reduced fees will allow consumers to spend more.

Developments in China offer a preview of the future of payments. The country is developing a world-leading digital payments infrastructure. The value of online payments is equivalent to three-quarters of China's GDP, which is almost double the proportion in 2012. Today, nearly half of in-store purchases in China are made with a digital wallet, which is far above the levels in any other country.[3]

Trend 6: Cryptocurrencies Disintermediate Central and Commercial Banks

With bank accounts paying low interest rates, cryptocurrencies are becoming another treasury-management tool for companies. A few publicly traded companies have started converting cash in their treasuries into Bitcoin as an alternative store of value. For example, MicroStrategy, a business analytics company, stated, "Company leaders believe that Bitcoin, as the world's most widely adopted cryptocurrency, is a dependable store of value." They "continue to believe Bitcoin will provide the opportunity for better returns and preserve the value of our capital over time, compared to holding cash."[4]

The increased mainstream acceptance of cryptocurrencies is threatening financial stability, and central and commercial banks. Cryptocurrencies operate peer to peer, so they have the potential to disintermediate the banking system as we know it. Central banks are unlikely to give up their monopolies easily. For now, central bankers are reacting to the rise of cryptocurrencies by speeding up research and launching pilots for their own digital currencies.

Avoiding the Next Large-Scale Financial Crisis

These dramatic, rapid changes can be confusing for policymakers, making it difficult for them to develop long-term plans. For this reason it is important to study previous financial crises and revolutions. Understanding the past can help us avoid mistakes in the future. Below are three recommendations.

Regulate Early to Avoid Subprime Lending

A key element of the 2007–2008 financial crisis was subprime lending, which led millions of people into unsustainable financial situations. There are at least three ways to avoid making the same mistake: investing in citizen financial education, controlling commercial lending sales pitches, and limiting the power of new fintech.

In regard to financial education, the IMF demonstrates that spending on financial and health education reduces inequality by promoting upward, generational social mobility. Financial literacy efforts can help people rise above a paycheck-to-paycheck way of life and help them avoid high debts that lead to serious loss of wealth. Financial literacy basics (e.g., compound interest rates, mortgages, types of investments) should be taught in schools and could even be part of mathematics curricula.

It is also important to regulate against predatory lending, which often occurs with commercial lending sales pitches. During the 2007–2008 financial crisis, banks were rightly blamed for pushing people into debt. They often spread alluring messages that promoted debt through their brokers or branch networks. Today digital ads and social networks have become new springboards for start-up and established players to promote financial products. To protect consumers from loan sharks, financial services regulators should create specialized teams to monitor the commercial activity of financial companies and regulate the aggressive campaigns designed to push vulnerable populations into risky debt (such as payday loans) or investment gambling (such as leveraged trading activity).

Finally, policymakers should find ways to add transparency, consumer protections, security, and accountability to start-up fintech companies. These protections are well established for traditional banks, but many new fintech firms are relatively unregulated. Thus, if a fintech start-up firm goes out of business, or mismanages customer accounts, consumers could lose money and have little or no recourse.

Monitor Data Collection and Algorithms

In the film *Minority Report,* the government deploys psychics to predict future crimes, allowing police to swoop in before the crimes can be committed. This possibility is no longer mere fiction. In China, for example, law enforcement agencies stop "pre-crimes" by using algorithms and the country's immense surveillance infrastructure to identify potential dissidents. We are seeing a rapid development of methods based on Big Data about individuals' demographics, payment history, browser history, medical history, and social network connections. Powerful computers track correlations and causality to generate predictions about the likeliness of defaulting on debt and the propensity of diseases.

Likewise, as large companies increasingly gather consumer data and then use algorithms to sell products and services, governments should make sure that these powerful tools do not lead to unfair exclusion and pricing. The usage of such predictive methods could be harmful in several ways. First, they provide companies and governments with detailed knowledge about consumers. This information enables companies to tailor convincing messages related to spending and debt. We can imagine a person who has recently become unemployed receiving a message such as: "Running low on cash? XYZ company can cover your need." Similarly, if a health insurance company can predict a high likelihood of cancer or diabetes in individuals, then the company could deny insurance to those people or charge higher premium prices, putting the whole system of group insurance and solidarity at risk.[5]

To prevent these problems, the use of data must be regulated. Regulators should appoint specialized teams to test company algorithms and ensure they are competently designed, unbiased, and nonexploitative.

Increase Monitoring of Fintech Companies

Governments must monitor, regulate, and coordinate to avoid "too big to fail" or "too powerful to regulate" scenarios. Although financial regulation over banks has been strengthened since the 2007–2008 financial crisis, most fintech players operate below the radar and benefit from weak or no regulations. As we have seen in other industries (such as Uber, Airbnb), when a company grows to become a multinational leader, it becomes much harder to regulate. Fintech giants, such as Alipay in China, already manage too much money across countries, which increases systemic risks within the global financial system. Similarly, digital firms offer an opportunity to scale-up products across multiple countries, with giant companies, such as the GAFA companies, arbitraging and optimizing local fiscal systems.

In light of these critical risks, there is an urgent need to create a cross-regulator taskforce to discuss and monitor emerging unicorn companies before they become so big that authorities are not able to effectively impose regulations.

Covid-19 Is Catalyzing the Transition to a Cashless Society

This book was finalized in the middle of the Covid-19 crisis. At the time of this writing, we recognize that it is far too early to draw conclusions. However, we believe this pandemic—the fear it has created and the unprecedented government measures—is a catalyst for accelerating current trends in financial services.

Fear That the SARS-Cov-2 Spreads on Cash and Cards

There is little disagreement that physical currency can serve as a vector for transmitting some disease-causing pathogens, much like a mosquito. Studies have shown that the average European banknote contains 26,000 bacterial colonies, including strains such as E. coli and salmonella, which can cause food poisoning. Tests show that up to 94 percent of US dollar bills in circulation are contaminated with high levels of bacteria. Unpublished research by New York University's Center for Genomics and Systems Biology found about 3,000 types of bacteria residing on US notes, and even traces of cocaine. Although most bacteria on banknotes are harmless, tests have found some pathogens.

With the Covid-19 pandemic there has been strong public concern that cash and cards might transmit the virus. Globally the number of internet searches on "cash virus" surged to unusual levels, with the highest in Australia, Canada, France, Ireland, Singapore, Switzerland, the UK, and the United States. The human influenza virus has been found alive and infectious for up to seventeen days on banknotes.[6] A recent study suggested that SARS-CoV-2, the virus that causes Covid-19, "can persist on inanimate surfaces like metal, glass, or plastic for up to nine days, but can be efficiently inactivated by surface disinfection procedures."[7]

To bolster trust in cash and guarantee universal acceptance, several central banks have actively communicated that risk of surface transmission is low. The Bank of England has noted that "the risk posed by handling a polymer note is no greater than touching any other common surfaces such as handrails, doorknobs, or credit cards." The Bundesbank has advised the public that the risks of transmission through banknotes are minimal and that a sufficient supply of banknotes is guaranteed. The Bank of Canada has asked retailers to stop refusing cash payments. The South African Reserve Bank has counteracted scams by clarifying that there is no evidence of transmission by cash and it is not withdrawing cash from circulation.

Other central banks have taken additional precautionary measures, believing that handling cash is a potential risk factor in the Covid-19 pandemic. First, the People's Bank of China, and the central banks in South Korea, Hungary, and Kuwait began to disinfect and even destroy banknotes to mitigate the spread of the virus. The governments' decision to undertake such radical action suggests one of two conclusions: first, that leaders believe that currency can be an effective mode of Covid-19 transmission; second, they deem the investment required to disinfect, destroy, and reprint currency as worthwhile compared to the potential health care costs of spreading the disease.

Covid-19 Fuels Transition to Digital Payments

As a result of the fears described above, central banks or governments in India, Indonesia, Georgia, and several other countries have encouraged cashless payments.

The effect of the Covid-19 on payment systems in Asia could be seen sooner than in Europe and the United States, given the already high penetration rate of digital payments in Asia. By the end of 2020 there were around 855 million online payment users in China, up from 137 million in 2010. One reason for this rapid increase is that in China and Southeast Asian countries the young populations are significantly larger than those in Europe and the United States, and young populations are usually more open to adopting new technologies.[8]

But the Covid-19 pandemic could be a game changer in the West. Older people are the most vulnerable to this virus, and they are the people who most use cash. It seems likely that the risk of infection from cash will compel older generations to more frequently use digital payment alternatives.

According to our research, Americans and western Europeans are much more dependent on cash than are other parts of the world. It takes much longer to change the ingrained habits of people in a legacy system. In terms of disease control, this could be a significant problem, especially in cash-based societies where populations are aging, such as Germany, Japan, or the United States. To reduce physical contact and queuing at checkout, contactless card payment limits rose from £30 ($35) to £45 ($52) across most European countries in March 2020. This increase, coupled with worldwide lockdowns and social distancing measures, has driven more and more people to use cards over cash. In the UK the number of sellers accepting only digital payments in 2020 jumped from 8 percent in February to 50 percent in April.[9]

Over the medium to long term, concerns over handling cash will certainly add to the calls for central banks (CBs) to develop central bank digital currencies (CBDCs). Over the past two years, central banks around the world have multiplied their digital cash initiatives. In early 2021, 86 percent of CBs were developing a CBDC. The work goes far beyond research. About 60 percent of CBs were experimenting with proofs-of-concept, and 14 percent were already running pilot projects.

This process is already in motion. In April 2020 China began a CBDC trial. In February 2020 Sweden, a country where the amount of cash in circulation now is only 1 percent of GDP, began its first trial of the e-krona. Several countries have already launched their CBDCs, including the Bahamas and the Organization of Eastern Caribbean States. In the United States, the drafts of the first Covid-19 stimulus bill first included and then discarded the creation of digital dollar wallets.

Can the Fintech Revolution Reduce Inequalities?

Periods of profound "disruptive innovation" have always reshuffled the inequality map. For example, during the Industrial Revolution, European countries saw their entire populations benefit from improved GDPs and increased living standards. At the same time, the inequalities widened in comparison to the rest of the world.

As we have noted, disruptive innovation has always impacted economic inequality. The same is true with fintech disruptive innovations. Next we summarize the primary ways in which new fintech advances are influencing the inequality map around the world.

Overcoming Pain Points: Fintech Solutions in Advanced Economies

First, developing countries struggle to close many remaining gaps in access to banking services. Millions of people (not only millennials) in advanced economies lack bank accounts. In 2015, 7 percent of households did not have access to a checking or savings account. This suggests that about 15.6 million adults and 7.6 million children in the United States were unbanked. A primary reason for not having an account is the expensive bank fees. In response to this problem, after the 2007–2008 financial crisis many companies launched digital-only, branchless banks that offer simpler, cheaper accounts and card services. The German start-up N26 was created in 2015 with the objective to offer lower-income millennials more accessible banking services.

Second, freelance workers and others with unstable careers often lack access to credit.

Online peer-to-peer lending, crowdfunding, and crowd-investing platforms have been established to increase access to financing. This approach allows project leaders to connect with digital communities for the purpose of investing, acquiring funding, and borrowing outside traditional and institutional intermediaries (banks, asset managers, and so on). Since it was launched in 2009, Kickstarter has been regarded as the pioneer in this field, at least in terms of crowdfunding. But the Kickstarter's genesis occurred much earlier, in the early 2000s. Perry Chen, then a musician who was frustrated about not being able to invite two DJs to a jazz festival for lack of funds, came up with the idea of a fundraising platform that would let citizens express themselves. Today the company faces increasingly stiff competition. Online jackpots and specialized funding sites abound and multiply the alternatives to Kickstarter.

Third, there continues to be unequal access to the "revenue" from capital. Wealthy individuals have access to a wide range of investment opportunities, including investments in alternative asset management plans (such as hedge funds), whereas small investors typically hold more "vanilla" investments (such as bank deposits and government bonds). An investment of $100 in 1927 in T-bills would have yielded $2,082 in 2020 and the same investment in stock would have yielded $592,868.

On average, stocks have outperformed short- and long-term bonds during most periods over the last two centuries. Clearly, long-term dormant savings can add up to a lot of money. We also see that small differences in investment returns make a big difference over the long term, via the compounding effect. Regular savings, even in moderate amounts, can accumulate significant wealth. These facts apply to pension planning and complementary retirement investments. Even small differences in investment fees can make a big difference over time.

To provide lower-income populations with access to more lucrative investment products and financial advice, fintech innovators launched robo-advisors (automated online financial advice) as an alternative to traditional financial advisers. Robo-advisors are based on algorithms that consider the investor's profile and his or her relationship to risk, with different objectives and varying time horizons. The robo-advisor then offers an investment proposal that best suits the client's needs. Robo-advisors offer low and transparent fees, convenience, affordability, and other benefits. Many people who never thought they could invest can now begin.

Recommendations for Developed Countries

First, public services, such as tax collection or ID creation, could leverage new fintech payment and blockchain technologies. This should help civil servants move away from jobs that entail data gathering, inputs, and verification—freeing them to work more directly with citizens. Banks and insurance companies are already leveraging blockchain technologies to significantly improve back-office processes. Adopting these technologies at scale could help governments improve tax collection and reallocate civil servants to functions that offer higher value to citizens. In the short term, workers will likely fear change; many jobs could be replaced by algorithms. But in the long run, fintech can improve services to citizens and offer more rewarding jobs for public servants.

Second, it is important at this time to modernize fiscal and labor policies as the world enters the new era of peer-to-peer employment platforms and cross-border digital commerce. Governments need to rethink the definition of taxation and employment protections so as to include those people who work in freelance jobs. We envision the creation of a social security and insurance framework—including the collection of social contributions—for freelance platform workers. In the era of Big Data, it is possible for governments to gather income information, to facilitate tax computation, and even to automate tax collection directly from online work platforms.

Third, governments should join forces to gather data and collaborate against individual and corporate tax evasion. Blockchain offers a great backbone for the dematerialization, centralization, and management of citizen data. It can track financial flows (taxes, authentication, and social benefits) while keeping some data confidential. The US government has already started to force foreign banks to share data on US citizens through FATCA. This effort could be extended by and between other governments. Banks could share data through a common platform, which would allow governments to map the cross-national assets and revenues of individuals and corporations.

Pain Points and Fintech Solutions in Developing Countries

There are, of course, barriers in developing nations as they seek to implement the fintech recommendations described above. First, the lack of official documents impairs access to financial services. A functioning banking system is based on individual documentation (IDs). Account holders must have reliable identity data that can be verified. In developing countries, many people lack basic IDs and documentation to access financial services. Aadhaar in India is a good example of a government-led initiative that could act as an enabler for the broader fintech ecosystem. Aadhaar was a groundbreaking initiative that enabled the Indian government to develop an online database with information about 1.2 billion people. It was created with the goal of enrolling up to one million new users every day and is capable of handling 600 million transactions per day. By comparison, Visa processes 130 million transactions every day.

Second, many developing nations face endemic fraud and corruption, which is harmful to economic development. In emerging markets, bribery systems means that a large part of taxes and social redistribution is "captured" by government employees or other predatory individuals along the chain of money collection or redistribution. Digitalization of payments, which requires the right infrastructure (e-wallet and so on) allows governments and citizens to disintermediate money collection and redistribution, thereby diminishing bribery and theft. This type of fintech innovation keeps track of transactions, enabling governments to monitor and identify fraud and bribery. This would increase the funds available for redistribution, perhaps reduce taxes, and potentially unleash the economy for the benefit of people.

Third, many developing nations have limited commerce in rural areas, which reduces access in those regions to goods and the capacity to sell. E-commerce could be a solution. It could enable rural small businesses to sell goods far beyond local boundaries. By establishing online stores, for example, merchants could avoid the high sunk costs of opening physical shops and they could reduce fixed costs related to rent, staffing, and so on. Small business owners could increase sales by utilizing lost-cost search engine optimization, social media traffic, and online evaluations. Fintech, specifically digital payments, could help rural e-commerce merchants to easily receive payments from distant clients. China has also seen explosive growth across online e-commerce and social networking platforms. The nation provides payment services that are almost universally accepted within China. They are used by low- and high-income, rural and urban households alike. These platforms include Alipay, developed by the Alibaba Group's affiliate Ant Financial, and Tencent's Tenpay, which operates the social media platforms WeChat and QQ.

A fourth barrier is that many developing nations have large unbanked populations, especially in rural areas. Many citizens lack access to banking services and / or must travel long distances to access banks. As we showed in Chapter 6, for example, unbanked citizens usually do not earn a formal salary or income. Most are paid in cash. This condition prevents them from opening a traditional bank account. And even if they have such an account, bank transfers are expensive. People do not want to pay high bank fees to transfer extremely small amounts of money, say to distant and unbanked relatives. In Kenya, for example, people often turn to a risky alternative. They often entrust *matatus* (privately owned minibuses), drivers, or train conductors to deliver their money. Not surprisingly, the money often vanishes.

Fintech is helping these populations. Any citizen in Kenya can open a M-Pesa account with a valid ID and a phone number. Safaricom set a goal of enlisting 350,000 customers during the company's first year, but it ended up with 1.2 million. According to its 2017 report, Safaricom is serving "thirty million customers in ten countries and [offering] a range of services, including foreign transfers, loans, and health provisions."[10]

Fifth, the lack of infrastructures to create social services redistribution is a significant problem in developing nations. Citizens who most need social redistribution often lack IDs, addresses, and bank accounts. There is a clear need to have a simple, cost-effective identification system that enables citizens to transfer and store small payments. As we saw in Chapter 7, the United Nation's World Food Programme (WFP) Building Blocks initiative has helped distribute cash-for-food aid to over one hundred thousand Syrian refugees in Jordan. In 2017, the WFP transferred over \$1.3 billion in Building Blocks benefits. The use of blockchain since then has reduced bank fees involved in those transfers by 98 percent. This has saved the WFP millions of dollars that can now be used for higher purposes, such as expanding programs or offering greater benefits per recipient.

Recommendations for Developing Countries

Our first recommendation for emerging economies is to launch vast programs to digitize IDs and create a positive ecosystem for e-commerce and financial services. The Indian government led with way with its Aadhaar ID system, which also enabled more people to obtain bank accounts and other financial services. Taking a proactive role and creating a digital infrastructure will serve as a backbone for opening banking accounts, launching or revamping national health systems, and creating start-up services such as e-commerce, digital wallets, and payment solutions.[11]

Second, the public sector should develop partnerships with start-ups to invest in telecom and payment infrastructure for rural areas. In emerging economies, the combination of mobile, e-commerce, and digital payment options helps business expansion. This creates a virtuous cycle that leads to stronger economic growth, better development, and higher living standards. Governments should continue working with the private sector to develop PPPs (public-private partnerships) to offer access to broadband, e-commerce, and payment solutions in the most remote areas. We can envision governments offering public tender for start-ups to partially fund fintech projects in remote and poor areas of each country.

Finally, newly created fintech ecosystems are a great steppingstone for government services and wealth redistribution. As stated above, one of the biggest barriers to creating social security or other redistribution services is the lack of official identities among the most remote citizens. Without IDs and residential addresses, for example, citizens are not able to access government services and they become more susceptible to theft, loss, and corruption. Fintech solutions can help gather valuable data, such as addresses, and create digital wallets or other means for people to receive government benefits. Governments should continue to strengthen partnerships with private-sector fintech companies to deliver public services to citizens in remote areas. These services could be delivered through newly created payment infrastructures.

Dreaming of the Future

We conclude by thinking ahead and trying to identify some of the key themes and next waves of disruption. This list is by no mean exhaustive, but this is a first glimpse of . . . dreaming of the future.

The all-encompassing social network. An underlying trend is the convergence of social media, payments, and e-commerce. Facebook has been used as a springboard to launch and advertise businesses and services to its users. It is now taking the next step to develop its own digital currency. Facebook could become a cross-border closed market in which people can exchange goods and services with a new currency. On the other side of the world WeChat services include a mix of social media, instant messaging, e-commerce, and instant payments. It would overlap with Amazon, WhatsApp, and Apple Pay services, just to name a few.

The full-service bank at your fingertips. We could easily envision a deeper and stronger integration between various digital and mobile services, such as mobile banking, robo-advisors, card payments, money transfers and remittances, trading and investments, and aggregation of banking accounts. Apart from in China, these services are not all-in-one and would benefit from further integration under the same umbrella. In the end, full money management will be available from a single mobile and a single app—unless it becomes a chipset inserted into the body as in the movie *In Time.*

The revolution in government administration. The pandemic has put additional pressure on already weak government finances, forcing them to reduce costs. They will probably follow the footsteps of the banking and insurance industries by automating back-office jobs and significantly reducing staff (by 40 percent or more). As we saw in Chapter 7, government data management will become incredibly more efficient through blockchain and algorithms thereby allowing for better tax collection, social redistribution, and fraud prevention. Smaller countries like Estonia or the UAE are already at the forefront of better, faster, stronger government services. They are pioneering new technologies and ideas not only to save costs but to improve services to their citizens. Clearly, this revolution will also be a political challenge. And as government workers fear losing their jobs, the transition to fintech solutions could take longer as people retire.

The cross-border digital or cryptocurrencies become mainstream. The pandemic has hastened the decline of cash by four or five years. Now, the world has shifted from asking *whether* digital currencies will succeed, to *how and when* they will become mainstream. Both PayPal and Venmo added cryptocurrency capability to their wallets in 2021. Central banks will continue to develop a digital cash alternative. The Bahamas launched the first nationwide CBDC in October 2020, and both Sweden and China launched pilots in early 2020. We can envision cashless societies and fully digitalized national currencies (with mobile payments secured by fingerprints or personal chips) as well as new cross-border payments to support trade using Bitcoin, Facebook, or . . .

The twenty-first century fiscal revolution. The value-added tax (VAT) is now increasingly difficult to manage when goods and services are far from their consumption markets. Today, small and medium industries (SMEs) in France are using advertising services based anywhere in the world while advisors are based in Ireland. These advertising services are transacted through a self-service platform that was coded by engineers from Facebook in California or India. How and where could these services be taxed? In a globalized post-Covid area, where people will increasingly travel again, what will and should drive VAT? Will the VAT be directly charged to and collected from the end consumer based on nationality or geo-localization? Similarly, the employment contract as we know it today will likely become rare as the freelance economy expands. The Covid-19 pandemic has led people to get paid in one country for services offered in another country while being confined in a third country. This short-term problem is only the tip of the iceberg. Platforms like Upwork allow people to hire freelancers anywhere in the world to offer services to clients in other parts of the world. During the pandemic, many companies have announced that people could work remotely from wherever they want. How should income tax be collected and social services be offered in that context? Governments will have to define new ways to calculate income tax for the freelancers while relying on technology and cooperation with freelance platforms to enforce income tax payments and to avoid fraud.

Each of these possible scenarios is already disruptive, but the combination of them may forever change the world as we know it. In the previous millennium, people fought for land causing the emergence and reshuffling of countries. A country was simply "a territory with a legal system, currency, and language that bound people together by birth, upbringing, and community. It was administered by a government responsible for maintaining the system (law, security, infrastructure) and funded by taxing the economic activity generated by this ecosystem." Each of the pillars in the definition have already been challenged by global forces, such as access to information, international travel, and global trade—to name a few macro trends. This system will be challenged by the emergence of cross-border currencies, and by platforms for global marketplaces of goods and services. Estonia may be pioneer in the through-process of offering "e-citizenship." This notion will be increasingly challenged. So will the legitimacy and capacity of governments to operate within this new context.

Appendixes

APPENDIX A

Selected data from the Deutsche Bank Research dbDIG proprietary survey of over 3,600 customers.

TABLE A.1 Demographics of people who consider cash as their favorite means of payment

	CASH					
	France	*Germany*	*Italy*	*UK*	*US*	*China*
Base	18%	59%	33%	29%	33%	22%
Female	19%	58%	35%	27%	33%	16%
Male	16%	60%	31%	32%	32%	28%
18–34	27%	53%	40%	23%	37%	21%
35–54	12%	52%	33%	33%	30%	17%
55+	15%	71%	25%	33%	32%	51%
Rural/Countryside	14%	65%	42%	32%	40%	36%
Suburban	21%	56%	37%	29%	28%	22%
Urban	19%	59%	29%	28%	36%	21%
Up to €20,000	26%	72%	49%			
€20,000 to €29,999	23%	61%	29%			
€30,000 to €39,999	19%	63%	30%			
€40,000 to €49,999	11%	67%	21%			
€50,000 to €69,999	13%	47%	26%			
€70,000 to €99,999	8%	47%	18%			
€100,000+	11%	50%	33%			
Up to £20,000				37%		
£20,000 to £29,999				31%		
£30,000 to £49,999				29%		
£50,000 to £69,999				20%		
£70,000+				23%		

(Continued)

TABLE A.1   (Continued)

	France	Germany	Italy	UK	US	China
			CASH			
Up to $15,000					54%	
$15,000 to $24,999					38%	
$25,000 to $34,999					37%	
$35,000 to $49,999					36%	
$50,000 to $99,999					28%	
$100,000 to $149,999					18%	
$150,000+					20%	
Up to ¥119,999						31%
¥120,000 to ¥179,999						19%
¥180,000 to ¥239,999						17%
¥240,000 to ¥299,999						24%
¥300,000 to ¥449,999						16%
¥450,000 to ¥599,999						16%
¥600,000 to ¥999,999						6%
¥1,000,000+						6%

Data source: Marion Laboure and Jim Reid, "The Future of Payments Part I. Cash: The Dinosaur Will Survive . . . for Now," Deutsche Bank Research, Corporate Bank Research, 2020, https://www.dbresearch .com/PROD/RPS_EN-PROD/PROD0000000000504353.pdf.

Note: Cash carried in France, Germany, and Italy is denominated in euros, in China in renminbi, in the United states in dollars, and in the UK in sterling.

	CASH						NON CASH					
	France	Germany	Italy	UK	US	China	France	Germany	Italy	UK	US	China
Base	72%	61%	68%	69%	69%	58%	67%	56%	47%	62%	68%	46%
Female	58%	48%	58%	45%	53%	31%	52%	54%	51%	55%	48%	53%
Male	42%	52%	42%	55%	47%	69%	48%	46%	49%	45%	52%	47%
18–34	47%	21%	37%	20%	32%	37%	31%	28%	25%	31%	27%	49%
35–54	19%	31%	36%	36%	27%	36%	37%	46%	35%	35%	34%	46%
55+	34%	48%	27%	43%	41%	27%	32%	26%	40%	34%	39%	5%
Rural/Countryside	18%	25%	19%	21%	22%	7%	29%	21%	14%	18%	17%	3%
Suburban	31%	23%	20%	52%	44%	28%	21%	25%	17%	53%	54%	26%
Urban	51%	51%	62%	26%	33%	65%	50%	54%	69%	29%	29%	71%
Up to €20,000	22%	18%	28%				13%	8%	19%			
€20,000 to €29,999	22%	12%	18%				16%	16%	23%			
€30,000 to to €49,999	35%	41%	32%				43%	36%	31%			
€50,000 to €69,999	14%	16%	14%				15%	20%	19%			
€70,000+	7%	12%	8%				13%	20%	8%			
Up to £20,000				22%						20%		
£20,000 to £29,999				34%						26%		
£30,000 to £49,999				30%						31%		
£50,000 to £69,999				7%						15%		
£70,000+				7%						8%		
Up to $24,999					36%						16%	
$25,000 to $49,999					22%						21%	
$50,000 to $99,999					28%						36%	
$100,000+					15%						27%	
Up to ¥119,999						41%						21%
¥120,000 to ¥179,999						19%						28%
¥180,000 to ¥239,999						19%						26%
¥240,000 to ¥299,999						11%						6%
¥300,000 to ¥449,999						5%						7%
¥450,000 to ¥599,999						4%						2%
¥600,000 to ¥999,999						1%						5%
¥1,000,000+						0%						5%

Data source: Marion Laboure and Jim Reid, "The Future of Payments Part I. Cash: The Dinosaur Will Survive . . . for Now," Deutsche Bank Research, Corporate Bank Research, 2020, https://www.dbresearch.com/PROD/RPS_EN-PROD/PROD0000000000504353.pdf.

Note: Cash carried in France, Germany, and Italy is denominated in euros, in China in renminbi, in the United states in dollars, and in the UK in sterling.

TABLE A.3 On an average day, approximately how much cash do you tend to carry with you?

	FRANCE				GERMANY				ITALY			
	18–34	35–54	55+	Overall	18–34	35–54	55+	Overall	18–34	35–54	55+	Overall
€0—I don't usually carry cash with me	12%	5%	7%	8%	2%	1%	0%	1%	3%	0%	1%	2%
Between €1 and €10	17%	26%	17%	20%	14%	6%	4%	8%	9%	6%	8%	8%
Between €11 and €20	23%	21%	28%	24%	23%	17%	13%	17%	18%	17%	17%	18%
Between €21 and €30	13%	19%	18%	17%	17%	18%	9%	14%	24%	14%	13%	17%
Between €31 and €40	9%	8%	7%	8%	12%	9%	5%	8%	12%	8%	7%	9%
Between €41 and €50	8%	8%	11%	9%	12%	18%	22%	18%	17%	24%	23%	22%
Between €51 and €75	5%	4%	3%	4%	10%	8%	14%	11%	6%	11%	9%	9%
Between €76 and €100	4%	3%	3%	3%	6%	10%	18%	12%	6%	10%	12%	10%
Between €101 and €150	5%	2%	2%	3%	2%	4%	7%	5%	2%	8%	5%	5%
Between €151 and €200	3%	0%	1%	1%	1%	2%	6%	4%	0%	1%	1%	1%
More than €200	3%	0%	3%	2%	1%	3%	1%	2%	2%	1%	1%	1%
Don't know	2%	3%	1%	2%	0%	3%	0%	1%	0%	0%	1%	1%
Mean	€37.81	€25.08	€31.89	€31.52	€38.13	€51.85	€63.19	€52.29	€37.99	€49.90	€48.41	€45.93

212

	UK				US			
	18–34	35–54	55+	Overall	18–34	35–54	55+	Overall
£0/$0—I don't usually carry cash with me	22%	10%	5%	13%	9%	13%	9%	10%
Between £1/$1 and £10/$10	34%	30%	18%	27%	14%	17%	10%	14%
Between £11/$11 and £20/$20	17%	19%	26%	20%	18%	15%	20%	18%
Between £21/$21 and £30/$30	9%	16%	16%	14%	11%	10%	11%	10%
Between £31/$31 and £40/$40	6%	5%	6%	6%	7%	8%	9%	8%
Between £41/$41 and £50/$50	4%	8%	8%	7%	9%	10%	8%	9%
Between £51/$51 and £75/$75	2%	3%	6%	3%	5%	6%	7%	6%
Between £76/$76 and £100/$100	3%	4%	9%	5%	11%	7%	12%	10%
Between £101/$101 and £150/$150	2%	2%	3%	2%	7%	3%	6%	5%
Between £151/$151 and £200/$200	1%	0%	2%	1%	3%	4%	3%	3%
More than £200/$200	1%	1%	2%	1%	3%	3%	2%	3%
Don't know	1%	1%	0%	1%	3%	3%	3%	3%
Mean	£21	£26	£37	£28	$48.82	$44.86	$47.62	$47.04

(Continued)

TABLE A.3 (Continued)

	CHINA			
	18–34	*35–54*	*55+*	*Overall*
¥0—I don't usually carry cash with me	9%	7%	9%	8%
Between ¥1 and ¥25	13%	5%	2%	8%
Between ¥26 and ¥50	12%	12%	6%	12%
Between ¥51 and ¥75	7%	8%	9%	8%
Between ¥76 and ¥100	12%	14%	17%	14%
Between ¥101 and ¥150	6%	8%	8%	7%
Between¥151 and ¥200	8%	7%	9%	8%
Between ¥201 and ¥250	4%	3%	6%	4%
Between ¥251 and ¥300	4%	4%	4%	4%
Between ¥301 and ¥350	4%	3%	8%	4%
Between ¥351 and ¥400	3%	4%	6%	4%
Between ¥401 and ¥500	4%	6%	4%	5%
Between ¥501 and ¥600	4%	6%	4%	5%
Between ¥601 and ¥700	2%	2%	4%	2%
Between ¥701 and ¥800	1%	3%	0%	2%
Between ¥801 and ¥900	1%	3%	4%	2%
Between ¥900 and ¥1000	2%	2%	0%	2%
More than ¥1,000	2%	2%	0%	2%
Don't know	0%	3%	2%	2%
Mean	*¥ 207.26*	*¥ 257.62*	*¥ 216.80*	*¥ 231.02*

Data source: Marion Laboure and Jim Reid, "The Future of Payments Part I. Cash: The Dinosaur Will Survive . . . for Now," Deutsche Bank Research, Corporate Bank Research, 2020, https://www.dbresearch.com/PROD/RPS _EN-PROD/PROD0000000000504353.pdf.

Note: Cash carried in France, Germany, and Italy is denominated in euros, in China in renminbi, in the United states in dollars, and in the UK in sterling.

TABLE A.4   Which of the following, if any, are the main reasons for cash being your most preferred payment method?

	France	Germany	Italy	UK	US	China
Easier to monitor my spending	44%	51%	38%	46%	28%	25%
Faster to pay	40%	44%	41%	37%	43%	18%
Really convenient	41%	34%	44%	56%	37%	20%
Accepted almost everywhere	44%	46%	27%	47%	33%	15%
Secure method of paying	32%	49%	32%	34%	31%	20%
Don't want to give up cash	39%	48%	32%	37%	9%	17%
Purchases remain anonymous	29%	42%	19%	21%	22%	10%
Easier to tip	23%	32%	11%	20%	21%	12%
Avoid cyber attacks on my money	24%	19%	17%	24%	16%	15%
Easier to split a bill if needed	25%	18%	21%	17%	16%	9%
Don't like using plastic cards	10%	10%	18%	8%	10%	12%
Does not impact my credit rating	13%	11%	10%	6%	14%	14%
Can get a discount	7%	8%	13%	5%	7%	15%
Don't know how to use a smartphone	11%	6%	7%	5%	7%	12%
Places I usually go don't take card	5%	4%	8%	5%	6%	12%
Places I usually go don't take electronic payments	6%	4%	6%	6%	4%	17%
None of these	2%	2%	2%	1%	3%	6%

Data source: Marion Laboure and Jim Reid, "The Future of Payments Part I. Cash: The Dinosaur Will Survive . . . for Now," Deutsche Bank Research, Corporate Bank Research, 2020, https://www.dbresearch .com/PROD/RPS_EN-PROD/PROD0000000000504353.pdf.

Note: Cash carried in France, Germany, and Italy is denominated in euros, in China in renminbi, in the United states in dollars, and in the UK in sterling.

TABLE A.5 Demographics of people who prefer plastic cards and digital wallets payment methods

	PLASTIC CARDS (CONTACTLESS & CHIP AND PIN)						DIGITAL WALLETS (SMARTPHONE + WATCH)					
	France	Germany	Italy	UK	US	China	France	Germany	Italy	UK	US	China
Base	76%	33%	58%	62%	53%	16%	4%	7%	9%	8%	13%	50%
Female	73%	34%	58%	64%	55%	16%	3%	7%	7%	9%	11%	51%
Male	78%	31%	59%	61%	50%	16%	4%	7%	10%	6%	16%	47%
18–34	64%	31%	48%	58%	40%	17%	7%	14%	10%	18%	22%	54%
35–54	82%	40%	56%	63%	51%	17%	3%	8%	10%	5%	17%	47%
55+	81%	27%	69%	67%	64%	4%	1%	2%	6%	1%	2%	38%
Rural/Countryside	80%	30%	57%	65%	48%	14%	2%	5%	1%	4%	9%	46%
Suburban	74%	34%	55%	63%	59%	20%	4%	8%	8%	7%	11%	41%
Urban	74%	33%	59%	60%	43%	15%	4%	8%	11%	12%	20%	53%
Up to €20,000	67%	20%	41%				2%	4%	10%			
€20,000 to €29,999	72%	31%	63%				1%	8%	6%			
€30,000 to €39,999	75%	31%	62%				2%	6%	7%			
€40,000 to €49,999	84%	15%	64%				5%	18%	15%			
€50,000 to €69,999	79%	47%	64%				4%	6%	10%			
€70,000 to €99,999	88%	44%	73%				2%	9%	9%			
€100,000+	61%	39%	61%				28%	11%	6%			
Up to £20,000				56%						7%		
£20,000 to £29,999				61%						7%		
£30,000 to £49,999				63%						8%		
£50,000 to £69,999				69%						11%		
£70,000+				71%						6%		
Up to $15,000					27%						18%	
$15,000 to $24,999					48%						12%	
$25,000 to $34,999					48%						14%	
$35,000 to $49,999					48%						14%	
$50,000 to $99,999					58%						12%	

$100,000 to $149,999	71%	10%
$150,000+	61%	16%
Up to ¥119,999	16%	42%
¥120,000 to ¥179,999	15%	48%
¥180,000 to ¥239,999	17%	49%
¥240,000 to ¥299,999	16%	48%
¥300,000 to ¥449,999	13%	72%
¥450,000 to ¥599,999	5%	79%
¥600,000 to ¥999,999	28%	56%
¥1,000,000+	22%	67%

Data source: Marion Laboure and Jim Reid, "The Future of Payments Part II. Moving to Digital Wallets and the Extinction of Plastic Cards," Deutsche Bank Research, Corporate Bank Research, 2020, https://www.dbresearch.com/PROD/RPS_EN-PROD/PROD0000000000504508.pdf.

TABLE A.6   Favorite in-store payment method, by country

	Germany	US	Italy	UK	China	France
Cash	59%	33%	33%	29%	22%	18%
Contactless (with chip and pin) debit/credit card	22%	17%	46%	49%	16%	57%
Chip and pin (not contactless enabled) debit/credit card	10%	36%	12%	13%		19%
Digital Wallet	7%	13%	9%	8%	50%	4%
Check	1%	2%	0%	0%	13%	3%
Prefer dematerialized payments	40%	66%	67%	70%	66%	79%
Prefer cash & check payments	60%	34%	33%	30%	35%	21%

Data source: Marion Laboure and Jim Reid, "The Future of Payments Part II. Moving to Digital Wallets and the Extinction of Plastic Cards," Deutsche Bank Research, Corporate Bank Research, 2020, https://www.dbresearch.com/PROD/RPS_EN-PROD/PROD0000000000504508.pdf.

TABLE A.7   What percentage of these weekly in-store purchases do you pay for using the following methods?

	France	Germany	Italy	UK	US	China
Cash	25	57	43	33	35	23
Contactless debit/credit card	45	20	33	38	16	20
Chip and pin debit/credit card	18	14	14	20	34	
Check	7	1	1	1	2	14
Smartphone digital wallet	3	7	7	7	11	36
Smartwatch digital wallet	2	1	2	1	2	7

Data source: Marion Laboure and Jim Reid, "The Future of Payments Part II. Moving to Digital Wallets and the Extinction of Plastic Cards," Deutsche Bank Research, Corporate Bank Research, 2020, https://www.dbresearch.com/PROD/RPS_EN-PROD/PROD0000000000504508.pdf.

TABLE A.8   In the next six months, are you planning on using the following payment methods more, less, or about the same for small, regular in-store purchases?

	US	Germany	Italy	France	UK	China
Check	−12%	−16%	−33%	−28%	−25%	18%
Cash	11%	8%	−21%	−2%	−10%	16%
Chip and pin debit/credit card	21%	8%	30%	16%	14%	
Contactless debit/credit card	34%	25%	51%	33%	33%	21%
Smartphone digital wallet	33%	25%	32%	33%	29%	47%
Smartwatch digital wallet	23%	4%	14%	28%	20%	28%

Data source: Marion Laboure and Jim Reid, "The Future of Payments Part II. Moving to Digital Wallets and the Extinction of Plastic Cards," Deutsche Bank Research, Corporate Bank Research, 2020, https://www.dbresearch.com/PROD/RPS_EN-PROD/PROD0000000000504508.pdf.

TABLE A.9   Which, if any, of the following are the main reasons for a digital wallet being your most preferred payment method?

	France	Germany	Italy	UK	US	China
Really convenient	43%	55%	54%	51%	44%	43%
Means I have fewer things to carry	52%	27%	27%	47%	25%	28%
Saves time as I don't have to take my wallet out	38%	30%	37%	47%	28%	35%
Digital wallet is free	38%	20%	35%	38%	26%	27%
Don't need to worry about not having money on me	24%	32%	29%	43%	24%	29%
I'm going cashless / don't carry cash with me	24%	23%	23%	45%	28%	18%
Reduces the chances of me being robbed / mugged	38%	18%	23%	19%	21%	18%
Easier to see what I have spent money on	14%	27%	33%	28%	20%	27%
Offers extra security	29%	25%	25%	19%	26%	25%
Easier to manage my budget	38%	16%	21%	17%	23%	27%
Trying to lessen the amount of cards I have	29%	20%	13%	15%	18%	18%
Most places are going cashless	14%	27%	4%	21%	18%	23%
Most digital wallets offer discounts, rewards, and prizes	19%	20%	13%	11%	23%	26%
Helps organize my credit cards	19%	11%	15%	9%	9%	18%
Don't like using plastic cards	14%	18%	8%	6%	11%	12%
None of these	0%	7%	0%	0%	4%	1%

Data source: Marion Laboure and Jim Reid, "The Future of Payments Part II. Moving to Digital Wallets and the Extinction of Plastic Cards," Deutsche Bank Research, Corporate Bank Research, 2020, https://www.dbresearch.com/PROD/RPS_EN-PROD/PROD0000000000504508.pdf.

TABLE A.10 Demographics of people who prefer smartphones and tablet via an app vs. desktop computer or offline to conduct financial transactions

	SMARTPHONE/TABLET VIA AN APP						DESKTOP COMPUTER/OFFLINE					
	France	Germany	Italy	UK	US	China	France	Germany	Italy	UK	US	China
Base	32%	25%	34%	45%	44%	57%	59%	68%	54%	48%	49%	26%
Female	57%	58%	59%	59%	50%	51%	45%	48%	42%	44%	45%	47%
Male	43%	42%	41%	41%	50%	49%	55%	52%	58%	56%	55%	53%
18–34	48%	47%	49%	52%	39%	49%	25%	19%	16%	13%	24%	51%
35–54	42%	39%	37%	35%	39%	41%	29%	35%	40%	35%	28%	41%
55+	11%	14%	15%	13%	21%	10%	46%	45%	44%	52%	48%	8%
Rural/Countryside	27%	24%	17%	16%	15%	6%	28%	18%	14%	24%	15%	3%
Suburban	19%	29%	21%	51%	55%	25%	23%	26%	21%	52%	56%	30%
Urban	53%	47%	62%	33%	30%	68%	49%	57%	65%	24%	29%	67%
Up to €20,000	13%	12%	25%				15%	15%	15%			
€20,000 to €29,999	14%	17%	17%				18%	11%	19%			
€30,000 to €39,999	25%	31%	30%				23%	33%	30%			
€40,000 to €49,999	15%	8%	5%				16%	5%	6%			
€50,000 to €69,999	17%	13%	12%				16%	21%	19%			
€70,000 to €99,999	11%	16%	7%				8%	11%	9%			
€100,000+	4%	3%	4%				3%	3%	3%			
Up to £20,000				18%						23%		
£20,000 to £29,999				36%						29%		
£30,000 to £49,999				29%						24%		
£50,000 to £69,999				12%						12%		
£70,000+				5%						11%		
Up to $15,000					12%						10%	
$15,000 to $24,999					10%						10%	
$25,000 to $34,999					11%						11%	
$35,000 to $49,999					14%						9%	

$50,000 to $99,999	38%	30%
$100,000 to $149,999	7%	14%
$150,000+	9%	16%
Up to ¥119,999	30%	26%
¥120,000 to ¥179,999	22%	30%
¥180,000 to ¥239,999	23%	15%
¥240,000 to ¥299,999	9%	10%
¥300,000 to ¥449,999	6%	7%
¥450,000 to ¥599,999	3%	7%
¥600,000 to ¥999,999	3%	2%
¥1,000,000+	4%	3%

Data source: Marion Laboure and Jim Reid, "The Future of Payments Part II. Moving to Digital Wallets and the Extinction of Plastic Cards," Deutsche Bank Research, Corporate Bank Research. 2020, https://www.dbresearch.com/PROD/RPS_EN-PROD/PROD0000000000504508.pdf.

TABLE A.11   What are the main reasons you are now using your actual active card(s) less than you did 12 months ago?

	China	France	Germany	Italy	UK	US
Using a digital wallet more	38%	26%	21%	22%	18%	15%
Want to have fewer card(s)	22%	24%	24%	17%	12%	28%
I am using cash more	16%	26%	27%	27%	18%	17%
I only had the card(s) for a specific purpose	21%	15%	25%	15%	17%	18%
I was spending to much on my card(s)	17%	20%	15%	17%	18%	22%
Becoming easier for fraudsters to copy cards	20%	12%	14%	21%	11%	16%
Becoming more expensive to use when travelling	18%	16%	14%	12%	11%	9%
The reward programs are no longer appealing	21%	15%	8%	12%	9%	11%
Being charged to use my card(s)	18%	10%	11%	14%	9%	13%
Interest rate on the card increased	17%	10%	11%	12%	8%	15%
Victim of card fraud	15%	7%	7%	14%	11%	11%

Data source: Marion Laboure and Jim Reid, "The Future of Payments Part II. Moving to Digital Wallets and the Extinction of Plastic Cards," Deutsche Bank Research, Corporate Bank Research, 2020, https://www.dbresearch.com/PROD/RPS_EN-PROD/PROD0000000000504508.pdf.

APPENDIX B

Selected data from the Deutsche Bank Research dbDIG proprietary survey of over 3,600 customers.

TABLE B.1 Demography of citizens who prefer cash and dematerialized payment methods

	CASH						DEMATERIALIZED (PLASTIC CARDS+ DIGITAL WALLETS)					
	France	Germany	Italy	UK	US	China	France	Germany	Italy	UK	US	China
Base	18%	59%	33%	29%	33%	22%	79%	40%	67%	70%	66%	66%
Female	19%	58%	35%	27%	33%	16%	76%	41%	65%	73%	66%	67%
Male	16%	60%	31%	32%	32%	28%	83%	39%	69%	67%	66%	63%
18–34	27%	53%	40%	23%	37%	21%	70%	45%	58%	76%	62%	71%
35–54	12%	52%	33%	33%	30%	17%	86%	48%	67%	67%	69%	65%
55+	15%	71%	25%	33%	32%	51%	81%	29%	75%	67%	66%	42%
Rural/Countryside	14%	65%	42%	32%	40%	36%	81%	35%	58%	68%	57%	61%
Suburban	21%	56%	37%	29%	28%	22%	78%	42%	63%	70%	70%	61%
Urban	19%	59%	29%	28%	36%	21%	79%	41%	70%	72%	63%	68%
Up to €20,000	26%	72%	49%				69%	24%	51%			
€20,000 to €29,999	23%	61%	29%				73%	39%	70%			
€30,000 to €39,999	19%	63%	30%				77%	37%	69%			
€40,000 to €49,999	11%	67%	21%				89%	33%	79%			
€50,000 to €69,999	13%	47%	26%				83%	53%	74%			
€70,000 to €99,999	8%	47%	18%				90%	53%	82%			
€100,000+	11%	50%	33%				89%	50%	67%			
Up to £20,000				37%						63%		
£20,000 to £29,999				31%						67%		
£30,000 to £49,999				29%						71%		
£50,000 to £69,999				20%						80%		
£70,000+				23%						77%		
Up to $15,000					54%						45%	
$15,000 to $24,999					38%						60%	
$25,000 to $34,999					37%						62%	

$35,000 to $49,999	36%	62%
$50,000 to $99,999	28%	71%
$100,000 to $149,999	18%	81%
$150,000+	20%	77%
Up to ¥119,999	31%	58%
¥120,000 to ¥179,999	19%	63%
¥180,000 to ¥239,999	17%	66%
¥240,000 to ¥299,999	24%	64%
¥300,000 to ¥449,999	16%	84%
¥450,000 to ¥599,999	16%	84%
¥600,000 to ¥999,999	6%	83%
¥1,000,000+	6%	89%

Data source: Marion Laboure and Jim Reid, "The Future of Payments Part II. Moving to Digital Wallets and the Extinction of Plastic Cards," Deutsche Bank Research, Corporate Bank Research, 2020, https://www.dbresearch.com/PROD/RPS_EN-PROD/PROD0000000000504508.pdf.

TABLE B.2 Demography of citizens who prefer cash and dematerialized payment methods

To what extent do you agree or disagree with the following statements about cryptocurrencies (e.g., Bitcoin, Litecoin)? The following tables are the results for the US, the UK, German, France, and Italy.

	They are easy to purchase				They are good for the overall				They are volatile			
	18–34	35–54	55+	NET	18–34	35–54	55+	NET	18–34	35–54	55+	NET
Strongly agree	18%	13%	12%	14%	15%	8%	5%	10%	19%	25%	38%	27%
Somewhat agree	28%	25%	24%	26%	22%	16%	8%	16%	28%	30%	26%	28%
Neither agree nor disagre	31%	41%	40%	37%	40%	44%	38%	41%	36%	34%	27%	33%
Somewhat disagree	16%	15%	13%	15%	15%	17%	19%	17%	13%	7%	5%	8%
Strongly disagree	6%	6%	12%	8%	8%	14%	31%	17%	4%	4%	4%	4%
% Agree	46%	38%	35%	40%	37%	25%	13%	26%	47%	55%	64%	55%
% Disagree	23%	21%	25%	23%	23%	31%	49%	34%	17%	11%	10%	13%

	It is difficult to sell them				They are completely anonymous				They are unregulated			
	18–34	35–54	55+	NET	18–34	35–54	55+	NET	18–34	35–54	55+	NET
Strongly agree	14%	14%	18%	15%	17%	15%	19%	17%	18%	24%	33%	24%
Somewhat agree	23%	25%	25%	24%	26%	28%	28%	27%	26%	28%	35%	30%
Neither agree nor disagree	37%	43%	44%	41%	36%	41%	37%	38%	35%	35%	24%	32%
Somewhat disagree	17%	12%	8%	13%	15%	12%	9%	12%	14%	9%	5%	9%
Strongly disagree	9%	6%	4%	6%	6%	5%	7%	6%	6%	5%	3%	5%
% Agree	37%	39%	43%	40%	43%	42%	46%	44%	44%	52%	68%	54%
% Disagree	26%	18%	13%	19%	21%	17%	17%	18%	20%	14%	8%	14%

	It is easy to commit fraud using				They are difficult to understand				They are replacing cash			
	18–34	35–54	55+	NET	18–34	35–54	55+	NET	18–34	35–54	55+	NET
Strongly agree	21%	22%	31%	24%	20%	21%	33%	25%	12%	9%	7%	9%
Somewhat agree	29%	30%	30%	30%	30%	32%	34%	32%	22%	19%	13%	18%
Neither agree nor disagre	33%	37%	29%	33%	27%	32%	22%	27%	29%	32%	24%	29%

	18–34	35–54	55+	NET
Somewhat disagree	13%	8%	4%	9%
Strongly disagree	5%	4%	4%	4%
% Agree	50%	51%	62%	54%
% Disagree	18%	12%	9%	13%

They are replacing debit/credit

	18–34	35–54	55+	NET
Strongly agree	12%	9%	5%	9%
Somewhat agree	22%	15%	10%	16%
Neither agree nor disagree	31%	30%	26%	29%
Somewhat disagree	20%	22%	22%	21%
Strongly disagree	15%	23%	37%	25%
% Agree	34%	25%	15%	25%
% Disagree	36%	45%	59%	46%

	18–34	35–54	55+	NET
Somewhat disagree	14%	10%	6%	10%
Strongly disagree	9%	5%	4%	6%
% Agree	50%	53%	67%	57%
% Disagree	23%	15%	10%	16%

I will never invest in them

	18–34	35–54	55+	NET
Strongly agree	21%	27%	50%	33%
Somewhat agree	23%	26%	20%	23%
Neither agree nor disagree	33%	31%	21%	29%
Somewhat disagree	15%	10%	5%	10%
Strongly disagree	8%	6%	3%	5%
% Agree	45%	53%	70%	56%
% Disagree	22%	15%	9%	15%

	18–34	35–54	55+	NET
Somewhat disagree	21%	20%	20%	20%
Strongly disagree	16%	21%	36%	24%
% Agree	34%	28%	20%	27%
% Disagree	37%	41%	56%	44%

They are creating a financial bubble

	18–34	35–54	55+	NET
Strongly agree	13%	16%	25%	18%
Somewhat agree	28%	30%	33%	30%
Neither agree nor disagree	38%	41%	32%	37%
Somewhat disagree	13%	10%	6%	10%
Strongly disagree	7%	4%	4%	5%
% Agree	42%	46%	58%	48%
% Disagree	20%	13%	10%	15%

The following tables are the results for China.

They are easy to purchase

	18–34	35–54	55+	NET
Strongly agree	18%	13%	13%	15%
Somewhat agree	29%	28%	25%	28%
Neither agree nor disagree	30%	37%	38%	35%
Somewhat disagree	16%	16%	13%	15%
Strongly disagree	7%	6%	11%	8%
% Agree	47%	41%	38%	43%
% Disagree	23%	22%	25%	23%

They are good for the overall economy

	18–34	35–54	55+	NET
Strongly agree	16%	10%	6%	11%
Somewhat agree	24%	19%	8%	18%
Neither agree nor disagree	37%	41%	37%	38%
Somewhat disagree	16%	18%	19%	17%
Strongly disagree	8%	13%	30%	15%
% Agree	40%	29%	14%	29%
% Disagree	23%	30%	49%	33%

They are volatile

	18–34	35–54	55+	NET
Strongly agree	18%	23%	37%	25%
Somewhat agree	28%	29%	26%	28%
Neither agree nor disagree	36%	34%	27%	33%
Somewhat disagree	14%	9%	6%	10%
Strongly disagree	5%	5%	4%	4%
% Agree	46%	52%	63%	53%
% Disagree	18%	14%	10%	14%

(Continued)

TABLE B.2 (Continued)

	It is difficult to sell them				They are completely anonymous				They are unregulated			
	18–34	35–54	55+	NET	18–34	35–54	55+	NET	18–34	35–54	55+	NET
Strongly agree	14%	14%	18%	15%	17%	15%	18%	16%	18%	21%	32%	23%
Somewhat agree	25%	24%	26%	25%	26%	26%	28%	27%	28%	28%	35%	30%
Neither agree nor disagree	34%	40%	43%	38%	37%	39%	36%	37%	34%	34%	24%	31%
Somewhat disagree	19%	16%	9%	15%	15%	15%	10%	14%	13%	12%	6%	11%
Strongly disagree	8%	6%	5%	7%	5%	5%	7%	6%	7%	5%	4%	5%
% Agree	39%	38%	43%	40%	43%	41%	47%	43%	46%	49%	67%	53%
% Disagree	28%	22%	13%	22%	20%	20%	17%	20%	20%	17%	9%	16%

	It is easy to commit fraud using them				They are difficult to understand				They are replacing cash			
	18–34	35–54	55+	NET	18–34	35–54	55+	NET	18–34	35–54	55+	NET
Strongly agree	20%	20%	30%	22%	19%	20%	32%	23%	14%	10%	7%	11%
Somewhat agree	31%	29%	30%	30%	29%	30%	33%	31%	24%	20%	14%	20%
Neither agree nor disagree	30%	36%	30%	32%	27%	32%	23%	28%	29%	32%	23%	29%
Somewhat disagree	13%	10%	5%	10%	15%	12%	7%	12%	19%	19%	20%	20%
Strongly disagree	5%	5%	4%	5%	9%	6%	4%	7%	14%	18%	36%	21%
% Agree	51%	49%	61%	53%	48%	50%	65%	54%	38%	31%	21%	30%
% Disagree	19%	15%	10%	15%	25%	18%	11%	19%	34%	37%	56%	41%

	They are replacing debit/credit cards				I will never invest in them				They are creating a financial bubble			
	18–34	35–54	55+	NET	18–34	35–54	55+	NET	18–34	35–54	55+	NET
Strongly agree	13%	10%	5%	10%	19%	24%	48%	29%	14%	16%	24%	17%
Somewhat agree	24%	19%	11%	19%	25%	25%	21%	24%	30%	30%	34%	31%
Neither agree nor disagree	30%	31%	26%	29%	33%	31%	21%	29%	37%	39%	32%	37%
Somewhat disagree	19%	21%	22%	21%	15%	12%	6%	12%	13%	11%	6%	10%
Strongly disagree	13%	19%	36%	21%	9%	7%	3%	6%	6%	4%	4%	5%
% Agree	37%	29%	16%	28%	43%	50%	69%	53%	43%	46%	57%	48%
% Disagree	32%	41%	58%	42%	24%	19%	10%	18%	20%	15%	10%	15%

Data source: Marion Laboure and Jim Reid, "The Future of Payments Part III. Digital Currencies: The Ultimate Hard Power Tool," Deutsche Bank Research, Corporate Bank Research, 2020, https://www.dbresearch.com/PROD/RPS_EN-PROD/PROD0000000000504589.pdf.

TABLE B.3   Demography of citizens who have personally bought or sold cryptocurrency in the last 12 months

	18–34	35–54	55+	Overall
China	29%	26%	8%	26%
Italy	14%	6%	1%	7%
France	14%	5%	1%	6%
Germany	12%	6%	4%	7%
US	11%	9%	0%	7%
UK	8%	4%	1%	4%

Data source: Marion Laboure and Jim Reid, "The Future of Payments Part III. Digital Currencies: The Ultimate Hard Power Tool," Deutsche Bank Research, Corporate Bank Research, 2020, https://www.dbresearch.com /PROD/RPS_EN-PROD/PROD0000000000504589.pdf.

Notes

Introduction

1. Mergermarket, mergermarket.com.
2. Although scaling back risks can lead to lower returns, a reduction in profits does not automatically mean there has been a corresponding reduction in financial services firms' activity, such as when loans have increased over the period. Thomas Philippon, "On the Theory and Measurement of Financial Intermediation," *American Economic Review* 105, no. 4 (April 2015): 1408–1438.
3. Mergermarket, mergermarket.com.
4. It is worth noting that there are important variations between countries. In developing markets—in India, for example—financial inclusion has been dramatically improving.
5. Thomas Piketty, *Capital and Ideology* (Cambridge, MA: Harvard University Press, 2020).
6. Anthony Atkinson, Thomas Piketty, and Emmanuel Saez, "Top Incomes in the Long Run of History," *Journal of Economic Literature* 49, no. 1 (2011): 3–71.
7. World Bank, "Financial Inclusion," October 2, 2018, https://www.worldbank.org /en/topic/financialinclusion/overview.

1. Millennials—The Subprime Generation?

1. Marion Laboure and Juergen Braunstein, "The Great Stagnation," *Global Policy* opinion, October 11, 2016, https://www.globalpolicyjournal.com/blog/11/10 /2016/great-stagnation.
2. Richard Dobbs et al., "Poorer than Their Parents? Flat or Falling Incomes in Advanced Economies," McKinsey Global Institute, July 13, 2016, https://www .mckinsey.com/featured-insights/employment-and-growth/poorer-than-their -parents-a-new-perspective-on-income-inequality.
3. According to Harvard economists Carmen Reinhardt and Kenneth Rogoff, public debt greater than 90 percent of GDP could hinder future economic growth in advanced economies and is thus of primary policy concern. Higher debt could slow growth through various channels, including rising interest rates, lower

public investment, and confidence crises. Carmen Reinhardt and Kenneth Rogoff, "Growth in a Time of Debt," *American Economic Review, Papers & Proceedings* 100 (2010): 573–578.

4. Robert J. Shiller, *Irrational Exuberance* (Princeton: Princeton University Press, 2000).

5. Shiller, *Irrational Exuberance.*

6. According to this survey, the most expensive cities have become even less affordable in recent years. The survey used the median multiple (median house price divided by median household income) to compare observations in cities globally. Demographia, "Demographia International Housing Affordability Survey: 2021," http://demographia.com/dhi.pdf.

7. According to Realtors.com, the average age for first-time buyers is thirty-two in the United States. The average household income of first-time buyers $75,000. The average home purchased by this group cost $190,000. These buyers usually offered a 5 percent down payment. National Association of Realtors, "2019 Profile of Home Buyers and Sellers," https://www.nar.realtor/infographics/2019 -profile-of-home-buyers-sellers; National Association of Realtors, "Student Loan Debt and Housing Report 2017," https://www.nar.realtor/student-loan-debt.

8. Ministry of Housing, "Communities & Local Government, English Housing Survey, First-Time Buyers," https://assets.publishing.service.gov.uk/government /uploads/system/uploads/attachment_data/file/945013/2019-20_EHS_Headline _Report.pdf.

9. Dollar amounts have not been adjusted for inflation. However, tuition and fees at four-year national universities are significantly outpacing inflation. The total consumer price index inflation increased by 52.7 percent from August 1997 to August 2017, according to the US Bureau of Labor Statistics. Briana Boyington, "See 20 Years of Tuition Growth at National Universities," *U.S. News & World Report,* September 13, 2018.

10. The perimeter of some definitions is larger, including additional forms of employment—even a couple of hours—whereas other definitions are more restrictive. McKinsey research reveals that 20 to 30 percent of the working-age population in the United States and the EU-15, or up to 162 million individuals, engage in independent work. James Manyika et al., "Independent Work: Choice, Necessity, and the Gig Economy: Executive Summary," McKinsey Global Institute, October 2016, https://www.mckinsey.com/~/media/McKinsey /Featured%20Insights/Employment%20and%20Growth/Independent%20 work%20Choice%20necessity%20and%20the%20gig%20economy/Independent -Work-Choice-necessity-and-the-gig-economy-Executive-Summary.ashx.

11. Richard L. Hills, "William Lee and His Knitting Machine," *Journal of the Textile Institute* 80, no. 2 (1989): 169–184.

12. Karl Marx, *Capital: A Critique of Political Economy,* vol. 3: *The Process of Capitalist Production as a Whole,* ed. Frederick Engels, trans. of first German edition, 1894, by Ernest Untermann (Chicago: Charles H. Kerr, 1909). Karl Marx, *Grundrisse: Foundations of the Critique of Political Economy (Rough Draft)* (1858; orig. pub. 1939), trans. Martin Nicolaus (New York: Penguin, 1973; repr. 1993); James Sacra Albus, *Peoples' Capitalism: The Economics of the Robot Revolution* (Ken-

sington, MD: New World Books, 1976); Jeremy Rifkin, *The End of Work: The Decline of the Global Labor Force and the Dawn of the Post-Market Era* (New York: Putnam, 1995).

13. Berthold Herrendorf, Richard Rogerson, and Ákos Valentinyi, "Growth and Structural Transformation," in *Handbook of Economic Growth*, vol. 2, ed. Philippe Aghion and Steven N. Durlauf, 855–941 (Amsterdam: Elsevier, 2014); Benjamin N. Dennis and Talan B. İşcan, "Engel versus Baumol: Accounting for Structural Change Using Two Centuries of US Data," *Explorations in Economic History* 46, no. 2 (April 2009).

14. Daron Acemoglu and Pascual Restrepo, "Robots and Jobs: Evidence from US Labor Markets," NBER Working Paper 23285, National Bureau of Economic Research, Cambridge, MA, March 2017.

15. However, the minicomputers released in the 1960s could already be considered personal computers, as was the first Olivetti Programma 101 desktop computer marketed in 1965.

16. Customer service call centers barely existed before personal computers.

17. Perhaps not, but with the assistance of AI, tasks that might have taken two or three assistants in the past will take only one. There are already apps that can help with advice, mood, etc. These are rudimentary, for sure, but we are still in early days.

18. Daron Acemoglu and David Autor, "Skills, Tasks, and Technologies: Implications for Employment and Earnings," in *Handbook of Labor Economics*, vol. 4B, ed. David Card and Orley Ashenfelter, 1043–1171 (Amsterdam: Elsevier, 2011).

19. United Nations, Department of Economic and Social Affairs, Population Division, "World Population Ageing 2017—Highlights," 2017, https://www.un.org/en/development/desa/population/publications/pdf/ageing/WPA2017_Highlights.pdf.

20. The researchers say that there is a higher likelihood of automation for jobs that rely on "predictable physical activities"—such as food preparation, data processing, and data collection.

21. Federal Deposit Insurance Corporation, "How America Banks: Household Use of Banking and Financial Services," 2019 FDIC Survey, October 19, 2020, https://www.fdic.gov/analysis/household-survey/2019report.pdf.

22. Financially excluded persons are those who are currently not able or willing to fully participate in the banking services offered in their country. MasterCard, "The Road to Inclusion: MasterCard Financial Inclusion Survey, Key Learnings Report," December 5, 2016, https://newsroom.mastercard.com/wp-content/uploads/2016/12/Road-to-Inclusion_Mastercard-Financial-Inclusion-Survey-2016.pdf.

2. Banking in the Digital Era

1. For example, Daniela Gabor and Sally Brooks examine the importance of digital-based financial inclusion. They demonstrate that the "digital revolution adds new layers to the material cultures of financial(ised) inclusion, offering the state new ways of expanding the inclusion of the 'legible' and global finance new

forms of 'profiling' poor households into generators of financial assets." Daniela Gabor and Sally Brooks, "The Digital Revolution in Financial Inclusion: International Development in the Fintech Era," *New Political Economy* 22, no. 4 (2017): 423–436.

2. Arvind Krishnamurthy, "How Debt Markets Have Malfunctioned in the Crisis," *Journal of Economic Perspectives* 24, no. 1 (2010): 3–28. Markus K. Brunnermeier, "Deciphering the Liquidity and Credit Crunch 2007–2008," *Journal of Economic Perspectives* 23, no. 1 (2009): 77–100. Gary Gorton, *Slapped by the Invisible Hand* (Oxford: Oxford University Press, 2010). Mervyn King's reformed proposal centers around a new form of constraint for banks. It aims to force banks to insure the liquidity risks with central banks when they issue short-term liabilities. The central banks would then determine the "price" of this insurance by setting haircuts for all the bank's assets. In turn, the central bank would stand ready to provide liquidity by using the bank's assets as collateral. Mervyn King, *The End of Alchemy: Money, Banking and the Future of the Global Economy* (New York: W. W. Norton, 2016).

3. Tencent and other Chinese firms have massive centralized platforms that give them an edge in AI research and development by allowing them to collect huge stores of data that can be used to train machine-learning algorithms. Moreover, Chinese firms benefit from Chinese culture, which values privacy less.

4. The National Development and Reform Commission requires private enterprises to invest in overseas deals that are genuine and not meant to be used for transferring assets abroad or for money laundering. Private firms are required to report investment plans to the government, and to seek approval if the investments involve sensitive countries or industries. Investment in projects that fit within the scope of the One Belt One Road endeavor is strongly encouraged.

5. Juergen Braunstein, Marion Laboure, and Clara Volintiru, "Will Digital Currencies Become the Next (Broadly Accepted) Currencies?," *Global Policy*, January 25, 2018, https://www.globalpolicyjournal.com/blog/25/01/2018/will -digital-currencies-become-next-broadly-accepted-currencies.

6. Marion Laboure, Haiyang Zhang, and Juergen Braunstein, "The Rise of Silicon China," *Project Syndicate,* April 3, 3018, https://www.project-syndicate.org /commentary/china-artificial-intelligence-research-development-by-marion -laboure-1-et-al-2018-04?barrier=accesspaylog.

7. Alt, Beck, and Smits showed that businesses are experiencing three levels of transformation: (1) Internal: Fintech drives businesses to change focus from internal processes toward a customer-centric perspective; (2) Business Network: Businesses in the fintech era become more networked with specialized external partners while competition intensifies with lower margins; (3) External: "Regulation shifts away from low-equity requirements, low levels of supervision, and high protection from national legislation toward stricter rules for held equity, more supervision on an international level, and less protection offered by national laws." R. Alt, R. Beck, and M. T. Smits, "FinTech and the Transformation of the Financial Industry," *Electron Markets* 28 (2018): 235–243.

8. KPMG, "Digital Payments—Analyzing the Cyber Landscape," April 2017, https://assets.kpmg/content/dam/kpmg/in/pdf/2017/04/Digital_payments _Analysing_the_cyber_landscape.pdf.

9. Citigroup, "Digital Disruption Revisited: What Fintech VC Investments Tells Us about a Changing Industry," January 2017, https://ir.citi.com/FIanoC50Aw5 dWM7kPzoLKU3buhKF1LETHM1deMYw1%2F2zNzWFg8zmYw%3 D%3D.

10. Rob Walker, "The Trivialities and Transcendence of Kickstarter," *New York Times,* August 7, 2011; Harry McKracken, "Kickstarter," *Time,* August 16, 2011; Steven Snyder, "Kickstarter," *Time,* November 11, 2010.

11. Kickstarter, Kickstarter Official Stats, https://www.kickstarter.com/help/stats.

12. Murray Newlands, "Why CommonBond Will Make You Forget Everything You Thought You Knew about Student Loans," *Forbes,* November 4, 2015.

13. Lending Club, "Why Lending Club?," 2018, https://www.lendingclub.com /investing/alternative-assets/why-lending-club.

14. Peter Gomber and his colleagues showed that (1) "it will be difficult for larger incumbent firms to match small entrepreneurial start-up firms at producing value-creating fintech applications with high innovation, without major spending to acquire knowledgeable human capital that is in such short supply in the market place"; and that (2) "the fintech sector is likely to experience significant adjustment and evolution a time passes and it matures into a typical industry sector." Peter Gomber et al., "On the Fintech Revolution: Interpreting the Forces of Innovation, Disruption, and Transformation in Financial Services," *Journal of Management Information Systems* 35 (2018): 220–265.

15. Brett King, *Bank 4.0: Banking Everywhere, Never at a Bank* (Singapore: Marshall Cavendish Business, 2018).

16. Alex Tapscott and Don Tapscott, "How Blockchain Is Changing Finance," *Harvard Business Review,* March 3, 2017, https://hbr.org/2017/03/how -blockchain-is-changing-finance.

3. The Emergence of Robo-Advisors

1. Kathleen Shaputis, *The Crowded Nest Syndrome: Surviving the Return of Adult Children* (Olympia, WA: Clutter Fairy, 2003).

2. International Monetary Fund, "The Challenge of Public Pension Reform in Advanced and Emerging Economies," December 28, 2011, https://www.imf.org /external/np/pp/eng/2011/122811.pdf.

3. Seth D. Harris and Alan B. Krueger, "A Proposal for Modernizing Labor Laws for Twenty-First Century Work: The 'Independent Worker,'" The Hamilton Project, December 7, 2015, https://www.hamiltonproject.org/papers/modernizing _labor_laws_for_twenty_first_century_work_independent_worker; Seth D. Harris, "Workers, Protections, and Benefits in the U.S. Gig Economy," *Global Law Review* 1, no. 17 (July 12, 2018).

4. For independent contractors, companies are not responsible for health care, unemployment insurance benefits, workers' compensation, overtime, or minimum wages. This also means that workers are on the hook for both the employer and the employee share of Social Security and Medicare taxes.

5. Marco della Cava, "Uber to Offer Drivers Retirement Plan Help," *USA Today,* August 24, 2016; Betterment, "Understanding Betterment for Business 401(k)

Accounts," 2018, https://www.betterment.com/resources/understanding
-betterment-for-business-401k-accounts/.

6. Claudia Goldin and Lawrence F. Katz, *The Race between Education and Technology* (Cambridge, MA: Harvard University Press, 2010).

7. Goldin and Katz, *The Race.*

8. Emmie Martin, "Here's How Much More Expensive It Is for You to Go to College than It Was for Your Parents," CNBC, November 29, 2017, https://www .cnbc.com/2017/11/29/how-much-college-tuition-has-increased-from-1988-to -2018.html.

9. Phil Izzo, "Congratulations to Class of 2014, Most Indebted Ever," *Wall Street Journal,* May 16, 2014, https://blogs.wsj.com/numbers/congatulations-to-class-of -2014-the-most-indebted-ever-1368/.

10. As we explained in Chapter 2, three main factors drive long-term economic growth: accumulation of capital stock, increases in labor inputs (such as workers or the number of hours worked), and technological advancement. Theoretically and empirically, economists have shown that technological progress is the main driver of long-run economic growth. This is explained by the concept of diminishing returns and can be traced back to the concerns of early economists such as Johann Heinrich von Thünen, Jacques Turgot, Adam Smith (*The Wealth of Nations*), James Steuart, Thomas Robert Malthus, and David Ricardo. The law of returns stipulates that, holding other input factors constant, the additional output obtained by adding one extra input unit of capital or labor will eventually decline. As a result, a country cannot maintain its long-run growth simply by accumulating more capital or labor. This means that technological progress is the main driver of long-run growth.

11. The few key determinants of private savings include disposable income, growth of income, stage of life, uncertainty about the future, public policies, availability of credit, and the interest rate level. Countries that saw strong economic growth over the last few decades are now seeing an even faster increase in income than in spending. It is time for people to readjust their expectations of future income and adapt their consumption patterns. Consequently, these countries are seeing high levels of net household savings. China, for instance, has net household savings of 37 percent of total household disposable income. On the other end of the spectrum, Greece, which has faced economic difficulties since 2008, is suffering from dissaving (spending more than earnings) estimated at 16 percent of disposable income in 2016, according to the OECD. Not surprisingly, countries that experienced a recent crisis (such as Greece, Italy, Portugal, or Spain) have a level of private savings close to or below 0 percent.

12. Private savings, also referred to as net household savings, are defined by the OECD as "the subtraction of household consumption expenditure from household disposable income, plus the change in net equity of households in pension funds." This definition seems odd because it excludes the change in net equity in stocks and bonds outside of pension funds, and in housing. In other words, this corresponds to gross disposable income, which has not been spent. Dimitris Christelis, Michael Ehrmann, and Dimitris Georgarakos, "Exploring

Differences in Household Debt across Euro Area Countries and the United States," Bank of Canada, 2015, https://www.bankofcanada.ca/wp-content /uploads/2015/05/wp2015-16.pdf.

13. Bank of America, "2018 Better Money Habits Millennial Report," Winter 2018, https://bettermoneyhabits.bankofamerica.com/content/dam/bmh/pdf/ar6vnln9 -boa-bmh-millennial-report-winter-2018-final2.pdf.

14. Bank of America, "2018 Better Money Habits."

15. Fisch and her colleagues emphasize that many people lack basic financial literacy and thus are more prone to make poor financial decisions. Mitchell and Lusardi emphasize that the safest bet in that specific context is to let professional advisors manage the money. Jill Fisch, Tess Wilkinson-Ryan, and Kristin Firth, "The Knowledge Gap in Workplace Retirement Investing and the Role of Professional Advisors," *Duke Law Journal* 66, no. 3 (2016): 633–672; Olivia S. Mitchell and Annamaria Lusardi, *Financial Literacy: Implications for Retirement Security and the Financial Marketplace* (Oxford: Oxford University Press, 2011).

16. Statista, "Development of Assets of Global Exchange Traded Funds (ETFs) from 2003 to 2020," accessed February 18, 2021, https://www.statista.com/statistics /224579/worldwide-etf-assets-under-management-since-1997/.

17. According to S&P Dow Jones Indices and SPIVA® US Scorecard, "84.23 percent of large-cap managers, 85.06 percent of mid-cap managers, and 91.17 percent of small-cap managers lagged behind their respective benchmarks." S&P Dow Jones Indices, "SPIVA U.S. Scorecard," 2018, https://www.spglobal.com/spdji/en /documents/spiva/spiva-us-year-end-2018.pdf.

18. Jill Fisch, Marion Laboure, and John Turner, "The Emergence of the Robo-Advisor," in *The Disruptive Impact of Fintech on Retirement Systems,* ed. Julie Agnew and Olivia S. Mitchell (Oxford: Oxford University Press, 2019).

19. Thomas Philippon, "On Fintech and Financial Inclusion," NBER Working Paper No. 26330, September 2019, http://www.nber.org/papers/w26330; Robert Bartlett et al., "Consumer-Lending Discrimination in the FinTech Era," NBER Working Paper No. 25943, June 2019, https://www.nber.org/papers/w25943; Isil Erel and Jack Liebersohn, "Does FinTech Substitute for Banks? Evidence from the Paycheck Protection Program," NBER Working Paper No. 27659, August 2020, http://www.nber.org/papers/w27659.pdf; Bruce Carlin, Arna Olafsson, and Michaela Pagel, "FinTech Adoption across Generations: Financial Fitness in the Information Age," NBER Working Paper No. 23798, September 2017, https://www.nber.org/papers/w23798.

20. Organisation for Economic Cooperation and Development (OECD), "Technology and Pensions: The Potential for FinTech to Transform the Way Pensions Operate and How Governments Are Supporting Its Development," 2017, http://www.oecd.org/pensions/Technology-and-Pensions-2017.pdf.

21. Wealthfront, "How Does Tax-Loss Harvesting Relate to Rebalancing?," June 18, 2018, https://support.wealthfront.com/hc/en-us/articles/209348586-How-does -tax-loss-harvesting-relate-to-rebalancing. TIAA Institute investigated the use of online plans in Jonathan Reuter and David Richardson, "New Evidence on the Demand for Advice within Retirement Plans," *Trends and Issues,* April 2017,

https://origin-www.tiaainstitute.org/sites/default/files/presentations/2017-12
/TIAA%20Institute_Reuter_New%20Evidence%20Demand%20for%20Advice
_T%26I_April%202017.pdf.

22. Government Accountability Office, "401(k) Plans: Improved Regulation Could Better Protect Participants from Conflicts of Interest," January 28, 2011, http://www.gao.gov/products/GAO-11-119.

23. Ernst & Young, "Global FinTech Adoption Index 2019," https://www.ey.com/en _om/ey-global-fintech-adoption-index.

24. Larry Ludwig, "The Rise of the Robo-Advisors: Should You Use One?," Investor Junkie, March 13, 2018, https://investorjunkie.com/35919/robo-advisors/.

25. Jill Fisch, Marion Laboure, and John Turner, "The Emergence of the Robo-Advisor," in *The Disruptive Impact of Fintech on Retirement Systems*, ed. Julie Agnew and Olivia S. Mitchell (Oxford: Oxford University Press, 2019).

26. This may also be true for human advisors to some extent.

27. Michael Kitces, "Adopting a Two-Dimensional Risk Tolerance Assessment Process," Kitces blog, January 25, 2017, https://www.kitces.com/blog/tolerisk-aligning-risk -tolerance-and-risk-capacity-on-two-dimensions/?utm_source=Nerd%E2%80%9 9s+Eye+View+%7C+Kitces.com&utm_campaign=ec884c7469-NEV_MAILCHIMP _LIST&utm_medium=email&utm_term=0_4c81298299-ec884c7469-57149837.

28. Oisin Breen, "The New Class of Robos Lay Siege to 'Antiquated' Target-Date-Funds (TDF) Market," RIABiz, October 7, 2019, https://riabiz.com/a/2019/10/8 /new-class-of-robos-lay-siege-to-antiquated-target-date-funds-tdf-market-even -defender-of-the-401k-citadel-vanguard-sees-handwriting-on-the-wall.

29. Anthony Atkinson, Thomas Piketty, and Emmanuel Saez, "Top Incomes in the Long Run of History," *Journal of Economic Literature* 49, no. 1 (2011): 3–71; Thomas Piketty, *Capital in the Twenty-First Century* (Cambridge, MA: Harvard University Press, 2014).

30. International Monetary Fund, "IMF Annual Report 2017: Promoting Inclusive Growth," 2017, https://www.imf.org/external/pubs/ft/ar/2017/eng/pdfs/IMF -AR17-English.pdf.

31. Jesse Bricker et al., "Changes in US Family Finances from 2010–2013: Evidence from the Survey of Consumer Finances," *Federal Reserve Bulletin* 100, no. 4 (2014): 1–41, https://www.federalreserve.gov/pubs/bulletin/2014/pdf/scf14.pdf.

32. James Choi, David Laibson, and Brigitte Madrian, "Why Does the Law of One Price Fail: An Experiment on Index Mutual Funds," *Review of Financial Studies* 23, no. 4 (2010): 1405–1432; Justine S. Hastings, Olivia S. Mitchell, and Eric T. Chyn, "Fees, Framing, and Financial Literacy in the Choice of Pension Manager," Pension Research Council WP2010-09, November 26, 2011, https://ssrn .com/abstract=1678077.

33. Sandro Ambuehl, B. Douglas Bernheim, and Annamaria Lusardi, "The Effect of Financial Education on the Quality of Decision Making," Global Financial Literacy Excellence Center, Working Paper 2015-4, 2015, https://gflec.org/wp -content/uploads/2016/08/WP-2015-4-The-Effect-of-Financial-Education-on -the-Quality-of-Decision-Making.pdf?x37611.

34. Michael Kitces, "How 'Robo' Technology Tools Are Causing Fee Deflation but Not Fee Compression," 2018, https://www.kitces.com/blog/fee-compression-fee

-deflation-robo-advisor-cost-savings-productivity-efficiency/?utm_source=Nerd
%E2%80%99s+Eye+View+%7C+Kitces.com&utm_campaign=7267c0cd54-NEV
_MAILCHIMP_LIST&utm_medium=email&utm_term=0_4c81298299
-7267c0cd54-57149837.

35. Alicia H. Munnell, Jean-Pierre Aubrey, and Caroline V. Crawford, "Investment
     Returns: Defined Benefit vs. Defined Contribution Plans," Center for Retirement
     Research, December 2015, http://crr.bc.edu/wp-content/uploads/2015/12/IB_15
     -21.pdf.
36. US Department of Labor, Employee Benefits Security Administration, "A Look
     at 401(k) Plan Fees," 2016, http://www.dol.gov/ebsa/publications/401k_employee
     .html.
37. Juergen Braunstein and Marion Laboure, "Democratizing Finance: The Digital
     Wealth Management Revolution," VOX CEPR Policy Portal, 2017, https://voxeu
     .org/article/digital-wealth-management-revolution.
38. Braunstein and Laboure, "Democratizing Finance."
39. Nathaniel Lee "Why Robo-Advisors Are Striving toward a 'Hybrid Model,' as
     the Industry Passes the $460 Billion Mark," CNBC.com, April 12, 2021,
     https://www.cnbc.com/2021/04/12/why-robo-advisors-may-never-replace
     -human-financial-advisors.html.

4. The Digitalization of Public Services

1. Republic of Estonia, "The New Digital Nation," https://e-resident.gov.ee.
2. Sten Tamkivi, "Lessons from the World's Most Tech-Savvy Government,"
    Atlantic, January 24, 2014, https://www.theatlantic.com/international/archive
    /2014/01/lessons-from-the-worlds-most-tech-savvy-government/283341/.
3. The value-added tax, or VAT, is also known in some countries as a goods and
    services tax (GST).
4. The number of cryptocurrency users has been estimated by Garrick Hileman and
    Michel Rauchs in "Global Cryptocurrency Benchmarking Study," Cambridge Centre
    for Alternative Finance, 2017. https://www.jbs.cam.ac.uk/wp-content/uploads
    /2020/08/2017-04-20-global-cryptocurrency-benchmarking-study.pdf.
5. International Monetary Fund, "Public Finance Goes Digital," March 2018,
    http://www.imf.org/externa l/pubs/ft/fandd/2018/03/pdf/gupta.pdf.
6. In terms like "e-administration" and "e-government," the prefix *e-* means
    "electronic."
7. Like banks, governments could automate processes. Banks have enhanced many
    customer-facing, front-end operations with digital solutions. Online banking,
    for example, offers consumers enormous convenience, and the rise of mobile
    payments is slowly eliminating the need for cash. More information on Pay By
    Plate MA in Boston can be found at Commonwealth of Massachusetts, Depart-
    ment of Transportation, https://www.ezdrivema.com/paybyplatema.
8. United Nations, "E-Government Survey 2020," 2021, https://publicadministration
    .un.org/egovkb/Portals/egovkb/Documents/un/2020-Survey/2020%20UN%20E
    -Government%20Survey%20(Full%20Report).pdf. Mathematically, the index
    EGDI is a weighted average of three normalized scores on three of the most

important dimensions of e-government: scope and quality of online services, development status of telecommunications infrastructure, and inherent human capital.

9. Emirates 24/7, "Sheikh Mohammed Directs Government Departments to Place Dubai 10 Years Ahead of All Other Cities," February 15, 2017, https://www.emirates247.com/news/government/sheikh-mohammed-directs-government-departments-to-place-dubai-10-years-ahead-of-all-other-cities-2017-02-15-1.648147.

10. Jamye Harrison and Amos Cheong, "Commentary: Singapore's New Headache of Fewer Public Transport Commuters," October 21, 2020, https://www.channelnewsasia.com/news/commentary/public-transport-mrt-bus-capacity-breakdown-covid-car-share-13329340.

11. Satoshi Nakamoto invented the blockchain in 2008 as a public transaction ledger for the cryptocurrency Bitcoin. Whereas commercial banks typically charge fees for transactions and services, blockchain technology is relatively cheaper. Blockchain could address current issues and help low- and middle-income individuals engage in more transactions. Satoshi Nakamoto, "Bitcoin: A Peer-to-Peer Electronic Cash System," https://bitcoin.org/bitcoin.pdf.

12. Tapscott and Tapscott (2016) describe various applications of blockchain technology. Blockchain has the potential to "record virtually everything of value to humankind, from birth and death certificates to insurance claims, land titles, and even votes." Quoted from Amazon.com, description of Don Tapscott and Alex Tapscott, *Blockchain Revolution: How the Technology behind Bitcoin Is Changing Money, Business, and the World* (New York: Penguin Random House, 2016), https://www.amazon.co.uk/Blockchain-Revolution-Technology-Changing-Business/dp/1101980133.

13. Some governments may be reluctant to adopt blockchain. In contrast to the decentralized nature of blockchain, a centrally controlled platform also offers benefits. According to Mattila (2016), most firms realize that a single or centralized platform is "undoubtedly" easier to construct and popularize. However, firms are often scared of decentralized platforms because they are inherently hard to control. In this case, companies may opt to create their own platforms despite the drawbacks of having suboptimal performance. Juri Mattila, "The Blockchain Phenomenon—The Disruptive Potential of Distributed Consensus Architectures," ETLA Working Papers 38, The Research Institute of the Finnish Economy, 2016, https://ideas.repec.org/p/rif/wpaper/38.html.

14. International Monetary Fund, "Money, Transformed: The Future of Currency in a Digital World," *Finance and Development,* June 2018, https://www.imf.org/external/pubs/ft/fandd/2018/06/pdf/fd0618.pdf.

15. The Conversation, "Why a Blockchain Startup Called Govcoin Wants to 'Disrupt' the UK's Welfare State," November 27, 2017, https://theconversation.com/why-a-blockchain-startup-called-govcoin-wants-to-disrupt-the-uks-welfare-state-88176.

16. Suparna Dutt D'Cunha, "Dubai Sets Its Sights on Becoming the World's First Blockchain-Powered Government," *Forbes,* December 18, 2017, https://www.forbes.com/sites/suparnadutt/2017/12/18/dubai-sets-sights-on-becoming-the-worlds-first-blockchain-powered-government/#13705c90454b.

17. Aaron Smith, "Shared, Collaborative and On Demand: The New Digital Economy," Pew Research Center, May 2016, https://www.pewresearch.org /internet/2016/05/19/the-new-digital-economy/.
18. Typically, high-net-worth individuals are defined as holding financial assets (excluding their primary residence) with a value greater than $1 million. Wealthy individuals pay, on average, lower taxes because they can optimize and benefit from more favorable treatment. Moreover, not all countries have taxes on non-inventory assets; there are significant variations among those countries that do. The tax on financial gains may be lower in some countries than the tax on work income. Low taxation on capital is usually justified as a measure to incentivize investments. However, because the capital gains mostly come from the wealthiest individuals, this can contribute to an increased gap between the top income earners and the rest of the population.
19. IMF, "Corruption, Taxes and Compliance," IMF Working Paper WP/17/255, 2017, https://www.imf.org/~/media/Files/Publications/WP/2017/wp17255.ashx.
20. The International Criminal Police Organization, more commonly known as Interpol, is an international organization that facilitates international police cooperation among 194 countries (as of 2021).
21. OECD, "Statement on a Two-Pillar Solution to Address the Tax Challenges Arising from the Digitalisation of the Economy," 2021, https://www.oecd.org /tax/beps/statement-on-a-two-pillar-solution-to-address-the-tax-challenges -arising-from-the-digitalisation-of-the-economy-july-2021.pdf.
22. Small, open economies such as Luxembourg, Ireland, and the Cayman Islands are particularly favored for their tax allegiance toward multinationals and wealthy individuals. Ireland and Luxembourg benefit from attractive corporate tax business models. Once a company has set up its headquarters in one of the EU countries, this company can access the whole EU market. To compensate for the EU's rules on digital products in 2015, the Luxembourg standard VAT rose from 15 percent to 17 percent on January 1, 2015. The reduced VAT rates also rose from 12 percent to 14 percent, and from 6 percent to 8 percent, respectively. The third reduced VAT rate of 3 percent remained unchanged. Luxembourg's prime minister, Xavier Bettel, announced that the measure would help raise €350 million. For more details, refer to: European Union, "Directives," *Journal Officiel de l'Union Européenne* (February 20, 2008), http://eurlex.europa.eu/LexUriServ /LexUriServ.do?uri=OJ:L:2008:044:0011:0022:FR:PDF.

5. A Macroeconomic View of Growth, Inequality, and Financial Exclusion

1. The share of employees in manufacturing relative to total employment has steadily declined since the 1960s. Employment growth in industries such as construction, finance, insurance, real estate, and service industries have played a significant role in reducing manufacturing's overall share of US employment.
2. Homi Kharas, "The Unprecedented Expansion of the Global Middle Class," Global Economy and Development at Brookings Working Papers 100, 2017, https://www.brookings.edu/wp-content/uploads/2017/02/global_20170228 _global-middle-class.pdf.

3. Diego Alejo Vázquez Pimentel et al., "Reward Work, Not Wealth," Oxfam International, January 2018, https://www-cdn.oxfam.org/s3fs-public/file _attachments/bp-reward-work-not-wealth-220118-en.pdf.

4. Mara Hvistendahl, "While Emerging Economies Boom, Equality Goes Bust," *Science* 23, no. 344 (2014): 832–835.

5. For more details on the distinguishing constraints on financial inclusion and their impacts on GDP, TFP, and inequality, see: Era Dabla-Norris et al., "Causes and Consequences of Income Inequality: A Global Perspective," *IMF Staff Discussion Notes* 15, no. 13 (2015): 1; Era Dabla-Norris et al., "Distinguishing Constraints on Financial Inclusion and Their Impact on GDP, TFP, and the Distribution of Income," NBER Working Paper No. 20821, 2019, https://www.nber.org/system /files/working_papers/w20821/w20821.pdf.

6. Martin P. Andersson and Andrés F. Palacio Chaverra, "Structural Change and Income Inequality: Agricultural Development and Inter-Sectoral Dualism in the Developing World, 1960–2010," *OASIS*, no. 23 (2016): 99.

7. Unlike South Africa, which has less than a 10 percent share of employment in agriculture, Columbia and China have close to 20 percent and India has over 40 percent. Andersson and Chavera, in "Structural Change" (2016), examined structural changes to see the effect of sectoral workforce shifts on income inequality. After looking at fifty years of data for twenty-seven countries in Asia, Africa, and Latin America, they concluded that the gap between the productivities of agriculture and non-agriculture is positively associated with income inequality. The Food and Agriculture Organization of the United Nations, in its 2017 report titled "The State of Food and Agriculture: Leveraging Food Systems for Inclusive Rural Transformation," mentioned that the agricultural sector employs more than 1.3 billion people, 97 percent of whom live in developing countries.

8. Andersson and Chaverra, "Structural Change," 99.

9. Castaneda Aguilar et al., "Who Are the Poor in the Developing World?," Policy Research Working Paper No. WPS 7844, 2016, http://documents.worldbank.org /curated/en/187011475416542282/Who-are-the-poor-in-the-developing-world.

10. Hanan G. Jacoby, "Access to Markets and the Benefits of Rural Roads," *Economic Journal* 110, no. 465 (2000): 713–737.

11. Christine Zhen-Wei Quiang et al., "Economic Impacts of Broadband" (World Bank, 2009), https://siteresources.worldbank.org/EXTIC4D/Resources/IC4D _Broadband_35_50.pdf; Joakim Reiter, "4 Ways Governments Can Develop Digital Infrastructure," World Economic Forum, 2017, https://www.weforum.org /agenda/2017/09/governments-develop-digital-infrastructure-vodafone/; Rob Matheson, "Study: Mobile-Money Services Lift Kenyans Out of Poverty," MIT News, Dec. 8, 2016, http://news.mit.edu/2016/mobile-money-kenyans-out -poverty-1208.

12. Timo Henckel and Warwick Mckibbon, "The Economics of Infrastructure in a Globalized World: Issues, Lessons, and Future Challenges," Brookings Institute, 2010, https://www.brookings.edu/research/the-economics-of-infrastructure-in-a -globalized-world-issues-lessons-and-future-challenges/.

13. In Asia, when per capita GDP rises above $3,000 there is a logarithmic increase, with education expenditures converging toward 5 percent in high-income

countries. In Latin America, educational spending is relatively stable between 3 percent and 5 percent of GDP, and then rises toward 6 percent and above as per capita GDP increases above $6,000 (following a logarithmic trend). Education expenditure varies most in Africa, particularly between low-income countries. Following a logarithmic trend with respect to the country's GDP per capita, the proportion of public expenditure spent on education starts at around 2 percent of GDP in countries such as Congo, Ethiopia, and Gambia, and reaches around 10 percent of GDP or more in countries such as Lesotho and Zimbabwe. Marion Laboure and Emmanuelle Taugourdeau, "Does Government Expenditure Matter for Economic Growth?," *Global Policy* 9, no. 2 (2018): 203–215.

14. Financial deepening can influence the economic situation of both individuals and societies, including producing lower rates of income inequality. George R. Clarke, Lixin Colin Xu, and Heng-Fu Zou, "Finance and Income Inequality: What Do the Data Tell Us?," *Southern Economic Journal* 72, no. 3 (2006): 578; Thorsten Beck, Asli Demirgüç-Kunt, and Ross Levine, "Finance, Inequality and the Poor," *Journal of Economic Growth* 12, no. 1 (2007): 27–49.

15. Chakravarty and Pal suggest that economic development, as measured by a nation's per capita income, is positively associated with that state's level of financial inclusion. Mohammed and Uraguchi suggest that low rates of financial inclusion have direct negative impacts on health, education, and gender equality. Satya R. Chakravarty and Rupayan Pal, "Financial Inclusion in India: An Axiomatic Approach," *Journal of Policy Modeling* 35, no. 5 (2013): 813–837; Essam Yassin Mohammed and Zenebe Bashaw Uraguchi, *Financial Inclusion for Poverty Alleviation: Issues and Case Studies for Sustainable Development* (United Kingdom: Routledge, 2017), 12.

16. Asian Development Bank Institute, "Accelerating Financial Inclusion in South-East Asia with Digital Finance," IDEAS, Working Paper Series from Repec, 2017, https://ideas.repec.org/p/ess/wpaper/id11723.html.

17. Claire Yurong Hong, Xiaomeng Lu, and Jun Pan, "FinTech Adoption and Household Risk-Taking," NBER Working Paper No. 28063, November 2020, http://www.nber.org/papers/w28063.

18. Susanne Chishti and Janos Barberis, *The Fintech Book: The Financial Technology Handbook for Investors, Entrepreneurs, and Visionaries* (West Sussex: John Wiley & Sons, 2016).

19. Oksana Kabakova and Evgeny Plaksenkov, "Analysis of Factors Affecting Financial Inclusion: Ecosystem View," *Journal of Business Research* 89 (August 1, 2018): 198–205.

20. The value of economic activity is high, with GDP at $350 billion in 2014. Per capita GDP growth rates have risen from negative rates to an average of 1.6 percent per annum since 1994 (when apartheid ended). Per capita GDP is only about 10 percent higher than it was in 1980. During the same period, other developing countries have seen much higher increases in income levels, almost twice as much in recent years. Unemployment rates have persistently stayed above 20 percent in the country. Youth unemployment is at 50 percent, the highest in the emerging world, and the overall unemployment rate is 2 percent higher than it was in 1994, when apartheid formally ended.

21. Ruchir Sharma, *The Liberation Dividend* (Oxford: Oxford University Press, 2014).

22. Asli Demirguc-Kunt and Leora Klapper, "Measuring Financial Inclusion: The Global Findex Database," World Bank, Policy Research Working Paper WPS 6025, 2012, http://documents.worldbank.org/curated/en/453121468331738740/Measuring-financial-inclusion-the-Global-Findex-Database.

23. Demirguc-Kunt and Klapper, "Measuring Financial Inclusion."

24. Demirguc-Kunt and Klapper, "Measuring Financial Inclusion."

25. Asli Demirguc-Kunt, Leora Klapper, Dorothe Singer, Peter Van Oudheusden, "The Global Findex Database 2014: Measuring Financial Inclusion around the World," World Bank, Policy Research Working Paper WPS 7255, 2015, http://documents.worldbank.org/curated/en/187761468179367706/The-Global-Findex-Database-2014-measuring-financial-inclusion-around-the-world.

26. In China, there remains a significant urban-rural divide in personal income, economic growth, and financial market developments. The shortage of local financial institutions in rural regions is another underlying constraint that prevents financial inclusion. Yubing Sui and Geng Niu, "The Urban-Rural Gap of Chinese Household Finance," *Emerging Markets Finance and Trade* 54, no. 2 (2017), 377–392; Zhu Bao, Shiting Zhai, and Jing He, "Is the Development of China's Financial Inclusion Sustainable? Evidence from a Perspective of Balance," *Sustainability* 10 (2018): 1200.

27. Pete Sparreboom and Eric Duflos, "Financial Inclusion in the People's Republic of China: An Analysis of Existing Research and Public Data," China Papers on Inclusiveness, No. 7, August 2012, http://documents1.worldbank.org/curated/en/677591468025160550/text/75149020120CGA0Box0374307B00PUBLIC0.txt.

28. Chen and Jin, in a 2017 report, state that even though 53 percent of households in rural China used credit, only 20 percent had credit from formal sources. Zibei Chen and Minchao Jin, "Financial Inclusion in China: Use of Credit," *Journal of Family and Economic Issues* 38, no. 4 (2017): 528–540.

29. Shijun Chai et al., "Social Networks and Informal Financial Inclusion in China," *Asia Pacific Journal of Management* 36, no. 36 (2019): 305–319.

30. Ben Walsh, "Fintech Lending Booms: Is That a Good Thing?," *Barrons*, September 24, 2018; Sara Hsu, "China's Fintech Giants Have the Money and Means to Dominate Despite the Wider Slowdown," *Forbes*, August 31, 2018.

31. The Treasury of the Australian Government, "Economic Benefits of Fintech," 2016, https://treasury.gov.au/publication/backing-australian-Fintech/economic-benefits-of-Fintech/.

32. International Monetary Fund. "Colombia: Staff Report for the 2015 Article IV Consultation: IMF Staff Country Reports: Colombia—2015 Article IV Consultation-Press Release; Staff Report, and Statement by the Executive Director for Colombia," 2015, http://www.elibrary.imf.org/view/IMF002/22588-9781513530215/22588-9781513530215/22588-9781513530215.xml.

33. Real GDP fell 4.2 percent. The unemployment rate was 20 percent, and 60 percent of the population was below the poverty line. *Poverty line* is defined as people living under $4 a day, PPP. The middle class came down to 11 percent, from 20 percent. Cord, Genoni, and Rodriguez-Castelan estimate that between 2002 and 2013 transfers accounted for 16.8 percent of the reduction in moderate

poverty (US$4 per day, PPP) in the country. The Gini coefficient improved only marginally since 2000, from 58.7 to 55.9 percent in 2010, when the lowest quintile held only 3 percent of the income share. In Colombia, the Gini coefficient declined by about 3.4 percentage points from 2002 to 2012, even as the rest of Latin America on average achieved a 5.8 percentage point reduction over this period. Louise J. Cord, Maria Eugenia Genoni, and Carlos Rodriguez-Castelan, "Shared Prosperity and Poverty Eradication in Latin America and the Caribbean," World Bank, 2015, http://documents.worldbank.org/curated/en /122581468188648941/Shared-prosperity-and-poverty-eradication-in-Latin -America-and-the-Caribbean.

34. Ulf Thoene and Álvaro Turriago-Hoyos, "Financial Inclusion in Colombia: A Scoping Literature Review," *Intangible Capital* 13, no. 3 (2017): 582–614.

35. Ernst & Young, "Global FinTech Adoption Index 2019," https://www.ey.com/en _om/ey-global-fintech-adoption-index.

36. The mobile penetration in Russia was 89 percent in 2017 and was forecasted to be 90 percent in 2025. In the list shown here for each nation, the 2017 percentage is shown first, and the 2025 forecast is shown second. China: 84/85; Indonesia: 73/77; Brazil: 68/75; Mexico: 63/72; India: 53/63; Bangladesh: 51/60; Nigeria: 43/55; Pakistan: 39/50. GSM Association, "The Mobile Economy 2018," 2018, https://www.gsmaintelligence.com/videos/mobile-economy-2018/.

37. Harvard Business School Professor of Economics Julie Battilana's research on power dynamics shows that existing power dynamics made leading social change even more challenging. People come to accept existing power differences and then take them for granted. Existing norms are reinforced by powerful individuals and organizations that gain from maintaining the status quo, and by those with limited power, the people who end up accepting their lower status positions. Leaders of change get stuck when their underestimation of power hierarchies befuddles their intentions, and when their overestimation of power hierarchies paralyzes their actions. Julie Battilana and Marissa Kimsey, "Should You Agitate, Innovate, or Orchestrate?," *Stanford Social Innovation Review*, September 18, 2017, https://ssir.org/articles/entry/should_you_agitate_innovate_or_orchestrate.

38. Josh Horwitz, "Alibaba's Customers Can Now Get a Loan Based on Their Online Shopping History," *Quartz*, June 25, 2015, https://qz.com/436889/alibabas -customers-can-now-get-a-loan-based-on-their-online-shopping-history/.

39. To establish a new Aadhaar card, individuals must present photo identity cards that contain name and photo. There are at least twenty commonly used forms of ID that can be used to obtain an Aadhaar card (passport; ration card; PDS photo card; PAN card; driving license; voter ID; NREGS job card; government photo ID cards or PSU issued service photo identity card; arms license; photo ID issued by a recognized educational institution; photo credit card; photo bank ATM card; Kissan photo passbook; pensioner photo card; freedom fighter photo card; ECHS/CGHS photo card; certificate of identity that has photo issued by an officer or Tehsildar on a letterhead; address card that has name and photo issued by the Department of Posts; disability ID card or handicapped medical certificate that is issued by the respective state or union territory government or administrators).

40. Tania Lopez and Adalbert Winkler, "The Challenge of Rural Financial Inclusion—Evidence from Microfinance," *Applied Economics* 50, no. 14 (March 22, 2018): 1555–1577.

41. Saifullahi Sani Ibrahim, Huseyin Ozdeser, and Behiye Cavusoglu, "Financial Inclusion as a Pathway to Welfare Enhancement and Income Equality: Micro-Level Evidence from Nigeria," *Development Southern Africa* 36, no. 3 (2019): 390–407.

42. Patrick Schueffel, "Taming the Beast: A Scientific Definition of Fintech," *Journal of Innovation Management; Porto Portugal* 4, no. 4 (2016): 32–54.

6. Fintech, Financial Inclusion, and Economic Infrastructure

1. Where no source is mentioned this section draws extensively on Asli Demirgüç-Kunt et al., "Measuring Financial Inclusion and the Fintech Revolution," Global Findex Database, 2017, https://openknowledge.worldbank.org/handle/10986/29510.

2. In high-income economies, 94 percent of adults have an account; in developing economies, 63 percent do. Demirgüç-Kunt et al., "Measuring Financial Inclusion."

3. Demirgüç-Kunt et al., "Measuring Financial Inclusion."

4. Robert Allen, "Technology and the Great Divergence: Global Economic Development since 1820," *Explorations in Economic History* 49, no. 1 (2012): 1–16.

5. Demirgüç-Kunt et al., "Measuring Financial Inclusion."

6. Asli Demirgüç-Kunt et al., "Measuring Financial Inclusion and the Fintech Revolution," Global Findex Database, 2017, https://globalfindex.worldbank.org/sites/globalfindex/files/2018-04/2017%20Findex%20full%20report_0.pdf. Microfinance institutions are available in developing and industrialized nations.

7. Stefan Dercon, Tessa Bold, and Cesar Calvo, "Insurance for the Poor?," UNICEF Social Policy, 2018, https://www.unicef.org/socialpolicy/files/Insurance_for_the_Poor.pdf.

8. James C. Brau, Craig Merrill, and Kim B. Staking, "Insurance Theory and Challenges Facing the Development of Microinsurance Markets," *Journal of Developmental Entrepreneurship* 16, no. 4 (2011): 411–440.

9. Saibal Ghosh and Deepak Vinod, "What Constrains Financial Inclusion for Women? Evidence from Indian Micro Data," *World Development* 92 (2017): 60–81.

10. Ross Levine shows that financial inclusion mobilizes savings for investment and helps people harness resources that promote specialization and innovation. Abiola Babajide and colleagues show that in the long term, financial inclusion should boost economic growth and productivity through increased availability of capital, increased transaction volume, betterment of resource allocation, improved risk management, and the reduction of information asymmetries. Ross Levine, "Financial Development and Economic Growth: Views and Agenda," *Journal of Economic Literature* 35 (1997): 688–726; Abiola Babajide, Folasade Adegboye, and Alexander Omankhanlen, "Financial Inclusion and Economic Growth in

Nigeria," *International Journal of Economics and Financial Issues* 5, no. 3 (2015): 629–637.

11. Jose de Luna Martinez, "Financial Inclusion in Malaysia: Distilling Lessons for Other Countries," World Bank Knowledge and Research, 2017, http://pubdocs .worldbank.org/en/298451495431805248/Financial-Inclusion-in-Malaysia -Report-Slides.pdf.

12. Ratna Sahay et al., "Financial Inclusion: Can It Meet Multiple Macroeconomic Goals?," IMF Staff Discussion Note, SDN/15/17, 2015, https://www.imf.org/en /Publications/Staff-Discussion-Notes/Issues/2016/12/31/Financial-Inclusion -Can-it-Meet-Multiple-Macroeconomic-Goals-43163.

13. Lawrence Okoye et al., "Financial Inclusion as a Strategy for Enhanced Economic Growth and Development," *Journal of Internet Banking and Commerce* 22, no. S8 (2017).

14. Babajide et al., "Financial Inclusion." Collecting accurate, representative data in developing settings is a challenge. There is often a dearth of administrative data. Also, it is in the country's best interest to report findings that paint them in a positive light. (For this reason, the most vulnerable and excluded groups are often excluded.) The data often lack rigor and representativeness, even today. Going back one or two decades, data collection and analysis were even worse.

15. Dipasha Sharma, "Nexus between Financial Inclusion and Economic Growth: Evidence from the Emerging Indian Economy," *Journal of Financial Economic Policy* 8, no. 1 (2015): 13–36.

16. The seventy-four emerging economies are: China; India; Brazil; Indonesia; South Africa; Colombia; Turkey; Mexico; Russia; Malaysia; Thailand; Argentina; Bangladesh; Botswana; Chile; Costa Rica; Ecuador; Iran; Mozambique; Myanmar; Niger; Nigeria; Pakistan; Ukraine; Uruguay; Zimbabwe; Afghanistan; Angola; Albania; Burundi; Benin; Belarus; Belize; Bhutan; Botswana; Djibouti; Dominica; Algeria; Estonia; Micronesia, Fed. Sts.; Georgia; Ghana; Guinea; The Gambia; Guinea-Bissau; Honduras; Croatia; Iran, Islamic Rep.; Iraq; Kazakhstan; Kenya; Kyrgyz Republic; Morocco; Moldova; Madagascar; Maldives; Macedonia, FYR; Mali; Malta; Myanmar; Mozambique; Mauritania; Mauritius; Panama; Peru; Philippines; Paraguay; Romania; Rwanda; Sao Tome and Principe; Suriname; Slovak Republic; Slovenia; and Zambia. Although World Bank Financial Index data spans only three observations per country, the sample was extended to a fourteen-year range by including alternative measures of financial inclusion. The dependent variables GDP per capita and GDP growth intend to reflect the changing levels of individual wealth. All variables are time-series data, and the relationships were analyzed using both ordinary least squares (OLS) and fixed effects regressions.

17. Although results overall indicate a strong, positive association between measures of banking penetration/accessibility and GDP per capita, the link between such indicators and GDP growth is slightly negative or not statistically significant, like the results reported in Okoye et al., "Financial Inclusion." It is noteworthy that regressions with both year and state fixed effects (not included in tables) are far from statistically significant. The linear models suggest that increasing financial inclusion

has the potential to raise global living standards and reduce global income inequality. However, the literature reveals contradictory results on the direction of causality. There is a strong possibility of reverse or bidirectional causality; that is, high per capita income may simultaneously allow for greater financial inclusion. Other considerations in this analysis include lag effects and scarcity of data. Increased account ownership or bank presence theoretically may improve growth, but the effects would likely take a substantial amount of time to manifest within the economy. Because account ownership is measured only every three years, it is challenging to measure the impact of financial inclusion on economic growth.

18. GSMA Intelligence, "Global Mobile Trends 2021," 2019, https://data .gsmaintelligence.com/api-web/v2/research-file-download?id=58621970&file =141220-Global-Mobile-Trends.pdf.

19. For more details on global consumer transactions carried out in cash, refer to the following sources: Susanne Chishti and Janos Barberis, *The Fintech Book* (West Sussex: John Wiley, 2016); World Bank, "Measuring Financial Inclusion and the Fintech Revolution," Global Findex Database, 2017, http://documents.worldbank .org/curated/en/187761468179367706/The-Global-Findex-Database-2014 -measuring-financial-inclusion-around-the-world.

20. Arvind Gupta and Philip Auerswald, "How India Is Moving toward a Digital-First Economy," *Harvard Business Review,* November 8, 2017, https://hbr.org /2017/11/how-india-is-moving-toward-a-digital-first-economy.

21. India Ministry of Finance, "Finance Ministry: Demonetization Immensely Beneficial to Indian Economy and People," August 2017, http://pib.nic.in/newsite /PrintRelease.aspx?relid=170378.

22. Gupta and Auerswald, "How India Is Moving."

23. "Know Your Customer" is the process of a bank verifying the identity of its clients and assessing potential risks of illegal intentions for the relationship.

24. Varadharajan Sridhar, *The Telecom Revolution in India: Technology, Regulation and Policy* (Oxford: Oxford University Press, 2011).

25. Ernst & Young, "Global FinTech Adoption Index 2019," https://www.ey.com/en _om/ey-global-fintech-adoption-index.

26. Ernst & Young, "Fintech Adoption Index 2019."

27. Ernst & Young, "Fintech Adoption Index 2019."

28. Chishti and Barberis, *The Fintech Book.*

29. Andrew Meola, "These Are the Five Best Remittance Companies in the World," *Business Insider,* July 11, 2016, https://www.businessinsider.com/these-are-the -five-best-remittance-companies-in-the-world-2016-7; Ben Schiller, "The Fight for the $400 Billion Business of Immigrants Sending Money Home," Fast Company, 2018, https://www.fastcompany.com/3067778/the-blockchain-is -going-to-save-immigrants-millions-in-remittance-fees.

30. Businessline, "Digital Payments Will Touch $500B in India by 2020, Says Report," 2016, https://www.thehindubusinessline.com/money-and-banking/digital -payments-will-touch-500-b-in-india-by-2020-says-report/article8898112.ece.

31. Safaricom, "M-Pesa Rates, M-Pesa Tariffs, M-Pesa Withdrawal Charges, M-Pesa Transaction Fees," 2018, https://www.safaricom.co.ke/personal/m-pesa /getting-started/m-pesa-rates.

32. Anybody can open an account with a valid ID and a phone number. This excludes those without ID, which is a prevalent issue in many developing economies.
33. Safaricom, "M-Pesa Rates."
34. Ignacio Mas and Daniel Radcliffe, "Mobile Payments Go Viral: M-Pesa in Kenya," *Capco Institute's Journal of Financial Transformation* 32 (August 2011): 169.
35. CNN, "M-Pesa: Kenya's Mobile Money Success Story Turns 10," 2017, https://edition.cnn.com/2017/02/21/africa/mpesa-10th-anniversary/index.html.
36. Mas and Radcliffe, "Mobile Payments Go Viral."
37. Rob Matheson, "Study: Mobile-Money Services Lift Kenyans Out of Poverty," MIT News, December 8, 2016, http://news.mit.edu/2016/mobile-money-kenyans-out-poverty-1208.
38. Aaron Meyer, Francisco Rivadeneyra, and Samantha Sohal, "Fintech: Is This Time Different? A Framework for Assessing Risks and Opportunities for Central Banks," Bank of Canada Staff Discussion Paper 2017–2010, July 2017, https://www.bankofcanada.ca/2017/07/staff-discussion-paper-2017-10/.
39. Pratim Datta, "A Preliminary Study of Ecommerce Adoption in Developing Countries," *Information Systems Journal* 21, no. 1 (January 1, 2011): 3–32.
40. Tyler Aveni and Joep Roest, "China's Alipay and WeChat Pay: Reaching Rural Users," CGAP, 2017, http://www.cgap.org/sites/default/files/researches/documents/Brief-Chinas-Alipay-and-WeChat-Pay-Dec-2017.pdf.

7. The Interplay of Fintech and Government

1. Maslow's hierarchy of needs is a theory in psychology proposed by Abraham Maslow in his 1943 paper "A Theory of Human Motivation." Maslow used the terms *physiological, safety, belonging* and *love, social needs* or *esteem*, and *self-actualization* to describe the pattern through which human motivations generally move. This means that for motivation to occur at the next level, each level must be satisfied within the individual. Abraham H. Maslow, "A Theory of Human Motivation," *Psychological Review* 50, no. 4 (1943): 370–396.
2. Marion Laboure and Emmanuelle Taugourdeau, "Does Government Expenditure Matter for Economic Growth?," *Global Policy* 9, no. 2 (2018): 203–215.
3. The three core sub-models—conservative, liberal, and social democratic—are developed in Gosta Esping-Andersen, *The Three Worlds of Welfare Capitalism* (West Sussex: John Wiley, 2013).
4. For further information on Wagner's law, see Adolph Wagner, *Grundlegung der Politischen Oekonomie*, vol. 1: *Grundlagen der Volkswirtschaft* (Leipzig: C. F. Winter, 1892).
5. While Barro holds that economic growth is primarily the result of endogenous forces, Myles shows that, for instance, subsidies for research and development or education can increase growth rates by increasing the incentive to innovate. Robert. J. Barro, "Government Spending in a Simple Model of Endogenous Growth," *Journal of Political Economy* 98, no. 5 (1990): 103–126; Gareth D. Myles, "Economic Growth and the Role of Taxation Theory," OECD Economics Department Working Paper 713, 2009, https://ideas.repec.org/p/oec/ecoaaa/713-en.html.

6. Wilensky found that a certain level of economic development and revenue is required to divert limited resources from productive use (investment) to welfare. Laboure and Taugourdeau found a positive association between public spending and the economic growth rates of low-income countries, whereas they found negative associations across higher-income countries. Harold L. Wilensky, *Industrial Society and Social Welfare: The Impact of Industrialization on the Supply and Organization of Social Welfare Services in the United States* (New York: Russell Sage Foundation, 1958); Laboure and Taugourdeau, "Does Government Expenditure Matter?," 203–215.

7. Mridula Ghai, "A Model for Universal Social Security Coverage: The Experience of the BRICs Countries," *International Social Security Review* 68, no. 3 (July 1, 2015): 99–118.

8. Labor contracts in these nations are often informal, and income and wealth inequality are high. Thomas Scharping showed that China's one-child-per-family policies introduced in 1979 corresponded with significant increased longevity. All the estimates come from World Bank staff estimates based on age distributions of the United Nations Population Division's World Population Prospects, 2017. Mukul G. Asher and Azad Singh Bali, "Social Security Reform and Economic Development: The Case of India," in *Reforming Pensions in Developing and Transition Countries*, ed. Katja Hujo (London: Palgrave Macmillan, 2014), 158–186; Thomas Scharping, *Birth Control in China 1949–2000: Population Policy and Demographic Development* (London: Routledge, 2003); World Bank, "Age-Dependency Ratio—China," https://data.worldbank.org/indicator/SP.POP.DPND.OL?locations=CN.

9. Katja Hujo, "Reforming Pensions in Developing and Transition Countries: Conclusions," in Hujo, *Reforming Pensions*, 311–335; Katja Hujo and Mariana Rulli, "Towards More Inclusive Protection: A Comparative Analysis of the Political Process and Socio-Economic Impact of Pension Re-Reforms in Argentina and Chile," in Hujo, *Reforming Pensions*, 278–310.

10. Lianquan Fang, "Towards Universal Coverage: A Macro Analysis of China's Public Pension Reform," in Hujo, *Reforming Pensions*, 187–219.

11. Fang, "Towards Universal Coverage."

12. Hujo, "Reforming Pensions"; Hujo and Rulli, "Towards More Inclusive Protection."

13. Asli Demirgüç-Kunt et al., "Measuring Financial Inclusion and the Fintech Revolution," https://www.google.com/url?sa=t&rct=j&q=&esrc=s&source=web&cd=&cad=rja&uact=8&ved=2ahUKEwjj1Y-09rbuAhUPqxoKHdOyAn0QFjAAegQIBhAC&url=https%3A%2F%2Fopenknowledge.worldbank.org%2Fbitstream%2Fhandle%2F10986%2F29510%2F9781464812590.pdf&usg=AOvVaw2WXJPhlKkiGJ5gRHaA6_jN.

14. Benjamin Olken and Rohini Pande, "Corruption in Developing Countries," *Annual Review of Economics* 4 (2012): 479–509.

15. Paul DiMaggio et al., "Social Implications of the Internet," *Annual Review of Sociology* 27, no. 1 (August 1, 2001): 307–336.

16. Andreas Freund, "Automated, Decentralized Trust: A Path to Financial Inclusion," in *Handbook of Blockchain, Digital Finance, and Inclusion*, ed. David Lee Kuo Chuen and Robert Deng, vol. 1 (Amsterdam: Elsevier, 2017).

17. Susanne Chishti and Janos Barberis, *The Fintech Book: The Financial Technology Handbook for Investors, Entrepreneurs, and Visionaries* (West Sussex: John Wiley & Sons, 2016).
18. "Know Your Customer" (KYC) is the name given to the process of verifying the identity of a company's customers. The term is also used to refer to the banking regulations that govern these activities. KYC processes are used by companies of all sizes to ensure customer compliance with anticorruption laws and to verify their integrity and integrity. It also aims to prevent identity theft, tax evasion, money laundering, and terrorist financing. These processes are typically done through data collection and analysis, verification of list presence (such as that of politically exposed persons), behavioral and transactional analysis, and so on.
19. For further information on the blockchain's decentralized trust, see Freund, "Automated, Decentralized Trust."
20. Freund, "Automated, Decentralized Trust."
21. Asian Development Bank Institute, "Accelerating Financial Inclusion in Southeast Asia with Digital Finance," IDEAS, 2018, http://dx.doi.org/10.22617 /RPT178622-2.
22. Demirgüç-Kunt et al., "Measuring Financial Inclusion."
23. "e-KYC" stands for "electronic Know Your Customer." This term is generally used by the Indian government's Aadhaar initiative. The principle behind it is that a person with only an Aadhaar number and a fingerprint can open a bank account. The Aadhaar biometric system would provide enough electronic identification and documentation to replace the previous KYC system that required paper documentation. Cyn-Young Park and Rogelio Jr V. Mercado, "Financial Inclusion: New Measurement and Cross-Country Impact Assessment," ADB Economics Working Paper Series 539, March 15, 2018, http://dx .doi.org.ezp-prod1.hul.harvard.edu/10.22617/WPS189270-2.
24. Pratim Datta, "A Preliminary Study of Ecommerce Adoption in Developing Countries," *Information Systems Journal* 21, no. 1 (2011): 3–32; Aakanksha Joshi, "Mandatory Aadhaar Linking: Confusion, Chaos and Complications," WTD News, December 1, 2017, http://wtdnews.com/mandatory-aadhaar-linking -confusion-chaos-complications/.
25. Yvonne Braun, "Pensions Dashboard: The Next Frontier in Fintech," Professional Pensions, 2016, https://www.professionalpensions.com/professional-pensions /opinion/2442942/pensions-dashboard-the-next-frontier-in-fintech.
26. Demirguc-Kunt et al., "Measuring Financial Inclusion."
27. Chishti and Barberis, *The Fintech Book*, 66.
28. Alliance for Financial Inclusion, "Fintech for Financial Inclusion: A Framework for Digital Financial Transformation," Intergovernmental Group of Twenty-Four, 2018, https://www.g24.org/wp-content/uploads/2018/09/G-24-AFI_FinTech _Special_Report_AW_digital.pdf.
29. Alliance for Financial Inclusion, "Fintech for Financial Inclusion."
30. Ernst & Young, "Global FinTech Adoption Index 2019," https://www.ey.com/en _om/ey-global-fintech-adoption-index.

31. M. Mostak Ahamed and Sushanta K. Mallick, "Is Financial Inclusion Good for Bank Stability? International Evidence," *Journal of Economic Behavior & Organization* (August 1, 2017).

32. Kok Lian Woo, "How Chinese Commercial Banks Innovate: Process and Practice," *Journal of Innovation Management* 5, no. 2 (2017): 81–110.

33. For further information on the European Union, see European Banking Authority, "EBA's Approach to Financial Technology (Fintech)," 2017, https://eba .europa.eu/regulation-and-policy/other-topics/approach-to-financial-technology -fintech; European Banking Authority, "EBA Report on the Impact of Fintech on Incumbent Credit Institutions' Business Models," 2018, https://www.eba .europa.eu/file/28458.

34. A primary aim of a sandbox is to align compliance and regulation with the rapid growth of fintech companies without drowning them in rules, while also not compromising customer security. Another goal is to attract the attention of different players, such as banks, private equity, and venture capital funds, in the hopes of securing investment. Regulatory uncertainty discourages investment. Investors are hesitant to invest in a company that is working in an unregulated landscape because regulatory bodies can suddenly deem its operations illegal, either forcing it to drastically change the business or shut it down. Similarly, investors do not necessarily want to invest in an overregulated market. We've mentioned that overregulation can hinder innovation, affecting a company's growth rate and ability to achieve a worthwhile return on investment. Fintech start-ups participating in regulatory sandbox initiatives can therefore potentially convince investors who previously have been hesitant to invest that they are working to comply with regulatory obligations and on their product or service innovations. In Europe the Authority for the Financial Market (AFM) and De Nederlandsche Bank (DNB) in Holland combined forces for a regulatory sandbox, and Denmark's Financial Supervisory Authority (Finanstilsynet) launched the FT Lab. Apart from Britain, these are the only two European countries that offer a fintech sandbox program. With Britain's decision to leave the EU, the European Union's banking watchdog indicated that there is an urgent need for a cross-border sandbox and innovation hub that will nurture the continued growth of fintech start-ups in the EU. In 2015 the UK Financial Conduct Authority (FCA) launched the first regulatory sandbox for Fintech start-ups, called Project Innovate. The program was rolled out in phases (or "cohorts," as they call them), with companies applying to be part of each stage. The sandbox seeks to provide firms with the ability to test products and services in a controlled environment; reduced time-to-market at potentially lower cost; support in identifying appropriate consumer protection safeguards to build into new products and services; and better access to finance. The Monetary Authority of Singapore (MAS) launched their fintech sandbox in 2016 to encourage more fintech experimentation and innovation. "The regulatory sandbox will enable FIs as well as fintech players to experiment with innovative financial products or services in the production environment but within a well-defined space and duration. It shall also include appropriate safeguards to contain the consequences of failure and maintain the overall safety and soundness of the financial system."

Regulatory sandboxes have been extensively developed in Ivo Jenik and Kate Lauer, "Regulatory Sandboxes and Financial Inclusion," CGAP Working Paper, 2017, https://www.cgap.org/sites/default/files/Working-Paper-Regulatory -Sandboxes-Oct-2017.pdf.

35. Jayati Ghosh, "Microfinance and the Challenge of Financial Inclusion for Development," *Cambridge Journal of Economics* 37, no. 6 (October 2013): 1203–1219.

8. Toward a Cashless Society

For more details on this chapter, please see Appendix A.

1. Marion Laboure and Jim Reid, "The Future of Payments Part I. Cash: The Dinosaur Will Survive . . . for Now," Deutsche Bank Research, Corporate Bank Research, 2020, https://www.dbresearch.com/PROD/RPS_EN-PROD /PROD0000000000504353.pdf; Marion Laboure and Jim Reid, "The Future of Payments Part II. Moving to Digital Wallets and the Extinction of Plastic Cards," Deutsche Bank Research, Corporate Bank Research, 2020, https://www .dbresearch.com/PROD/RPS_EN-PROD/PROD0000000000504508.pdf.

2. Jack Lefler, *Las Cruces Sun-News* (NM), July 24, 1968; Neil Ardley, *World of Tomorrow: School, Work and Play* (Franklin Watts, 1981); "The End of the Cash Era," *The Economist,* February 15, 2017, https://www.economist.com/leaders/2007/02/15 /the-end-of-the-cash-era; Laboure and Reid, "The Future of Payments Part I."

3. With the exception of Sweden, where the use of physical cash is actually de-clining. According to a nationwide survey conducted by the Sveriges Riksbank—the Swedish central bank—only 18 percent of Swedes reported using cash recently, compared to 40 percent of Swedes in 2010. Factors that help include Sweden's strong broadband coverage, even in remote areas; small, tech-savvy population; and deeper trust in institutions and new technologies.

4. One exception is Sweden, where the use of physical cash is declining substan-tially. According to a nationwide survey conducted by the Sveriges Riksbank— the Swedish central bank—only 18 percent of Swedes reported using cash com-pared to 40 percent in 2010. Purchases are usually done as digital transaction by cards, online, or by using Swish, Sweden's most popular mobile payment app. The following factors help: strong broadband coverage, even in remote areas; a small, tech-savvy population; and a deeper trust in institutions and new technologies.

5. Mathew Scott, "WeChat Is a Way of Life for 900 Million Daily Users," *INTHEBLACK,* May 1, 2018, https://www.intheblack.com/articles /2018/05/01/wechat-super-app.

6. Constance Emmanuelli et al., "Elevating Customer Experience Excellence in the Next Normal," McKinsey & Company, May 21, 2020, https://www.mckinsey .com/business-functions/operations/our-insights/elevating-customer-experience -excellence-in-the-next-normal.

7. In advanced economies, the collection and use of data are more challenging due to data protection regulations. In the European Union, the General Data Protection Regulation (GDPR) regulates individuals' data and privacy. Similarly,

in California, the California Consumer Privacy Act (CCPA) is a state statute intended to enhance privacy rights and consumer protection for residents of California. Alessandra Tanda and Cristiana-Maria Schena, "FinTech, BigTech and Banks Digitalisation and Its Impact on Banking Business Models," Palgrave Macmillan, Palgrave Pivot Analysis, 2019, https://www.palgrave.com/gp/book/9783030224257.

9. Digital Currencies

For more details on this chapter, please see Appendix B.

1. The Bank of International Settlements defined three examples of current technological and design features of cryptocurrency assets relative to traditional assets: (1) They are digital and virtual in nature; (2) they rely on cryptography and advanced mathematical techniques to restrict the transmission of data to the intended parties; (3) they use distributed ledger technology.

2. But it is bad for AI developers, who face hurdles accessing the data they need to train their algorithms. The European Union has codified and put into practice "right to be forgotten" since 2006.

3. That suits Chinese technology firms just fine. The legal framework in China allows tech firms to collect a wide range of user data for a wide range of purposes, such as constructing social-scoring systems, like Alibaba's Sesame Credit.

4. Marion Laboure and Jim Reid, "The Future of Payments: Series 2, Part I. Post Covid-19: What Executives Are Thinking and Doing," Deutsche Bank Research, January 13, 2021, https://www.dbresearch.com/PROD/RPS_EN-PROD/PROD0000000000515432.pdf.

5. The UK has just started the consultation process, and the government follows a staggered consultation approach with individual focus on the different categories and purposes of cryptocurrencies. The Chinese government has high interest in establishing and strengthening the digital yuan. We find targeted regulatory actions to support that. For example, in 2017, in response to Bitcoin peaks, the government increased already strict scrutiny over cryptocurrencies as the People's Bank of China (PBoC) prepared to launch its own digital currency. In October 2020, PBoC outlawed the issuance of private digital currencies. In India, cryptocurrencies are no longer banned but regulatory activities are very much prohibitive. For example, exchanges are legal, but the government has made it difficult for them to operate. We will see more activity throughout 2021. In Japan there were lots of regulatory activities related to cryptocurrencies in 2020. They were mainly focused on adoption of payment and financial services, and on exchange rules for cryptocurrencies.

6. Raphael Auer and Stijn Claessens, "Cryptocurrencies: Why Not (to) Regulate?," in *The Economics of Fintech and Digital Currencies*, ed. Antonio Fatás (London: CEPR Press, 2019), 83–90.

7. "Stablecoins" are designed to minimize volatility. The value of stablecoins can be pegged to an existing asset, such as a commodity, or to an existing currency (or a basket). This approach makes cryptocurrencies more useful for transaction and settlement processing on a business network using a distributed ledger technology

such as blockchain, which reduces traditional infrastructure expenses and operational costs. Since 2017, over two hundred stablecoins have been created. Diem plans to use stablecoins pegged to fiat currencies like the dollar, the euro, and sterling.

8. Libra Association, "Cover Letter," White Paper 2.0, April 2020, https://wp.diem.com/en-United States/wp-content/uploads/sites/23/2020/04/Libra_WhitePaperV2_April2020.pdf.

9. Mathew Scott, "WeChat Is a Way of Life for 900 Million Daily Users," *INTHEBLACK,* May 1, 2018, https://www.intheblack.com/articles/2018/05/01/wechat-super-app.

10. Cash as a means of payment has declined while cash as a store of value has increased. The rise of cash in circulation over the last twenty years is almost entirely due to high-denomination notes. It is also estimated that two-thirds of USD 100 notes are held outside the United States, which indicates they are not used for ordinary transactions.

11. BIS, "Central Bank Group to Assess Potential Cases for Central Bank Digital Currencies," January 20, 2021, https://www.bis.org/press/p200121.htm.

12. BIS, "The Technology of Retail Central Bank Digital Currency," *BIS Quarterly Review* (March 2020), https://www.bis.org/publ/qtrpdf/r_qt2003j.pdf.

13. For example, the Riksbank—the Swedish central bank—launched in 2017 its e-krona project and reported on how to straddle the difficult line between anonymity, public backing, and compliance with anti–money laundering laws and regulations designed to prevent the financing of terrorism.

14. In other words, a CBDC would (1) be a third form of central bank money that exists next to cash and reserves; (2) try to combine the advantages of world reserves, which are already digital but available only to banks, and cash, which is available to everyone, but physical; and (3) be digital and available to everyone. Clearly, a digital currency is not the same as paper cash. CBDCs are complementary to cash; they are not supposed to replace cash in most advanced economies. Cash has specific properties that only allow it to be transmitted peer-to-peer. In other words, cash transactions are not traceable. They are anonymous.

15. The digital yuan is a digital form of cash (digital banknotes and coins). Technically speaking, it is part of M0, which is the most liquid form of money supply in the economy. The e-RMB is issued and backed by the country's central bank.

16. China has a high number of banked people (80 percent in 2017) compared to the other emerging economies; however, due to its large population, China has the highest number of unbanked people in the world. According to the World Bank, 224 million Chinese people were unbanked in 2017.

17. This is also why Alipay (for example) and PBoC wallet are different.

Conclusion

1. McKinsey Global Institute, "Jobs Lost, Jobs Gained: Workforce Transitions in a Time of Automation," 2017, https://www.mckinsey.com/~/media/McKinsey/Industries/Public%20and%20Social%20Sector/Our%20Insights/What%20the%20future%20of%20work%20will%20mean%20for%20jobs%20skills%20

and%20wages/MGI-Jobs-Lost-Jobs-Gained-Executive-summary-December-6 -2017.pdf.

2. Håkan Samuelson, "What Percentage of Trading Is Algorithmic?," The Robust Trader, April 13, 2021, https://therobusttrader.com/what-percentage-of-trading -is-algorithmic/.

3. Marion Laboure, "The Future of Payments—Part II: Moving to Digital Wallets and the Extinction of Plastic Cards," Deutsche Bank Research, January 2020, https://www.dbresearch.com/PROD/RPS_EN-PROD/PROD0000000000 504508/The_Future_of_Payments_-_Part_II__Moving_to_Digita.PDF ?undefined&realload=a1HFAwdhjWXerPnNISwUv0bV4mRYc3deOAE 65DtWxYBptW1woTBcexqb63HwiF5TfNDUeDNidtne2zDZjhYhqw==.

4. MicroStrategy, "MicroStrategy Announces Over $1B in Total Bitcoin Purchases in 2020," December 21, 2020, https://www.microstrategy.com/en/company /company-videos/microstrategy-announces-over-1b-in-total-bitcoin-purchases-in -2020.

5. Yet, this is not far from our current system. They do deny or charge high pre- miums to individuals with high risks. So, the fact that big data convey more information plays along with this method, and legally it would be hard to argue against it unless the whole risk model is challenged.

6. Yves Thomas et al., "Survival of Influenza Virus on Banknotes," *Applied and Environmental Microbiolology* 75, no. 10 (2008): 3002–3007; Danielle Westhoff Smith et al., "Ebola Virus Stability under Hospital and Environmental Condi- tions," *Journal of Infectious Diseases* 214, no. 3 (October 2016): S142–S144.

7. G. Kampf et al., "Persistence of Coronaviruses on Inanimate Surfaces and Their Inactivation with Biocidal Agents," *Journal of Hospital Infection* 104, no. 3 (February 6, 2020): 246–251.

8. Statista, "Number of Online Payment Users in China from 2009 to De- cember 2020," 2021, https://www.statista.com/statistics/248900/number-of -online-payment-users-in-china/.

9. Marion Laboure, "The Steps Required to Promote Digital Currencies," *Konzept*, no. 19 (November 10, 2020): 49, https://www.dbresearch.com/PROD/RPS_EN -PROD/PROD0000000000513741/The_steps_required_to_promote_digital _currencies.pdf?undefined&realload=Z1UoWbB1mtD3cSx9d4vGVuqiviOWpcu U3CROwUgPdXagCMcNMCv50wkIGQrJLq0QIC4eRQ99e9lBNH4q- wowLVQ==.

10. CNN, "M-Pesa: Kenya's Mobile Money Success Story Turns 10," 2017, https:// edition.cnn.com/2017/02/21/africa/mpesa-10th-anniversary/index.html.

11. Thierry Isckia has investigated the role of platforms in the emergence and development of broader ecosystems. The development of platforms shapes the nature of relationships between partners engaged in an open innovation process. The more open the platform, the more it will improve collaboration between business partners. Aadhaar is a typical example. The Indian government initially created the platform to help citizens establish IDs, but it has since been opened to banks and to a broader network of application developers. In the future, start-ups could develop ATM withdrawal mechanisms or e-commerce authentication systems that use a fingerprint or iris scan. Thierry Isckia, "Amazon's Evolving

Ecosystem: A Cyber-Bookstore and Application Service Provider," *Canadian Journal of Administrative Sciences* 26, no. 4 (2009): 332–343; Thierry Isckia and Denis Lescop, "Open Innovation within Business Ecosystems: A Tale from Amazon.com," *Communications & Strategies* 74, no. 1 (2009): 37–54; Ben Letaifa, Anne Gratacap, and Thierry Isckia, *Understanding Business Ecosystems: How Firms Succeed in the New World of Convergence* (Louvain-la-Neuve: De Boeck, 2015).

Acknowledgments

The purpose of this book is to contribute to the practical and academic understanding of financial technology and its overall economic impact, with a specific focus on inclusive growth and inequality. We also describe the dynamics that are shaping fintech services, including regulations, governance structures, and investment practices. The book could not have been published without the help of many people.

The team at Harvard University Press was truly exceptional. Our first editor, Jeff Dean, shared our passion for the topic right from the beginning. His guidance, feedback, and good judgment helped us to structure *Democratizing Finance* into an informative, instructive, inspiring, and entertaining narrative. When Jeff left his position, we were fortunate to work with Ian Malcolm, who supported and brought this book into the world. We are grateful for his commitment, interest, and precious help. Many thanks to James Brandt, Olivia Woods, Stephanie Vyce, and Brian Ostrander, who were always available when needed.

MARION LABOURE This book would never have reached completion without Kenneth Rogoff and Juergen Braunstein. While I studied and worked at Harvard, Ken gave me the most interesting and challenging years I could imagine, as well as a great platform for professional growth. Juergen introduced us to Harvard University Press, which led to this book's publication. Juergen and I published numerous articles together in the *Economist, Project Syndicate*, VoxEU, *Le Monde, Global Policy,* the *Financial Times*, and the *New York Times*. Nicolas and I are indebted to Juergen for the title. In fact, he reminded us that, by writing the book, we were democratizing economics and finance—making it accessible to undergraduates and midcareer students.

Many others have been instrumental in the effort to publish this book. At Harvard University, I was fortunate to have been surrounded by supportive colleagues. I am profoundly grateful to Dante Roscini, Dorian Klein, Lawrence Summers, Mervyn King, Laura Wilcox, Julie Battilana, Patrick Schena, Prajapati Trivedi, Anup K. Pujari, Shiva Kumar, Rachel Deyette Werkema, Robert Lawrence, Kessely Hong, Hans-Helmut Kotz, and Sigmar Gabriel. They all provided me with key insights into the relationship between financial services and inequality.

I would like to thank my colleagues at Deutsche Bank for their invaluable support and insights over the last two years. In particular, I am thankful for David Folkerts-Landau, Jim Reid, Peter Hooper, Pam Finelli, Isaure De-Vaumas, Gurdon Wattles, Christoph Woermann, Raghu Gulati, Dixit Joshi, Christiana Riley, Markus Mueller, Stefan Hoops, Christian Sewing, Benjamin Madjar, Anthony Chaimowitz, Yann Couronneaud, Jessica Hakansson, Hanswolf Hohn, Luke Templeman, Tim Tait, Astrid Poussel, Mallika Sachdeva, Michal Jezek, Henry Allen, and Clarissa Dann.

This book draws from my research at the École Normale Supérieure and Harvard. It is also built on my previous experiences at the European Commission, Barclays, the Central Bank of Luxembourg, and the International Monetary Fund. I am grateful to my colleagues at the European Commission: Vitor Gaspar, Martin Larch, and Agnès Hubert, for supervising my work and remaining great friends over the years; at the Central Bank of Luxembourg: Gaston Reinesh for inviting me into the BCL research department while pursuing my PhD, and Muriel Bouchet and Olivier Delobbe for supervising my work; at Barclays Capital: Laurence Boone for offering me my first job in investment banking, and Julian Callow, Eldar Vakhitov, Francois Cabau for being great friends and keeping in touch; at the International Monetary Fund: Vitor Gaspar and David Coady for inviting me into the Fiscal Affairs department; at the École Normale Supérieure: Emmanuelle Taugourdeau for being a great supervisor and mentor when I was juggling with a full-time job and my writing work; at the Consumer Electronics Show: Xavier Dalloz and André Lamotte for their support and invitations to the CES; and my great fellow authors: John Turner, Yael Hadass, Sally Shen, Patrick Schena, Eva-Maria Nag, for their support and insights in this academic journey.

A special word of thanks goes to Vitor Gaspar, for his encouragement, advice, and insights since we met at the European Commission fifteen years ago. He kindly invited me to the International Monetary Fund to deepen my research.

NICOLAS DEFFRENNES   Lionel Melka was the first person to initiate me into the world of mergers and acquisitions, and financial services, which is the arena in which I began my career. Many years later, he was the first to encourage Marion and I to write books, and he played an essential role in my entrepreneurial journey. He has been a true source of inspiration all along.

This book could not have been written without the financial services and banking experiences that I acquired during my years at AnaCap Financial Partners. I would like to thank my mentors Joe Giannamore, Finlay McFadyen, Steve Barry, Chris Patrick, and Justin Sulger. I am also grateful for my peers and colleagues, such as Alison Ip, Christian Schuller, Paolo Savini-Nicci, Nassim Cherchali, Ian Wilkins, Stijn Proost, and Alex Mills. A special mention goes to Philip Monks, who built Aldermore Bank from the ground up. Lifelong friends such as Alison Ip, Nicolas Vrillaud, Aurelien Cristini, Nawar Cristini, Nicolas Trindade, and Pierre Viandaz have made this journey a joy.

My years at McKinsey gave me invaluable insights into how consumers engage with the digitalization of financial services. I would like to thank the leaders of the Consumer and Digital Consumer initiative, including Natalie Rémy, Olivier Sibony, Clarisse Magnin, Nicolo Galante, Franck Laizet, Karim Tadjeddine, Arnaud Minvielle, and Hortense de la Boutetière. I formed lasting friendships there with Fabrice Bocquet, Cyrielle Villepelet, Charles Best, Gary Roth, Catherine Abi-Habib, Boris Dragovic, David Ben Porat, and Philipp Hillenbrand.

I could not have written this book in a meaningful way without direct experiences in the world of start-ups and innovation. My entrepreneurial journey, which gave me an insider's view, would not have happened without good friends, co-entrepreneurs, and angels. Among them are Sylvie Barbossa, Thierry Prévot, Ivan Massonnat, Siméon Péllissier, Engelbert Heitkamp, Thomas Melkebeke, Pierre Viandaz, James Butler, Valerian Déjours, and Ismail Drissi.

We would also thank Glenn McMahan, who did a fantastic work in editing this book. Glenn was always available when needed, and he was always optimistic and confident. Nicolas Moreau, Preeti Sahai, Rangesh Vittal, James Butler, and Rachel Hathaway also contributed to shaping this book with their edits, insights, comments, and research.

Finally, our thanks go to family and friends, whose unrelenting support and encouragement brought us to the end of this journey. The book could not have been completed without the sustained tolerance and all-round support of our families. For these and many other reasons, this book is lovingly dedicated to Philippe Laboure, Christiane Laboure, Claire Laboure, Clementine Laboure, Huguette Laboure, Denis Laboure, Alexandre Boittin, Charlotte Creuzot, Régis Fanget, Julien Allard, Olivier Deffrennes, Colette Bernard, Marie-Therese Bernard, Sophie Deffrennes, Benoit Deffrennes, Helene Deffrennes, Guillaume Deffrennes, Nicolet Verdier, Laurie Meynet, Mieko Deffrennes, Julien Feruglio, and Charles Deffrennes.

Index